THE
ENFORCER

THE ENFORCER

ALBERT DONOGHUE
AND
MARTIN SHORT

BLAKE

Published by John Blake Publishing Ltd,
3, Bramber Court, 2 Bramber Road,
London W14 9PB, England

www.johnblakepublishing.co.uk

First published John Blake Publishing in 2002

ISBN 978-1-85782-525-1

British Library Cataloguing-in-Publication Data:

A catalogue record for this book is available from the British Library.

Typset by T2

Printed and bound in Great Britain by CPI Bookmarque

3 5 7 9 10 8 6 4

Papers used by John Blake Publishing are natural, recyclable products
made from wood grown in sustainable forests. The manufacturing processes
conform to the environmental regulations of the country of origin.

‖CONTENTS

ACKNOWLEDGEMENTS

I must thank all the people with whom I made the *Gangsters* series, which first put Albert Donoghue on British television in 1994. They are Allen Jewhurst, Simon Wells and Mark Stokes of the Leeds-based production company, Chameleon. I'm also indebted to Gill Wells for transcribing my original filmed interview with Albert. It follows that I'm deeply grateful to Paul Corley, then of Carlton, who commissioned *Gangsters*.

Twenty-five years ago, the solicitor Victor Lissack gave me a copy of Albert's statement against the Krays. Victor is long dead but I still 'owe' him. I also 'owe' a lot of underworld folk, both friends and foes of the Krays. Over these twenty-five years I have enjoyed the confidence of many of the principal players in this story. You know who you are. My thanks, even though I'm aware that much of what Albert says will displease you.

Most of all I'm indebted to Big Albert himself who, incidentally, talks with a Cockney twang rather than an Irish lilt. I have put this shrewd, sardonic man through repeated six-hour grillings, stretched over many months. He tells me this has been worse than being cross-examined in the Old Bailey during the Frank Mitchell murder trial. Trying to stitch the resulting mass of material into a seamless garment has been my contribution to this book. The failings are also mine. The life is Albert's. The lessons are for society.

Martin Short

▌INTRODUCTION

by Martin Short

They could scarcely read, write or count, and they were rotten shots, yet in the 1960s Ronnie and Reggie Kray became Britain's most notorious gang bosses for centuries: feared and hated, respected and despised, adored and ridiculed. Some 30 years on, it's time to strip off the myth, fantasy and invention that has raised them almost to role-model hero status and lay bare the grubby reality.

This is the story of one man who saw Ronnie and Reggie Kray close to, nose-to-nose, almost incessantly for three and a half searing years at their manic-depressive height – or depth, according to your point of view. He was their strongest henchman and their senior collector of protection money throughout their final baroque years, when they murdered two men, ordered a third murder and planned another dozen gangland executions. Despite the evidence of his own eyes, Donoghue stood by them all the way through to their final arrest and beyond. He broke away only when they told him to take the rap for a murder he had not committed. At this point he turned Queen's Evidence and helped send them both to jail for 30 years.

In view of his brutal initiation by gunshot into the 'Firm', it strikes me as strange that they could ever have felt sure of his loyalty. Charlie Kray has expressed the same view to me: 'I said to Reggie once, "If this happened, Donoghue will never forget it. He'll be an enemy. He'll work for you, but he'll always be an enemy." And Reggie said, "No, I don't think so. He's all right, Donoghue. He knows it was one of them things." '

Donoghue is adamant that when he joined the Firm in 1964, Charlie greeted him with the warmest of handshakes. He claims it wouldn't have seemed at all odd to Charlie that the Twins' newest lieutenant had a hole in his plastered foot through their brutality, because ritual humiliation was their standard recruiting method. Indeed it was their way of securing loyalty, and it had worked remarkably well since 1954 when they began their rapid and strangely irresistible rise in a profession in which London's Eastenders had been ferociously competitive for generations.

This book explains how the Twins' rare blend of low cunning and high violence enabled them to subvert and command criminals of far greater brain, strength and courage than their own. It shows how they maintained gangland supremacy for well over a decade through extraordinary attention to the petty detail of their Firm's organization – the collection of tribute, the gathering of intelligence, the application of intimidation, the infliction of punishment, the exacting of revenge, the distribution of charity and even the handling of public relations. Albert's tale also explains how this finely tuned gangland machine blew up in farce and chaos due to an over-consumption of Stematol, gin, brown ale and newspaper headlines.

With the benefit of hindsight, it seems astonishing that the Firm lasted as long as it did. It was brilliantly organized in an instinctive way, but hopelessly disarrayed when it came to expansion. It was like thousands of highly successful legitimate businesses that grow too big for their founders to run on the lines that made them big in the first place. As Donoghue argues, Ronnie and Reggie should have been pensioned off to their country mansion as early as 1965 so junior members of the Firm could marry their greater management skills to the Twins' matchless reputation for violence and produce better financial rewards for everyone on the board, the Twins included.

Albert joined the Firm ten years after Ronnie and Reggie first set themselves up as gangland businessmen. For readers who don't know what they had achieved by then, here is the briefest summary of their early lives and crimes. If you want to know more, there are a dozen books that tell their story from various angles. They were born on 24 October 1933, Reggie ten minutes ahead of Ronnie. At that time their mother and father, Violet and Old Charlie, were living in Hoxton with their first son Charlie, who was four years older than the Twins. In 1939 the family moved half a mile to 178 Vallance Road, Bethnal Green, a terraced house that the Twins themselves called a dump but that in the 1950s and early 1960s was good enough to serve as Fort Vallance, their command HQ. The roots of their criminal careers lay in the merger of two family traditions: boxing through their mother's father (all three brothers enjoyed short careers as professional boxers) and villainy through their own father, a totter who spent much of his life running from both the civilian and military police. For dodging the army right from the start of World War II, Old Charlie was on the trot for 12 years.

The Twins were to spend nine months of their own ignominious conscription in an army jail for desertion. Even while they were AWOL they could not stay out of trouble and were given a one-month sentence for assaulting a policeman. On their release in 1954 they served a brief criminal apprenticeship with Jack 'Spot' Comer, who was then gang boss of the East End and much of the West End too. But the Twins never had any intention of working for anybody except themselves, so when Spotty was gang-knifed by other villains into premature retirement in 1956, Ronnie and Reggie rapidly moved in to fill the vacuum.

They muscled in on a ramshackle billiard hall in Mile End called the Regal, which became a base for diverse extortion rackets and for conquering neighbouring East End crime territories. They were continually committing acts of extreme violence but few victims dared testify, either because they were villains themselves or they feared even worse retribution. Soon many local businessmen, mostly bent but a few straight, were paying for the privilege of not having the Twins' bully-boys smash up their property. In 1956 Ronnie's massive contribution to underworld imperialism was interrupted by a three-year jail sentence for his role in the bayonetting and stabbing of a lone victim called Terry Martin.

It was due only to the vigilance of one of his fellow inmates in Winchester Prison that Ronnie's violent insanity was first diagnosed. In February 1958 he was certified as needing psychiatric treatment and transferred to Long Grove mental hospital in Epsom. He soon contrived to escape by having Reggie visit him and take his place, while he was driven off in the car that was waiting to take Reggie home. Five months later the crime reporter Norman Lucas cleverly persuaded Ronnie to give himself up. In 1959 after a few months of deceptively good behaviour back in Long Grove, he was released back into a community that would have been far better off without him.

By now his brothers had set up in a club in Bow Road called the Double R, which, it seems, fulfilled Reggie's dream of a plush and 'properly run' drinking establishment. Properly run meant that within two years it went bust. No matter, by then the Twins had bullied their way into a share of the Regency Club in Stoke Newington. In autumn 1960 they intimidated the owner of a lucrative Knightsbridge casino, Esmeralda's Barn, into selling it to them for a fraction of its value. Untold wealth should now have poured in, but soon it was Reggie's turn to get into trouble with the law. Through a clumsy sidekick he was dragged into a pathetic attempt at demanding money with menaces from a shopkeeper in West Hampstead, far from Kray territory. The police pounced, and Reggie was jailed for 18 months. Soon after his release in 1962 the Twins set up another East End club of their own, the Kentucky. Along with Esmeralda's Barn, this was still going in October 1964 when Albert Donoghue was recruited on to the Firm.

What did other people think of Albert at that time? The Twins' original biographer, John Pearson, who first met them in October 1967, described Albert as 'one of the enigmas of the Firm and an Irishman, but he never talked much, never gave himself away.' Leonard 'Nipper' Read, the detective who led the Metropolitan

Police squad that eventually destroyed the Firm, recalls Donoghue as 'a big cold person' who 'offered to become an informer, but even then he confessed without emotion. It was the same at the trial: he was cold, absolutely cold . . . uncharismatic.'

Another member of the Firm who gave evidence against the Krays, Scotch Jack Dickson, recalls Donoghue as 'broad and fair-looking' and says, 'We got on well.' Understandably, the Krays – all dead now – took a less sympathetic view. Charlie Kray has described Donoghue as one of 'the insects, creeping and crawling to the spider', Nipper Read. He said, 'First one, then another Judas stepped forward to buy his freedom with a pocketful of lies.' Again, Charlie claimed he saw it all coming. One night in the Carpenters' Arms, a pub they bought in 1967 when all their clubs had gone bust, he said he shouted at the Twins in front of all the Firm, 'You won't get any loyalty from them when the Old Bill gets lively. They'll grass you up as fast as you like.' Donoghue, who would surely have been present if 'all the Firm were there', cannot remember Charlie ever shouting anything of the sort.

Reggie Kray described Donoghue as one of the people who 'were only too happy to ride with us when the going was good' but who 'let us down badly' in the end. They 'weren't around any more... They just ran away.' Ronnie Kray claimed that Donoghue 'told unforgivable lies in court'.

That's really what you would expect the Twins to say. Less predictable, and far more revealing, are the observations of Tony Lambrianou, who was jailed with the Twins for the murder of Jack 'the Hat' McVitie. To Tony, Albert was 'a very deep bloke and one of the few we all felt we could rely on. Everybody respected him. I liked him.' He says he was surprised by Albert's 'betrayal': 'Of all the people in the Firm, Donoghue was the last person I would have expected to go against us. I could not believe it.'

This book explains how that 'betrayal' came about, and why Donoghue asserts it was the Krays who grassed him, not the other way round. In the end he felt his loyalty wasn't worth him doing time for their crime – and that might have been 20 or even 30 years in jail. Instead he did less time than a traffic offender might get today. And he still holds his head up in the East End.

▌PROLOGUE

Fire and Hire

By the early Sixties I was an active criminal on a good little team. Our main business was payroll snatches.

We operated out of Bow, two miles east of Bethnal Green, the heart of Kray territory. We knew the Krays but had little to do with them. We were our own bosses.

Around this time I got to know a man named Lennie Hamilton. He was a sort of valet, a batman for one of the guys on our payroll team, Harry Abrahams. Lennie wasn't a robber, but on the weekends he used to look after this guy's kids while we went over to Paddington to mix with the working girls. Late one Sunday night – so late, it was Monday morning – we came home to find this Lennie sitting there looking dreadful. Lennie had a dark complexion and black stubble, so we couldn't help noticing these fresh grooves in his face, which looked as if they'd been cut into his cheeks. His hair was badly burnt, and one of his eyes looked as if it had been almost poked out.

We said, 'What's happened, Lennie?' and he told us how somebody had sat him down, tied him to a chair and burnt his face with a cold steel, a poker-shaped tool you sharpen knives on. So we said, 'Who was it? We'll go and see 'em,' but he wouldn't tell us. Eventually I got fed up trying to coax him into giving us the names, so I said, 'If somebody had done that to me, I wouldn't be sitting here talking about it, I'd go out and blow his head off!' And off I went.

Later we found out that the man who'd used the poker on Lennie was Ronnie Kray. We knew Ronnie had a reputation for violence, but we weren't softies either. So me and Harry phoned the Twins and went round to their house in Vallance Road to find out what this branding was all about. We knew that Ronnie and Reggie liked to deliver symbolic messages, so what did they mean by doing this to Lennie? If this was a message, we wanted to know, were they signalling that they were going to war with our team or what?

Just in case the war had already started, we decided to go tooled-up, so I was carrying a shooter. When we got to the house this gun nearly came out of my trousers. I'm fumbling about, trying to put it back so clumsily they could have thought I was making a deliberate signal. They must have known what was there but nothing happened. They could see if they had made a move, somebody would have got shot. This was what we'd gone round there for, to have a shoot-out. They probably knew that, so Ronnie said, 'Well, it's no good crying over spilt milk. What's happened has happened. Lennie got a bit flash, and that's the end of it. Just leave it.' It was more or less peace talk, and it was agreed that nothing else would be done.

Within a couple of months of the Lennie Hamilton incident, I got nicked for a failed payroll snatch. I got a three-year sentence, but in those days there was no parole. You did the straight two years, and, if you were good, you got one year's remission. Now while I was away, someone who was close to this little Lennie has gone and told the Kray Twins that I'd said, 'If they'd done that to me, I'd have blown their heads off.'

But at the moment when I'd said that, I didn't realize it was the Twins who'd done Lennie because he had refused to tell me, only they had been told I knew it was them all along. So, unknown to me, all the time I was away, they must have been thinking I was still planning to gun them down. Mind you, if I had know right from the start that it was the Twins, I would have still thought the same, but I wouldn't have said so.

So when I come home after my two years, I know nothing of what the Twins have been told. Then I hear they're looking for me, but I have no reason to suspect anything. I'm also a bit skint so, just like any East End con fresh out of jail at that time, I go round to the Twins' local pub, the Crown and Anchor, because it was known that if you were short of money, you could go and get a few quid off them. So I walk in the Crown, go up to the bar, and within ten minutes people are drifting away from me. Now I know something is going to happen. Next thing, 'Bang!' I get shot in the back of the leg. Reggie Kray did that.

Of course, I have to go to hospital because the bullet's stayed in – if it goes straight through you it's probably all right. Then I get out of the hospital. I'm in plaster, and I'm sitting in a little drinking club in Mile End, and this guy Bill Ackerman comes in – he's a bit of a gofer for the Krays – and he says, 'The Firm's looking for you.' He mentions a few faces – Big Tommy Brown, Johnny Squibb – and says, 'They're all looking for you.' I say, 'What for?' He says, 'The Twins want to see you.' So they've been sending these delivery boys to collect me, and so I tell Bill, 'Well, they know where I live, I got my leg in plaster, I can't run . . . I might as well go round their house. Take me round there!'

Now Ackerman's so scared he nearly has to change his underpants, but to me this was common sense. So he drops me at their house and scuttles off while I knock on the door. Reggie shows me into the front room, and I find myself sitting with all three Krays: Reggie, Ronnie and Charlie. They say, 'How do you feel – apart from the pain?' I say as a peacemaking gesture, 'Well, if I'd have been in your position and someone had told me the nonsense you'd heard over Hamilton I'd have probably done the same as you.' So they say, 'OK, what we do, we put you on a pension [that was their word for wages] and, when you're fit, come and get your money with us.'

So that's it! Now I'm 'on the Firm'.

1: A CRIMINAL EDUCATION

I was born on the fifth of November 1935, Bonfire Night. I came into this world with a bang, and I'll probably go out with one. Not that they celebrate Bonfire Night where I was born. In Dublin they don't burn effigies of Guy Fawkes, the Catholic who tried to blow up parliament and kill a Protestant king of England. Instead they think he's a great Guy.

My family was Catholic working class. I was the third of four children. All the others were girls. In those days Ireland was a very poor country, and life must have been scrappy for the Donoghues. When I was one year old my father Joe brought all of us to London and set up home in the East End. He must have thought prospects were better in England, but he never had the chance to enjoy them. He was in the British merchant navy and used to ship out of Belfast, but on a trip home to Dublin he fell ill of pneumonia and had to be taken to hospital. He seemed to recover and came back to England, but he died soon after. I was just three years old. I have no memory of him.

My mother was now a single parent with four kids to support, but she had her mother with her, and her brothers were already living in Hammersmith, which was the centre of London's Irish community at that time. On one occasion these uncles came over from Hammersmith to see us. They brought along another Irishman called John Barry. They introduced him to Mum, the couple got on well, and, two years after my father's death, they got married.

By now Britain was at war with Germany. I suppose Mum could have taken us all back to Ireland, which stayed out of the war, but that might not have been too healthy because a couple of my uncles were serving in the Royal Navy and my stepfather John Barry had joined the Royal Artillery. Thousands of Irishmen fought for Britain in World War II, but this was seen as treachery by staunch Republicans. My mother could have had a lot of trouble in Dublin so she stayed put in Stepney.

Soon there were a lot more of us at home. My mum finished up with 12 children: me and my three Donoghue sisters, and eight younger kids by Barry. He must have made her pregnant every time he came back on leave. In between births she had to earn a living. She did some bus-conducting and an ambulance run. It would have been tough for her in the best of circumstances, but during the Blitz we were twice bombed out of our homes: first out of Pitsea Street in Stepney, then we moved to Head Street until it happened there too. The family was always on the move, in and out of temporary accommodation.

Not that I knew much about that because soon after war broke out, my two older sisters and I had been evacuated to Devon. I was tucked away there from when I was four until I was eight. At that time we were in Okehampton on the edge of Dartmoor. Today it may sound idyllic. Back then it seemed to me as remote as the moon.

The first time evacuee children arrived in any place, they would be taken off the train to the local church hall, where people would circle round looking to choose kids who, presumably, seemed sweet, docile and reasonably well brought up. I was always left till last, so I must have looked a right little ruffian. We were all called 'Townies', which was really a codeword for 'rough and rowdy urchin', and when your billet – the folks you were staying with – got fed up with you, you were shipped on somewhere else. I was billeted at four different homes in Okehampton. Only in the last place was I staying in the same house as my sisters. The call must have gone out, 'Who's willing to take these kids?' People probably didn't mind the two girl Donoghues. I would have been the problem, not least because I was very protective of them, and I would get into all sorts of scraps on their part.

Once my mother sent us a letter saying that our stepfather John Barry was now stationed at an army camp near Newton Abbot, not far from Okehampton. In fact it's 20 miles but I didn't know that, so one day me and Micky Holland, my little friend from the East End, who was billeted with me, set off down the road with the intention of walking all the way there. We didn't know where we were going, I guess we just followed the white line in the middle of the road.

After a couple of miles Micky couldn't keep it in and badly needed to go to the toilet, so we knocked at the nearest cottage. It was occupied by a couple of nice old ladies who made us welcome. One cleaned up poor Micky, while the other gave me a huge apple. Next thing we were put on a bus back to Okehampton, where we were met by a big red-faced bobby who took us back to our billet. The woman of the house pretended to be overjoyed to see us, gushed all over the copper and laid three places at the table. She dished out three huge portions of rabbit pie; the copper dug into his helping and said the food was so good, he wouldn't have run from this billet. We were terrified to touch the plates in front of us because we knew the drill. Sure enough, when the copper went, she whipped our portions back and took them away. This show of generosity was all done for his benefit. A clip around the ears was done for ours.

I was reunited with my sisters at my fourth billet, which was the home of a rag-and-bone man and his wife. They had a son who was an altar boy but he lacked the Christian spirit. They had an outside toilet, a cubicle privy in the garden, and on this particular day I've got the runs. This boy's in the toilet, and I'm banging at the door, but he's just sat in there. He's obviously finished, but he's taunting me through the door. So I've crapped myself. I could have been scarcely eight, if that, but when he came out, I set about him and broke his nose. It was more anger than expertise, and I just laced into him. Now I was branded a violent Townie. I got a good thrashing, and I was aimed down a flight of stone steps by the rag-and-bone man. I must have been in a state because I remember being tested for possible brain damage. One good thing came out of this. While the hospital was conducting these tests, they found out we had all contracted scabies. This was because he was making us work in his barn, helping him sort old rags. This constituted ill-treatment, and we were all shipped home.

So after four years in Devon we were back in London for only six weeks. Then it was off again, this time to Scarborough for two more years until the war was over. During those entire six years I scarcely saw my mother. I think this huge time apart was the reason why, later, we were never really able to establish a good relationship. A lot of mothers were evacuated with their kids and stayed with them, but we were farmed out throughout the time when kids usually become closest to their mothers. I remember missing her a lot even though she was hard, a typical tough Irishwoman. You give Irishmen a few bottles of whiskey, and they'll become sentimental and sing silly songs, but in their sober moments they're tough. They're not cruel, they're just firmer with their children than most other people are. The boys are brought up to be men and the girls as women, but both male and female can be as hard as nails. Over generations they've had to be hard to survive.

Being Irish in England was a toughening experience in itself. Even as a youngster I tasted discrimination. We had been evacuated to Devon as an entire Catholic primary school. In Ashburton our own priests and nuns continued to teach us in a self-contained school building handed to them for that purpose. This meant we were being educated in the one true faith during the day, while at night we ate and slept in Protestant homes. There were hardly any Catholics in Devon, and we were frowned on by the community at large. I'm sure it was because I was Catholic that I was kicked out of the cub scouts. We were particularly unacceptable because we were Irish. Even long after the War I saw signs saying ROOMS VACANT. NO DOGS, NO IRISH, in many parts of London. And you could always spot an Irishman. The working Irish all appeared to wear a uniform, consisting of a navy-blue serge suit. They always seemed to be big red-faced men, who kept themselves to themselves, so they were an easy target. The Irish, the Jews, the Blacks, everyone who was slightly different came up against this sort of thing.

I was in jeopardy from both sides. I was discriminated against as a Catholic, but I didn't think much of Catholicism myself! I certainly didn't think much of the nuns and priests who taught us in Devon. Right from when I was seven I knew I was different, because I was already thinking differently from the bulk of the kids in class. The teacher would say, 'Now, we're all going to do this,' and I'd question it. Whether I was just stroppy or what, if it didn't suit me I would kick up a fuss, and I wouldn't do it.

This was especially true if the lesson was religious instruction, which was always being popped into us Catholics. The nuns used to come out with all sorts of nonsense, like the story of Adam and Eve. I would say to the sister, 'So if it was only them people in the world, who did Adam marry? He must have married his sister. That's wrong.' 'Come out here!' she would shout – I'd sparked her off already – 'Troublemaker!'

I used to question everything in the Bible. I'd say, 'This is nonsense. I'm not having it!' I was already a rebel, but don't get me wrong. I wasn't suffering from any buzz. I wasn't doing this out of perversity. I was seeking knowledge. I'd ask genuine questions, but they would respond, 'You're being lippy.' If you asked a question that they couldn't handle, they lashed out. They were just bad teachers.

When the War ended, and all the evacuees came back to the East End, we Donoghue kids turned up at the ever expanding Barry household and just packed out the place. Looking after the 12 of us obviously took up all Mum's time. In those days working-class people didn't have washing machines or any other labour-saving devices – except children themselves.

While we were waiting for the entire family to be rehoused, I was shunted into a boarding school run by the Christian Brothers in Orpington, Kent. This was worse than anything I had encountered at the hands of the nuns. Here they used to torture you, they would cut your hair almost to the bone, and if you did anything they did not like, they would grab hold of your head and rub their thumbs up the back of the skull. They used to make the whole school run barefoot through a cornfield when it had just been cut and the stubble's sticking up like razor blades or a bed of nails. The first morning I did this my feet had a nice few gashes in them, until one brother, slightly less sadistic than the others, said, 'Slide your feet into it, and it won't hurt so much.'

The place was run throughout on the bully principle. The head boy was the toughest boy in the school. These Christian Brothers were fierce people. They all wore heavy skirted robes, with a thick and wide horsetack belt-strap around the waist and a huge metal ring. The two ends of this strap would hang loose right down to mid-calf. They were so long that they were frequently used for whacking kids without even having to be taken off. This was my first real taste of an 'institution', and, although I wasn't in this one for any anti-social behaviour, it had a lot in common with all the other places that I would be locked in for much of the rest of my life. I found that all these places employed drop-outs. Even the doctors were useless. You go and see them with a sprained wrist, and they give you a couple of aspirins. None of them seemed to be a normal adult. As a kid you have a picture of adults as conforming to a certain pattern of decent behaviour, but there was always something wrong with these people. They went to work in such institutions because they had failed at everything else.

One day my mum came on a visit to this Christian Brothers' outfit, and I insisted on leaving with her. I refused to stay. The head brother was trying to coax me to change my mind, but I said, 'No. I'm not staying, 'cos when you leave here, Mum, these people are going to thrash me all round the place.'

This emotional blackmail worked, and my mother brought me

home. By now the family were living east of Stepney, in Bow, where I spent most of my next few years and rapidly established a reputation for being able to handle myself. This started at Catholic primary school, where I was always scrapping in the playground and making a nuisance of myself in class. I was tall for my age, and as you grow bigger, your reputation gets bigger too, if you're handy with your fists. Of course, all the other kids are growing, too, but if they start sticking their heads up and you manage to win a fight with them, then you go a step higher in the reputation ladder. It's a gradual thing, until suddenly you reach a stage where the professional villains start taking notice. They're always on the look-out for a bit of extra muscle.

Being quite big has got to help in this game, but that's not all there is to it. I know little guys who could knock the daylights out of me. What really matters is just how much you're prepared to stand. You could say to somebody, 'You're an ugly bastard,' and he'd stand for it. If you said it to the next guy, he'd want to knock you out. So do you want to stand and fight him? How much pain are you prepared to inflict? And – most important – how much pain are you willing to suffer in order to defeat him?

Don't get me wrong. I wasn't a school bully. We didn't go round bullying people, in fact we stopped bullying. I remember one incident in school when we decided to take out this big bully. He was another Irishman, what we call a 'black Irishman', with black curly hair and blue eyes. We decided to teach him a lesson. One afternoon after school we got somebody who was a bit fast on their feet to challenge him with a few insults. This provoked the bully into chasing him to the back of some bombed-out houses, where we ambushed him. We set about him as a team and gave him a good belt, a lashing. Suddenly his bullying stopped. He didn't need counselling or a social worker to make him stop, like they have in schools these days. The only thing he'd understand was a bloody good hiding himself. And we kids could reason this out because we were living in the same jungle as he was.

THE ENFORCER

The Catholic–Protestant thing didn't go away either. My primary shared a site with a Church of England primary, so there was a rope stretched down the middle of the playground: Catholics on one side, Protestants on the other. This way prejudice was being perpetuated by the authorities. Things were no better at my secondary school, which was wholly Catholic, and where, again, my irreverence kept getting me into trouble.

My partner in classroom crime was another second-generation Irish boy called Prendergast, and we would always get picked on. On Mondays they called a 'mass register'. The nuns would ask, 'Did you go to mass on Sunday? Hands up those who went to mass.' Well, of course, we all put our hands up, whether we'd gone or not, but without fail it would be just Prendergast and me who would be chosen for public execution: 'You two! Come out here! What mass did you go to?' This was a trick question, because for each religious season the priests wear different colour robes. So we would say, 'Half-past nine,' and the inevitable next question would be, 'What colour robes?' We'd guess, 'Purple.' Crack! We should have said green! And for this error the nuns would whack us. So, in the eyes of these oh-so-reverend sisters, me and Prendergast were definitely the bad guys of the class and doomed to boil for an eternity in Hell.

One day after a particularly bad spell my mother went down to the school, she had a rap with the nuns, and I was instantly transferred to a Protestant secondary modern. There I was two years behind academically, but I could baffle the CofE vicar with my knowledge of the scriptures, because they had been pumped into me since I was an infant. I knew all the mystical terms and their meanings – the Annunciation, the Temptation, the Crucifixion, the Resurrection – but I don't recall him asking about the Virgin Birth or the Immaculate Conception, neither of which the nuns had ever explained to my satisfaction.

By this time I had long been bored stiff with straight education, not just because of the follies of religion. I was now enjoying a criminal education on the streets, which commanded far more of my intellectual hunger than school ever did. Since the age of ten I had been a professional thief.

Older people who knew my game did not necessarily brand me either a pariah or a parasite because, in the East End in those days, thieving was almost as respected – and certainly more use to the community – as education, because everyone was so poor, no one could pay the full price for almost anything. Our house in Bow was right on the canal, so my school mates and I used to see these barges moored near by, piled with peanuts still in their shells. At the time a firm called Larkins used to sell a silly little bag containing a dozen of these peanuts for sixpence – well over £1.00 at today's prices. So, armed with a load of empty sacks, me and my mates used to slip on to the barges and fill the sacks with these peanuts. We would package them up ourselves and sell them to the neighbours. Now although we were poor, that's not why we did this. We didn't do this because we were deprived. This was a deliberate business venture.

Rationing was still on at the time, so an even greater money-spinner was tea. We would break into grocery shops and take their whole stock of tea, then go and sell it at eight shillings a pound door to door. Today you couldn't go round a block of flats brazenly selling stolen property. All right, you might get away with selling it to two or three people, but sooner or later someone's going to pop you in.

In those days everybody was involved in the black market, so no one could cast the first stone. You could just sell gear door to door, especially tea, cigarettes and booze. We even took orders from people. Whatever they wanted, we'd go and steal. There was no Fagin leading us astray. We were total freelances. Two or three of us would get together and break into a shop. Back then it had to be a really top-class place to have a bell or an alarm system. We'd just pick out a quiet grocer's. A lot of them were bomb damaged, so you could chip through the walls and clean them out. That was my early schooling, not listening to nuns and brothers. We were self-taught, and we were regarded by locals young and old as public servants.

Then we started going for cash. The best place for cash was when it was in transit or when we could run in somewhere and take it out of an office. Eventually we got over-confident, and our luck ran out. Someone informed on us. Even then it wasn't any of the 'honest citizens' we'd been supplying with tea or peanuts, it was one of our own thieving kind. Somebody 'at it' must have been picked up by the police, who pressured him into volunteering a few names to lighten his own load. My name was put in, I was implicated, then the police may have found pieces of evidence to justify rounding me up or pulling me in for questioning.

Once you were in the police station you were bound to get verballed. They would write down whatever they wanted, claim you had said it, then they'd make sure you put your signature at the bottom. The coppers used to say, 'Right, sit down, on with the boxing gloves.' But only they had the gloves. You didn't get any. What you got was a beating. That was the interview!

I had plenty of interviews like that. 'Smoke?' they'd say. 'Yeah.' Then they'd give you a fag and pull out a lighter or a match, so naturally you would lean forward to where the guy had the flame. Then, 'Bosh!' you'd get a smack in the chin. It was a trap. Now these coppers were applying the law of the jungle, just as we were doing in the playground, on the basis that a good smacking would teach us the error of our ways. But they were also looking for an immediate result: my signature on the confession. I was now supposed to be so terrified that I'd write the whole lot out, but I never did.

I still have no idea what started me so early on a life of professional crime. My mother's family was totally straight. So was my stepfather, John Barry. A couple of my brothers got into a little trouble in their teens. One went AWOL during national service but that was a jaunt really, and he soon gave himself up. He wound up liking the army, and he went on to become a respectable businessman.

In the entire Donoghue–Barry clan there were six of us boys. We were all brought up the same way, and I'm the only one who ended up a gangster. In some ways my start in life was better than most of theirs, so I don't believe crime has that much to do with poverty. A deprived childhood is not the sole cause. Is it something genetic? I don't know. What I do know is that I recognized very early the difference between right and wrong, and if I did something wrong, and I got caught, I might say, 'I wish I hadn't done that.' But whatever turned me into a juvenile thief and later into a professional villain, I don't think it was a psychiatric 'cry for help'. I wasn't suffering because my dad hadn't given me any oranges, or I hadn't read the *Beano*.

Over the tea thefts, some breaking and entering, and the odd robbery I was given every chance of probation, but I blew them all. I appeared so often in front of Mr Basil Henriques, the juvenile magistrate at Toynbee Hall in Aldgate, that he used to call me 'Albert', he knew me so well. Eventually my unstoppable criminal tendencies drove even him to believe I had to be put away, so at the age of twelve I was packed off to a remand home in Goldhawk Road, west London. It was called Stamford House, but Dotheboys Hall would have been more appropriate.

In theory a remand home was where juvenile offenders went for short periods while the powers-that-be decided what best to do with you. Inside you would be put through various tests, by doctors, psychiatrists and whatever they called social workers in those days. Then after three or four weeks, you would either get probation again or they would decide you were a hard nut and stick you in the next institution in the justice system, an approved school.

The people who dreamed up this system probably had decent, liberal intentions and believed this was a caring and humane way of coping with juvenile offenders. If so, they reckoned without the sheer evil of some of the people who worked in these places. My dominant memory of Stamford House in the late 1940s is of child sex abuse. It was rife, and the master who was worst of all was a man whom I shall call the Beast, in case he has had the undeserved good fortune to remain alive for another 45 years. If anyone should have been locked up, it was him. He was a screaming poof who used to select little favourites to be his tea-boy. As you might expect, the tea-boy's job was to take a cup into the Beast's study every morning. The door would be closed, and the kid would stay in there for up to an hour. We never saw behind the door, but we knew exactly what was going on. The Beast would take no more than five minutes to drink his tea, then he would be busy tampering with the tea-boy.

If you got one of these boys on their own, you would say, 'Oh, you been playing with the Beast's dick today?' Well, surely, if you made that sort of remark to someone who'd been up to no such thing, he would go, 'What?' and deny it. But with these people there was no such reaction, just one of shame. They would shrug their shoulders in a defeated kind of way. A normal person would have shaped up to fight you, or – if they weren't the fighting kind – they might have burst into tears and run away, but there was nothing like that with these kids. I didn't approach them aggressively. I did it in a protective way because I was having my own battles with the Beast, and I would have loved to expose him.

The trouble was that nothing any of us might say would be believed against a member of the staff. You imagine, if a young delinquent tried to make a complaint in those days against these sort of people. It was a Charles Dickens carry-on. It just wouldn't be listened to. Simple as that. There was another obstacle to getting these perverts dealt with. The kind of kids who suffer buggery and other forms of sex abuse are usually very quiet, withdrawn types. They are open to bullying, they invite it, they are walking victims, and it's them who are creamed off by perverted members of staff and get given these silly little jobs. If you complain and say, 'Why are these kids always being creamed off?' the staff's defence would be, 'We recognize that they're vulnerable, so we're doing it to protect them from the other boys.' Rubbish. They needed protecting from the staff!

I must have been an ugly kid because I was never approached in that way. It was always these little, sad and withdrawn kids that they would pick out because they were just the ones who would put up with it and would never complain. This went on in every 'reform' institution I attended. It was rampant. If anyone had fancied me as chicken meat, I wouldn't have stood for it. I would have got myself a tool and done the guy.

I did one pervert in the Bow Regal cinema when I was eleven. I was in this local fleapit with my young brother, we had a bottle of lemonade, and we were watching the picture. Then I looked over, and I saw this man's hand coming over the armrest towards my flies. So I did him with the lemonade bottle. Pow! The bottle exploded – they were made out of proper glass in those days – and the lights went up, and the manager came down. In the meantime this guy stole to the exit, so I said, 'There he goes!' They were so busy chasing him, they didn't bother to ask what had caused the explosion, and while all this was going on we disappeared out the other exit.

Stamford House wasn't run by Catholics. It came directly under the Home Office, the religion was Church of England, and the Beast wasn't a priest. The regime was stupid: you had to wear short trousers, you were allowed only two cigarettes a day, and you had to hand in your dog-end when you'd finished. There was a lot of regimentation and a lot of bullying. People were always shouting, 'Do this! Do that!' and if you didn't do it, you were in trouble, whether what you'd been asked to do was sensible or not. If you got caught whispering, it would be 'Scrub out the showers with a toothbrush!' I remember having to trim round the cricket pitch with nail scissors, giggling while I was doing it because it was so bloody stupid and wondering: What's this going to teach me? Not to sit anywhere near nail scissors in future?

That's the stupid discipline they came out with. And if they said, 'Get over there, do that!' and you said, 'Why?' you were on report, for dumb insolence. If you happened to look the guy in the eye, it was 'dumb insolence' again. Your punishment would be that you can't go to the film show – *The Reproductive Processes of the Butterfly*, that kind of film – or you didn't get an apple.

One time they put on a boxing show, with a lot of invited guests as well as all the inmates in the crowd. The staff's idea of a joke was to stick me and two other kids in the ring not only wearing gloves but also blindfolded with pillowcases over our heads. We had to feel round in the dark and strike either of the two other boys. This was all for the staff's benefit and amusement. Then I got one blow planted right on my nose, so I pulled off this pillowcase, and I set about the other two who can't see me because they're still wearing their pillowcases. While they're flailing about, I'm pounding them to pieces. So in jump the staff, they drag me out of the ring and tell me, 'You won't get your apple!' which was to have been the prize.

We could have done a lot of damage to each other by accident. You could get punched in the eye, the ear or the back of the head. But to the staff it was a show, which had the additional advantage of setting you against your colleagues, your fellow inmates. Divide and rule.

The Beast also dished out the physical beatings, and boy! he must have loved those, because he caned you on your bare arse. This was real pain for you and real pleasure for him. What a stupid way to discipline us. There are far more intelligent ways of punishing kids. You can stop their pocket money, stop their sweets, stop their cigarette ration, but in those days the cane was almost the first option for straightening out naughty boys like me.

I remember getting good stick from him, just as I remember the beatings all the way back to when I was with the Christian Brothers 50 years ago. I'd get lash after lash on my arms, and the pain would shoot right the way up, but all I was doing was concentrating. I wasn't going to cry. I would just stare at this twit who was dishing out the stick. That's all they knew: 'This boy's been naughty, I'll thrash him' – Charles Dickens stuff – not 'Sit down, lad. What's going wrong? What's up?' No. 'You've done wrong. You know the rules.' Crash.

Despite all this violence, it wasn't the system that turned me into a criminal. Indeed, the system as a whole was remarkably forgiving. I was given so many chances, but within months I'd get caught doing another crime, and they'd send me back to Stamford House, where I'd be greeted by the Beast going, 'Ooh, yes! Look who we've got here! Back again, Barry?!'

After each spell in there I would get probation, I'd go home to Bow, and I'd go back to Fairfield Road secondary modern school. I did pretty well there. The headmaster wanted me to do an extra term because he thought I had a bit of potential, so I stayed long enough for the state to give me a post-office savings book with £5 in it, as an encouragement to pursue an education. It didn't work. I quit school just before I reached fifteen, the formal leaving age. For a while I tried to go straight. I started an electrical engineering apprenticeship, but I was un-indentured. For nine weeks all I did was fit fluorescent lights in Boosey & Hawkes, the musical instrument store in Regent Street. I didn't learn anything. I was supposed to go to night-school, to do the paperwork and the practical, but the electrician was just using me so I dropped out.

Pretty soon I was back in trouble. This time the system gave up on me, and I was sentenced to approved school, but I hadn't seen the last of Stamford House. I was ordered back there one more time until a place came up at a Catholic approved school. I stuck it out for six weeks until I decided I'd had enough. I wouldn't stand for the beatings any more. I'd also had enough of that scumbag the Beast. He was bursting to get rid of me because he knew I knew what he was doing to other kids. I used to look him straight in the eye with contempt written all over my face. He must have thought, This bastard knows what I'm up to. He'd got to have felt some guilt or shame.

It got so bad that some of us attempted a break-out, but we were caught in the act. They had to drag me off barbed wire. I don't remember the pain, but I must have been in a state because I was deemed 'unfit for punishment'. In those days that meant I must have been badly injured.

Being unfit for punishment meant that they couldn't lace into me, so instead they put me on fatigue, washing down a dormitory wall. I was doing it with another guy but it was supposed to be silent work, and we were being supervised by an ex-prison screw. I was up a ladder, and when we thought the screw was out of earshot, this other guy said to me, 'What's going to happen when you *are* fit? They're going to give you a right seeing-to.' 'When I'm fit,' I said, 'if they start laying into me, I'm going to lay into one or two of them.' But the screw was standing just round the corner. He had heard all this, so he ordered me to get down from the ladder, he put my arm up my back, and he marched me off on report to the Beast.

Of course, the Beast was loving it as the screw told him what I'd said. A big smile came over his face as he sneered, 'Oh well, Barry, we've got you now!' That was it. He called a taxi and sent me to West London Magistrates' Court, to get an order stating I was 'out of control', and I should be sent immediately to approved school. The magistrate was no fool. He wound up giving *them* a lecture. Right in front of me he said, 'You're supposed to be looking after these children, it's your job to keep them under control, yet here you are asking me to make them "out of control".' But, whatever he thought, he did what the Beast asked. I was deemed too hot to handle at Stamford House, but as there was still no place for me at the approved school I was lined up for, I was packed off to prison. Wormwood Scrubs. I was fifteen.

You might think I would have been terrified in the Scrubs, but I thought it was heaven compared to Stamford House. I couldn't believe it: long trousers, smokes, books. It was liberation! Of course, if it happened nowadays that a kid of fifteen was put in the Scrubs, there'd be questions in the House of Commons and a big public outcry, but in those days you mixed with all the adult remand prisoners. They could have been in there for almost anything – not murders but violence, robbery, molesting – everyone was lumped together, unless they were peeled off for protection. So I walked round with these guys, and I mixed with them, although I had to use my head about who I mixed with. You think, Don't like the look of him, and pick your own company according to your experience and instincts. In jail I could have been assaulted, because these people were bigger, heavier and stronger than a fifteen-year-old. I might have been raped, but it would have had to be a violent assault. Then I would have peeled them off later and got my revenge. It didn't happen.

Eventually the Catholic approved-school vacancy came through. I was to go to St Benedict's in Mortimer near Reading. This was run by the De La Salle brothers, a teaching order. I had no fixed sentence, but I was there, on and off, until I was almost eighteen. An approved school is a bit like a private boarding school, only even more oppressive. You stay there for the whole term, then you go home for the holidays: a week at Easter, ten days in summer and a week at Christmas. St Benedict's was also a farm, which kept a lot of the boys occupied, but I did a joinery and decorating course. A few of us preferred the decorating so we suggested we'd be better suited if we stuck to that. The brothers agreed so we painted all the dormitories and the staff houses. I almost got a City and Guilds in painting and decorating, but my time was over before I could take it. Still, the skills came in very handy later with the Krays, in horrific circumstances.

Getting a trade was the one good thing about St Benedict's. Everything else was a fight for survival because it was run by bullies. In our days approved schools aped the grand public schools, with a system of prefects chosen from the senior boys to inflict discipline on everybody else. Naturally it's the tough guys who get put in charge because they know all the ropes. Also, by giving them a bit of authority, the headmaster hopes they'll give him less trouble. So the boy he chooses to be head boy is always the Boss because he's the strongest, the biggest, and it's him who passes down the head's orders. I could never take that.

For instance, at meal times we had to sit in groups of seven at oblong tables. There'd be three boys on each side and at one end would sit a senior boy who was the head of the table. The boys on the side were called the 'tops', 'middles' and 'bottoms'. If you were a new boy, you went 'bottom'. Your food was served in big bowls, which the head of the table would dish up. Out of the seven bowls the 'bottoms' were supposed to pick theirs last, but on my first day at St Benedict's I didn't know that. The pudding that day was spotted dick and custard. I just grabbed one and tucked straight in. *Now* I'd broken every rule. After that I had to have a fight with the guy on the head, but he had got there by acting. He couldn't really fight. All right, he shaped up to me as if he was going to give me a beating, so to start with, I stood back because of his reputation. But the way he shaped up, I was able to do him, which surprised me because I thought he was going to be good.

The point of this story is, that once I'd done him, I knew that I'd done the other five, too. They were psychologically defeated. From then on, all those rules about 'tops', 'middles' and 'bottoms' went away on our table because I was not going to stand for it. Some people will stand for it, just as the other five now stood for my insubordination. None of them dared have a go at me. So you do one, you've done six – another lesson that was to come in handy later on.

Then again there was the sexual abuse. Some Catholic brothers were just as bad as the Beast. In later years I'd see their victims in the nick. We called them 'Borstal poofs'. Borstal poofs were kids who couldn't stand up physically, who couldn't go through the system without buckling. Most boys would evolve through it, they'd gain some inner strength to survive, but these kids would become poofs because they needed someone to look after them. On the outside they'd become heterosexual adults and would probably get married and have kids, but if they were reconvicted and sent to prison they would become poofs again. Rather than stick up for themselves they would submit to sexual humiliation because they were frightened of everybody. Sick people.

In the nick you might use these guys as 'gofers'. You don't beat them up because only people lower down the criminal pecking order beat up molesters in jail. Everybody likes to have somebody lower than himself, and the molester is the lowest of the low. In prison anyone can pick on him, but I found that the cons who screamed the loudest and made the most fuss about these people had something similar to hide themselves. That's why they were making such a fuss.

The other thing that I couldn't stand at St Benedict's was the teaching. There was one brother who took a dislike to me. Now some of these kids he was having to teach were really dim, they couldn't write their name, or count, or anything. They came from Liverpool, Manchester, not just London, and they were not up to understanding whether this brother was talking sense or nonsense.

One day he's rabbiting on with these proverbs. To me they contradict each other. Then the bell goes and we're all standing up, and there's a nice little hush, and I say, 'Wise men make proverbs, only fools repeat them.' This brother goes livid! And he punches me! Now, if he'd been an intelligent man, he could have said, 'That's a proverb itself.' End of story. He could have smiled and walked away, but, no, he couldn't handle it. Once he'd punched me, I didn't say, 'Ooh, I've done something wrong again,' because I knew I hadn't done anything wrong. I just looked at him and thought, The man's an idiot. I was getting set to sort him out because he used to call us 'street Arabs'. He was just a violent psycho.

Believe it or not, I did eventually get a bit of official status at St Benedict's. In the school there were four houses, each named after a patron saint: Patrick, Andrew, George and David. There were 50 guys in each house, and as time went on, you came up through the bullying. The older boys would leave for the army or whatever, until you become the senior. That's how I wound up in charge of Andrew House, so even the brothers must have seen some good in me – or was it just that by then I was bigger and stronger than anyone else?

Whenever I got back to Bow, of course, it was business as usual. I did the kind of thing that's always recommended for keeping young chaps off the street, a little bit of club boxing, but I was never really into it. I used to cheat at training. It was just something to do, a bit of interest. But Friday and Saturday night it was guaranteed we'd have a fight on the streets. We'd go out looking for a fight. Terrible. By the time we were seventeen we were bad people. They talk about teenagers today but we were nuisances. Flash bastards.

We'd run into other guys with their girlfriends. Now a man who goes out all dressed up for a Saturday night out with his girlfriend doesn't necessarily want to take his coat off and fight, but with me he wouldn't get a chance to take his coat off. There was none of that 'come outside' business, it was done there and then. No 'gentleman' about it. The main difference then was that you didn't carry a tool. You didn't go out with a knife or hammer. You went out, and you had what they called a 'straightener'. Sometimes there'd be no kicking, just a straight fight. And, gradually, the more fights you won, the more you came to be noticed.

There's other little things. You would realize how easy it is to get money off people. Somebody's frightened of you, and you just mention to them that you happen to be skint, and they'll give you a fiver. Ah! you think to yourself, That's a good idea. So the next time you go into them for a tenner, and it develops from there. Or you want to borrow their car or nick their bird – all different things. Once you know you've got the beating of the man you take liberties.

On our manor there were little cafes and clubs dotted around. We would just go in and take these places over, and we wound up getting our dinner for free. These were the sort of things that prepare you for the protection game. Not that we ever protected anybody. We just demanded money off someone who had money and who was weaker than us. This was straight extortion, although we didn't use that term. We were just bully boys who went into places, and if the people were frightened and took a step backwards, then we would press our case.

We never preyed on honest, straight people because normally they would just pick up the phone and call the police. That has to be the end of it. But it's entirely different with someone who's a bit shifty anyway, who's up to something illegal. You might not even know *what* he's up to, but he's up to something, otherwise he wouldn't stand for you. That kind of guy just gives you your dinner every day, whenever you feel like it.

To me this was nothing unusual, it was a normal way of life. That's how we lived in those days. We could get away with it, but some people couldn't. Some people would walk in a cafe and say, 'I want a dinner,' and the cafe owner would laugh and say, 'Piss off.' That's the end of it. But if we walked into the same place, we'd just sit down, and dinner would be on the table in no time.

Compared with this easy, parasitical existence, I couldn't see that going straight had much to recommend it. To me the prime example of going straight was my stepfather, John Barry. When I was a nipper and he was in the army, he hadn't been about much. When he was demobbed, I used to wear his demob jackets at school. By then he was working in an iron foundry. Twelve hours a day, six days a week, for £12 a week. I used to look at him and think, What a way to live! Somehow our family scraped by on the money, but I thought this was a measly reward for so much work.

When I was seventeen it was time for me to have a talk with him. I was still using his surname. At all my schools I'd been known as Barry, although I'd used both Barry and Donoghue to try and fox the police. Now I had to tell him that, as I was the only male Donoghue left in our family, I was going to take that name. He was a very decent fellow and was quite OK about it. Then he said, 'What are you going to do for a living? Are you coming to work in the foundry?' I said, 'I'm not going to work in the foundry either. I'm going to get it my own way.' And that was the end of the discussion. He was a totally straight guy, but I wasn't.

In my last few terms at St Benedict's I calmed down and behaved myself. All I was looking to do now was cruise through without rocking the boat until I could get out. Every male still had to do conscription – military national service – so I knew that when I reached eighteen I would be leaving straight for the forces unless I did something really bad. In that case I'd be sent to a Borstal, the next stage in the system for young criminals. I couldn't face that. I'd had enough of penal institutions. I was ready to see a bit of the world.

2: FROM THE NAVY TO THE 'VILLE

It was now time for my army medical. If I passed, I would be given ten days' grace to choose a regiment, but I had a diseased bone in my ankle, which could not be operated on until I'd stopped growing. Years before, the surgeons at St Andrews Hospital in Bow had decided to deal with it when I was eighteen, so now they told me the operation would be done in a few weeks. This didn't impress the army, which refused to delay its medical. Their doctors took one look at my foot, gave me a 'grade 4' and deemed me unfit for military service.

In the meantime, during my last few weeks at St Benedict's and despite my best efforts, I had got into more trouble. Borstal was now looming ever nearer, especially as I had been rejected by the army. Then I overheard a mate of mine talking to his probation officer who was offering to recommend him for the merchant navy. I chipped in and asked the man to help me too. He said, 'I've got nothing to do with you, but you can go round all the offices of the shipping companies and ask if they have any jobs.'

That seemed a good idea, but I still had to go into St Andrews for my operation. It was successful, but the hospital couldn't guarantee it for more than five years and gave me a green card to say I was an invalid. This slaughtered my hopes of getting into the merchant navy, but, despite the foot, I went up to Union Castle's offices and said I wanted to sign on. I went before some committee, which asked me why I wanted to join. I said that my grandfather was still serving in the merchant navy (which he was), and my father had been in it too. I said I wanted to follow in their footsteps, but I wasn't joining for the glamour because I knew it was hard work. They seemed satisfied and sent me straight in for one of their medicals. I came back A1 – within ten weeks of the operation – so they said, 'Right: go home, pack your kit and be on the *Bloemfontein Castle*, King George V Dock, Canning Town, by eleven o'clock tonight.'

Bang! I was on a round trip to South Africa. I didn't even see my mother. I went home, she was out, so I just packed my kit and sailed away. The next time I saw her it was nine weeks later. She said, 'Where have you been, beJasus?' You see, before I left I had told my brothers where I was going, but they hadn't bothered to tell her. So she'd thought I must have been off on one of my trips to the nick.

I stayed in the merchant navy for two and a half years. I started as a UDH – 'utility deck hand' – which meant I was a deck labourer. I was matched off with a seaman, learning knots and other naval skills, and I wound up as an EDH – 'efficient deck hand'. By then I was looking to get out from the service. In August 1956 I paid off a ship in Dublin, a Shell tanker called the *SS Patella*. I had three days in Ireland, then I came back home. I was thinking of joining the Norwegian navy, which paid twice the money, because life at sea was suiting me fine, when something happened to change my mind.

I had been invited to the wedding of a friend of mine called Michael. During the reception I caught sight of a pretty young blonde who turned out to be just seventeen. When a selected few of us carried on the celebrations at a house, I found out the young lady's name. I asked her for a dance, we had a nice chat, and then I heard she'd been asking who I was. When she was told I was a sailor home from the sea, I must have seemed more exciting than if she had met me hanging round a street corner in Bow. We just clicked, and soon we were doing the usual things, going to the cinema and local dances, and it grew from there. She knew from the start that I was a tearaway. Perhaps this intrigued her, perhaps she thought I'd grow out of it. Either way, now I'd met this lady I didn't want to go back in the merchant navy. I was twenty-one, I wanted to stay in

London and, in a year or two, set up home. But how was I to earn a living? I tried a few straight jobs, but they were too much like hard work. Then I tried a 'job' of a different kind.

Although I'd been at sea for three years, the family had never moved out of Bow so I knew all the local villains, the 'chaps'. One day some of them approached me about going on a job. It was a robbery. I went on it, we broke open a safe, and it was a good earner. Then when the money was running out, it became a question of looking for something else. Now I was getting known as a 'game 'un' – someone who didn't mind 'going to work' – and I'd be invited to work with different firms. It could be 'on the pavement' – a street robbery – or it could mean going inside some premises, whatever. But, all the time, your bloody reputation is building up behind you. You become known as '*that* person' – not what you intended to be or what you'd like to be – you become known as a 'right good grafter'.

Now I started getting in with some of the big boys. We robbed a few banks and payrolls. The payroll team I used to work with consisted of people who had each created a reputation. One guy might come from the other side of London, but somebody local has been in the nick with him. He'll say, 'My mate Harry's good on the payment,' or 'He can open a safe,' or 'He can drive like Stirling Moss.' Each person gets word-of-mouth recommendation, you form the team, and then it's chemistry: you either get on with this person or you don't; you work with him or you don't.

You didn't take guns. You didn't need them. In those days a gun would have been counter-productive because the public were not educated to fear firearms as they are today. You must have read stories where little old ladies in post offices used to throw ink pots at guys with guns, because they didn't realize how dangerous a gun – or the person who's carrying the gun – can be. People just thought, This is an outrageous thug coming in to rob me. But if you ran up to a guy with a stick, it was different. He knew how much damage you could do him, and he wouldn't take risks. A stick was all you needed. So you would 'stick' people or threaten to 'stick' them, and that was it. Time up! Never a gun.

To get with the big boys, you had to have a certain code. This was something you learnt, it was part of your criminal upbringing. The code was, you didn't take liberties. If you took liberties, you didn't get that far. You were stopped along the line. Your education would cease, and that's where you'd stay, or you became staunch. Throughout your career you've been known to be a 'stand-up merchant': you don't speak to policemen, and nobody's had any funny results when they've been working with you. You have a criminal record, but, on the other side of the fence, you've got a clean record! With that, you can go as far as you like. In different circumstances I could have gone as far as I liked. Today I could have been sitting on the Costa del Sol. But, of course, my career was to come to a sudden halt at the end of the 1960s.

We weren't just doing robberies. We'd try anything. One Derby Day a mate knocked at my door and told me that three carloads of our chaps were going down to Epsom to take on a hood called Caney. He was a champion bare-knuckle fighter, and on Derby Day he and his gang planned to mug the 'pikeys' – the gypsies – at their camp on Epsom Downs. Well away from the course and barred to straight racegoers, the gypsies would run unlicensed fights in an open ring. There'd be prize money and a lot of gambling.

Caney had pulled this trick off at other race meetings. He himself would take on all comers to win the boxing prize. But if he looked like getting beaten, he'd still get the money because his gang would form a ring round the gypsies, steam in, beat them up and steal both the prize and the gambling kitty. This would add up to £1000, which was a huge sum in those days – equivalent to near £20,000 today. This particular day our scheme was to humiliate Caney. We were going to 'ring' his boys, do them and take the money ourselves! But when we got there, Caney must have heard we were around, because he didn't show. As for the pikeys, they told us nothing and kept a firm grip on the kitty. OK, that day we didn't make any money, but we'd proved our ascendancy over Caney, and we made sure that by the evening the story that he was scared stiff of us was all round the East End. No one was frightened of him any more.

We earned a bit of money as bookmakers ourselves. Harry Abrahams, Bunny Harris and me would often spend weekends at point-to-point races. We worked under a bookmaker's licence held by old George Mizel, the Hatton Garden jewel fence. We would go whenever there was a meeting and stand on a couple of boxes beside a post with Mizel's name on it and a board to write the odds on. This simple erection was called a bookmaker's 'joint', but although we could have put it up ourselves in seconds, we had to pay someone else for the service, just as we had to pay for the chalk and even the water to wipe the board clean between races. A guy would come round with a can, and you had to pay him. You weren't allowed to bring your own water!

This operation was all under the control of Albert Dimes, the Soho gangster who was known as the 'King of the Points'. Everybody in gambling knew 'Italian Albert', he had a lot of style and finesse about him – and even a lot of straight people knew he was a leading figure in London's underworld – yet there was nothing 'under' about this game. It was all out in the open and had even been okayed by the stewards, who were wonderful landed-gentry types. Here were some of the highest in the land in bed with the lowest!

Usually Dimes himself would be on the course, in action controlling the prices. Let's say he made the odds on the favourite 6–4, whereas previously it was 2–1, then his man Bobby Warren would come down the line, and you all had to change to 6–4. Bobby Warren was a heavy guy himself. He had been jailed for taking part in the ferocious knife attack on Jack Spot, another top gangster, in 1956. That was in revenge for Spot pulling a knife on Albert in the notorious battle of Frith Street in Soho. Mad Frankie Fraser was jailed along with Warren for cutting up Spot. When Fraser came out of jail a few years later for one of his short spells at liberty he was one south London face I'd be opposing on behalf of the Kray Twins.

THE ENFORCER

It was in connection with this racing game that I had my first experience of the Twins. While we were busy on the joint – doing the clerking, writing the odds and giving the spiel – another set of twins called the Browns used to come round rattling a tin for the 'Aways' – meaning, our criminal brethren currently locked away in jail. These Browns were tied in with the Dimes team and thought they could milk us, but one day we got pissed off, and we said, 'What's all this Aways business? My mate's just come out of the nick. He was away. He never got anything!'

So they started growling, but they could see me standing on the box with my hand in a bag. And I'm looking down at these two little guys, ready to pull out a hammer and give them a whack. But, as I found out later, you've always got to watch out with twins because they're used to working instinctively as a team. It's like having to watch two dogs instead of one. On this occasion the Browns could see we meant business, so they slunk off threatening, 'You'll hear about this!'

When we got back to the East End we had a word with George Mizel. Next thing there was a meet between the Dimes camp and Mizel's protectors, who happened to be the Kray Twins. This fact was conveyed to the Browns, who were told not to approach us for money any more. In return we would give them no problems.

I still had not met any of the Kray brothers, but the rising reputation of our payroll team in Bow had reached their ears. They knew Harry Abrahams – he used to work as a barman in their Double R club – but it wasn't our payroll jobs that caught their attention so much as our readiness to have a fight. They knew that there were eight or ten of us who didn't mind having a row, and now we were on a par with all the local top nuts. That's how you climb. Each time you do something, you get a different classification. Going up and up (or down and down, if you look at all this as a straight person) until you hit the big one.

One of our spectacular stunts was beating up the teddy boys.

They thought they were tough, so we used to show them how 'un-tough' they were. One night I pulled the so-called King of the Teddy Boys, whose name happened to be Curly King. I caught him bullying some old guy at a pie stall. Curly was with two or three supporters, and they picked on this ex-serviceman who still had his demob clothes on. He was obviously down on his luck, and you could see the man had suffered. He was standing there on his own, all quiet, and they picked on him. So I said, 'Oi! Why don't you leave him alone?' So Curly King said, 'Do you know who I am?' and I said, 'Yeah, I know who you are.'

If I'd have said, 'No,' he'd have come on strong at that point and threatened to do me, but now I've faced him down. He didn't dare come at me. This grand 'King of the Teddy Boys' has been made to back off. Now his cronies will spread this story throughout the East End. It will be embroidered. It will build and build. This way several episodes pile up, they will all combine until suddenly people are saying, 'Oh! You're so-and-so, the guy who did Curly, yeah, I remember.' And that's it! You're in the picture, in the frame. And, as soon as your reputation reaches a certain level, the Other Two – as the Kray Twins were called – get to hear of it, and they start showing a bit of interest. At the same time I was picking up a lot of info on the Twins, through a family coincidence.

In 1958 that pretty young blonde and I had moved in together. Our courtship was a bit like *Love on the Dole* or *Up the Junction*. We'd met at a wedding, but we would never get married, not even in a civil ceremony. In the East End in those days a formal marriage was the expected thing, whether you were Catholic or Protestant, as she was. At first we had intended to wed, but I always thought that I was going to do a lot of bird, that I'd be spending much of my life in prison. Even when I'd just come home from over two years 'going straight' at sea, I guessed I would soon become an active villain again. And when you go on the pavement and do robberies, anything can happen. Will a pack of coppers suddenly appear on the scene? Will anyone on either side get shot? If it wasn't going to be death, it was certain to be jail, as any villain with the slightest common sense knows, and I didn't think any marriage could survive the stress of the husband being locked up for years on end.

Instead we became man and wife in common law, which these days amounts to the same thing as a formal marriage. In 1961 she would give birth to our first child, a daughter. So where do the Krays come in? Well, by now, my wife's sister had married a guy called Bill (he was the brother of Michael at whose wedding my wife and I had met). Bill was teamed up with a guy called Charlie Cook. Together they were two of the toughest street fighters in the East End, but around this time the Kray Twins beat them both badly and cut them up in the Coach and Horses in Mile End. They were packed off to hospital, where the Twins sent someone in to ask, 'What do you want to do about this?' Charlie Cook was all for nicking them, but Bill said, 'Nah, leave it off. I'll see them when I get out.'

Despite this brutal encounter, Bill soon became a full member of the Kray Firm, so he was my 'in' to the Twins as early as 1958. Through him I knew they were well at it, levying money off other criminals and operating protection rackets. I also knew they were into counterfeit currency. This was when there were white fivers about. At today's prices each fiver would be worth £100. One day we were given a batch of forged white fivers, so we used one to pay for some petrol at a garage. In those days you had to sign the back of the note with your name and address. What we didn't know was that the guy at the garage took the registration number of our car as well.

When this guy found out the fiver was forged he called the police. They checked the car number and discovered that this old Standard belonged to Reggie Kray. My brother-in-law Bill had borrowed it from Reggie! This must have excited the police, because it certainly upset Reggie, who told Bill we had to come forward and say we were the guys in the car. Then we got called up to Ilford police station to go on an identity parade. We knew the form, so we took along a dozen East End mates of various sizes to stand on the parade alongside us. They weren't involved in this crime, but they looked as rough as we did, all broken-nosed thugs. Making up our own ID parade was allowed at the time. We didn't get picked out, but we each had to make a statement. Mine said, 'I passed the note unknowingly. I must have received it among my winnings at the dog-track.' Now the police couldn't do anything. To nick you, they had to catch you with at least two forged notes, but this was weeks later, and we'd got rid of them all. So no charges. We were away. It was over, except that this was my first direct brush with any member of the Kray family. I was now half-involved with what would become the most notorious crime gang in British history.

During the next few years I'd occasionally bump into the Twins. It must have been 1961 when I met Ronnie at Esmeralda's Barn, the Knightsbridge casino that they'd taken over, to talk about a man called Stevie Smith who was said to have strung himself up in Wandsworth Prison in suspicious circumstances, while I was in there for three months over a Saturday-night fight. I was struck by Ronnie's belief that he could get some official inquiry set up into this guy's death, when Ronnie himself was already a notorious ex-con with a substantial record. He obviously felt he had friends in high places.

I don't know what he felt about me, but I must have looked quite a useful character. I was a shade over six feet tall, and I'd been as fit as a fiddle ever since I was at sea. At the age of twenty-two. I weighed 12½ stone, and I was ready for anything. What I didn't realize was that, five years later, the forces of law and order would be ready for me and my friends on the payroll gang.

In 1962 we had an inside man at a printing firm in Bow. He told us that the payroll for the whole works was there every Friday morning, in an office three floors up a fire escape. He said that in the lunch hour there were just two stand-by staff on duty, and the safe was usually open because the workers could pop up any time on Fridays to claim their wages.

This sounds good to us except that, to get to this cash office, we have to go 200 yards inside the premises, and we can't take the car in. We have to be on foot, but that doesn't bother us too much because we are all physically fit. So this Friday we go in four-handed, but when we get into the office we find the safe is shut. So we have a little shout and holler to dominate and frighten the people into giving us the keys, but they go into a panic anyway. Next thing we know, lots of workers start pouring in.

We have a pitched battle to get out of the room, and we've still got to get the 200 yards to the street with all these people after us screaming, 'Shut the gate! Shut the gate!' So we join in shouting, 'Shut the gate! Shut the gate!' and nobody knows who's who. This way we manage to get out and away.

I thought I was pretty well clear. I had taken the care to wear a mask, because I lived right next to the place and knew a few people who worked there, but another guy from Hoxton didn't bother with a mask. About three weeks later I was arrested. One of the detectives was a Welshman who decided to play the religious card.

He said, 'You're a Catholic, aren't you?' I said I was brought up as one, so, right in front of me in this police cell with another copper looking on, he got on his knees and pleaded, 'I'm appealing to you, as one Catholic to another, to help me, and I'll help you.' Well, I looked at this, and then I looked at the other copper, and then I looked back at this guy still on his knees, and the bastard was grinning.

Then they put me on an ID parade, but this Welshman told me to get rid of the purple shirt I was wearing because it would make me stand out. I said, 'They'll be looking at my face, not my shirt,' so he said, 'Have it your own way, then!' and I went out on the parade wearing this shirt. Sure enough, the main witness, a woman in the wages office, picked me out. Anyway, I'm remanded to Brixton Prison – put in the 'warehouse' – for eight months. Next thing, I'm on trial. I'm convicted, and I get three years.

I went straight from the Old Bailey to Wandsworth Prison, but I hadn't been there long before my wife was giving birth to our second child, a boy, in Bancroft Hospital. She was in a pretty bad way, and I was worried if she would survive, especially when the prison governor was informed she was in a life-threatening situation. This meant I could be allowed out of prison to visit her. For most of the trip I was handcuffed to a screw, but as we reached the hospital, a big American car came past, and the driver honked the horn at me. The screw got the shakes and undid the cuffs. He thought I was going to escape or get shot. Either way, he didn't want to be anywhere near me. I had no idea who was in that car. All I wanted to do was see the missus and the baby. It turned out they were both in good shape and that the 'life-threatening situation' had been faked, just so I could come and see them.

In prison I wasn't interested in dragging out my sentence by taking on the system. I did not believe it was my duty to beat up screws, like some latter-day heroes of the British criminal scene. My scheme was to get out of my cell and make the days fly by doing whatever jobs were going, especially when I got a transfer to the 'Ville: Pentonville. I couldn't bear sitting there, sewing mailbags, eight stitches to the inch. That does your head in. So as soon as I could, I joined the fire party. Then I got a transfer to work in the prison hospital, initially as a stretcher-bearer.

Working in the hospital had many benefits. I was given my own cell there, with a proper mattress, but I was scarcely locked up in it because I was out working until nine at night. I'd cook the night screw's grub for him, and he always brought a bit extra so I got a decent sandwich for my own supper. Then I took on the job of dental orderly as well. All interesting stuff compared with those bloody mailbags.

Now I was a 'trusty', I wasn't despised by other inmates. Contrary to the impression you get from prison dramas, trusties are often well regarded by hard-nut convicts because they can get hold of all sorts of banned items and even set up smuggling runs. Another factor is that, although the screws trust you because you treat them decently, you keep up your status among the prisoners as a tough guy. You don't take any nonsense, and you sort out troublemakers in the usual physical way. But you do that out of sight, so that the screws still feel you're a good chap.

One of my fellow trusties was Harry MacKenney, the prison barber. He used to come to me for advice on his marital situation. He struck me as a big softie, he was always near to tears. I couldn't believe it later when I read about him turning into a serial contract killer in the 1970s. Even I shiver now when I think that 'Big H' – all six foot six of him – once held a razor round my throat, but with me he was just a pussycat.

From stretcher-bearer in the hospital I was promoted to 'observations': watching to make sure people didn't do silly things like hang themselves. In this job I'd see the court reports that officers and psychiatrists wrote about prisoners, especially ones due for removal to 'special hospitals' – mental jails like Rampton and Broadmoor. I used to go round with the screws carrying a great basket with all the different medicines. We'd go from cell to cell, checking not just on 'nutters' but also on quite sane individuals like epileptics or people with heart conditions. Every day the screw would unlock each man, give him his medication and his razor blade. He would say, 'Good morning, Davey!' but Davey might have had a rough night or received a bad letter, so he'd not be feeling too happy, and he'd just grunt. At this point the screw would write down 'unco-operative' or 'surly'. Now next morning this same Davey might be quite cheery. He'd say, 'All right, Guv'nor, how you doing?' but when the screw got back to his desk, he wouldn't write anything good. He'd write 'truculent' or overexcited'. When I read those things I thought, Whoever reads this is going to get the wrong idea. The magistrate is going to go 'Tut, tut tut! One minute this man is up, the next he's down, manic-depressive, lock him up!' when the guy isn't mad at all. He's just displaying the normal ups-and-downs we all go through.

Even ordinary prisoners have these reports written about them. They are kept throughout your correctional career, and they can be so cold and clinical, they are easily misinterpreted. You can wrongly get a reputation for being anti-authority, which does you no good at all. Reading hundreds of these reports also taught me what a screw would be looking for, if ever he approached me in a certain way. Every time I went to a new nick I'd be interviewed by a top screw, a deputy governor or a psychiatrist. They would ask a lot of questions, but now I knew what answers they wanted, and up to a point I could fake it.

Prison psychiatrists make you do intelligence tests. When I did them I used to score such a high IQ rating that several judges said, 'You could have been a successful businessman.' This was only because I'd been taking these tests all my life, and I knew half the questions. Many took the same basic form: 'If you were in a house with a southerly aspect on all four sides, where would you be?' Obviously, the North Pole! Thinking that way gets you an inflated IQ.

I suppose even the fact that I'd picked up the knack of doing these tests proved I had a certain intelligence, but with some prisoners you could explain a trick answer one day, and the next day you'd ask them the same question, and they'd go 'What?' They'd lost it already. That's why they would stay sewing mailbags, while other people would end up in the library. On such things the authorities build up their picture of you, which marks you throughout your prison life.

So I wasn't going to get branded 'unresponsive'. If I thought a screw had come up with a good suggestion to keep me busy, I would say, 'Yeah, that's a good idea.' I wasn't going to stick in my cell and read silly books. Sitting there being a 'hard con' is nonsense. By me playing a trusted role doing all these jobs, my time's flying. Now I just want to do my time and get out.

Quite soon I was out again. I'd served two years out of the three, and now I was back on the streets of the East End. The time I'd spent inside reading all those psychiatric reports quickly came in handy in another way: I knew what to look out for when I came up against Ronnie and Reggie Kray.

3: A FIRM BEGINNING

In August 1964 I came out of Pentonville. I wasn't in the mood to go straight back in again. My two-year stretch was that much of a deterrent, and I knew I'd get ten years, if I was caught on a robbery again. Not that I was getting any 'job' offers. It was all very quiet, and I was quiet, too, staying at home, getting to know our little girl again and our baby boy for the first time. I was keeping my head down but slowly picking up my connections in Bow.

Then I heard that a runner for the Kray Twins called Limehouse Willey was touring my local pubs like the Black Swan, saying, 'If you see Albert, tell him the Other Two want to see him.' As he'd said this not in a friendly way, making sure that everyone saw his dreadful scar, I decided that rather than wait for Willey to find me, I'd go down into the lions' den on my own and catch the Twins by surprise.

That's why, in October 1964, seven weeks after I'd walked out of jail, I walked into the Crown and Anchor, the Krays' local behind the family home in Vallance Road, Bethnal Green. Sure enough, Ronnie and Reggie Kray were there, along with Uncle Alf and plenty of other faces: Bobby Ramsey, Dukey Osbourne, Billy Maguire. There was a good crowd of Kray familiars, about 15 of them. Then I realized they had been expecting Limehouse Willey to bring me in. Later he said, 'I hope you didn't think I was trying to set you up,' but that's obviously what he had been doing, because when I walked in the Crown somebody said, 'Here he is!'

I was standing at the bar and shook hands with a few old mates. Then they started drifting away. Ater a bit no one would come near me, so I knew something was up. I looked around but realized I couldn't get away without making a bolt for it, so I decided to stick it out. I noticed that one or two people were passing in and out of the back room, and afterwards I realized they must have been waiting for the artillery. Suddenly there was a bang behind me, and I felt a pain in my left leg. I turned round and saw Reggie Kray with an automatic in his hand, and he was pulling the cocking action again.

Strange how, even when I'd just been shot and I could see Reggie getting ready to shoot me again, I was thinking to myself, What a prat! He's got an automatic. Doesn't he know the whole point of an automatic is that you don't have to reload it after each shot? You just keep pulling the trigger.

'What's that? A firework?' said some joker, breaking the silence. Not a bad crack, I thought. It was only a week or two to Guy Fawkes' night, so it could have passed for a firework.

I walked towards Reggie. He was acting as if he thought he had missed and wanted another pop, especially now I was on my feet and going for him. Even in this situation, I knew that the best form of defence is attack. Go forward, because if you're going to get shot, it doesn't matter how far away you are or which side of the room you're on. The only certainty is that you've got to be right on top of somebody to disarm him. So, if there was going to be any more shooting, I'd be there to make sure I had the gun.

But, as I say, twins act instinctively to protect each other. In no time Ronnie Kray had moved from the other end of the bar, stepped up in front of me, grabbed my two arms and brought them down by my sides. It's an old street fighter's technique. He said, 'What's a matter? Your leg hurt?' Then he took me outside and got hold of my arms again: 'What you doing here?'

I said, 'I've only been home two or three weeks, and I come over to see if I could get a few quid off you.' In fact, I had no intention of asking for money, but with Reggie still waving that gun about inside the pub, I had to come up with a good excuse to be there and to say something that would placate Ronnie. I was using a bit of that prison-hospital psychology.

'Are you sure it wasn't something else?' he asked, rubbing his hands over my pockets, giving me a little spin to see if I had a shooter. 'Right. We'll get somebody to take you to the hospital.'

Then Dukey Osbourne came out with another bloke called Bob the Painter, and they took me to Bow with the intention of depositing me at the gates of St Andrews Hospital but as soon as we hit Bow and the Black Swan I said, 'Drop me here,' because I had no intention of going straight to hospital. I wanted to go home and inspect the wound. If the bullet had gone right through, I could patch it up myself. Now, as I wanted to go home, I couldn't allow these henchmen of the man who shot me to take me there, because I didn't want them to know where I lived. Instead they were insisting, 'The Colonel told us to take you to the hospital.'

I said, 'Look! If you don't let me out, I'll do the pair of you.' 'Ooh!' 'It's how you want it!' I said. Now they had their doubts. If we had a big fight at this point, and the police came along and found them tackling a man who's just been shot, they would be in deep trouble in the courts. And they couldn't say that it was Reggie Kray who had shot me, because they would be in deep shit with both the Twins. So they looked at each other, then dropped me and drove away. I watched them go, then I cut through the flats and alleys towards Ashcombe House, the block of council flats off Devons Road, where we were living.

The leg was still good enough for me to reach home, but it was beginning to stiffen up. I told the wife I'd slipped and fallen off the open back platform of a bus, because I was still hoping I could treat the wound myself. Then I took a look at the leg and saw a hole above my ankle. Lower down, right next to the ankle, was the bullet itself. Shit. Now I *had* to go to the hospital. That wasn't a problem as it was only 200 yards from our home, but now I had to tell my wife I'd just had a row with someone who shot me. She took it calmly. It wasn't as if I was an honest citizen suddenly gunned down by total strangers. She knew I was a villain who was always in scrapes and battles. She may even have thought I deserved it.

So off I walked to St Andrews Hospital. When I got there, I saw a lot of police. They were there because a patrol car had knocked an Indian fellow off his bike, and there had to be an internal police investigation, but when they heard why I was there, one copper came over and asked me how I'd been hit. I told them I'd been walking along Bow Common Lane when a car cruised past me, and I was shot. I said I didn't know what it was all about. I also said that, even if I did know, I wouldn't tell him because I had a family to think about.

When the doctor had a look at me, it was clear that I'd have to stay in and have the bullet removed. While I was there I developed jaundice. They were feeding me penicillin streptomycin, and I got a liver reaction, leading to mild non-infectious hepatitis. Then the doctor gave me some good news. He said I could never be a junky because my liver reacted so badly. I was just allergic to the drugs.

The day after the shooting a Detective Sergeant Moorcock from Bow police station came to see me in hospital. I told him the same as I'd told the squad-car men, about being shot from a car. I wasn't revealing anything to any cops but, now I was stuck in hospital for what turned out to be five weeks, I told my wife I expected the mob that shot me to come after me again, so if anybody from that crowd came to the house, she was to let me know immediately.

The first guy to visit me that first night was my brother-in-law Bill. Of course, he knew where I lived, but he wasn't going to tell the Twins. They had contacted him to ask if he would collect my clothes in order to destroy that much of the forensic evidence. I said, 'They can take it, nothing's gonna happen.' He took that message back to them, but they weren't satisfied because soon a man called Bill Ackerman turned up at my home. First he arrives with a bunch of flowers for my wife, but she blanks him. She refuses the flowers and pisses him off: 'I want nothing to do with you. If you want to talk to Albert, go and talk to him. Don't come round to my house, and don't come anywhere near here when my kids are in!'

Then he comes to the hospital and makes a point of telling me, 'I took these to your wife,' which also means, 'Now we know where you live.' I'd already calculated they would find out where I lived because I wasn't low profile in Bow. You could ask anyone there, and they'd tell you where I lived, and the Twins were bound to have sent some little runner round to make inquiries. But by sending in their emissary Ackerman, they were just letting me know that they knew.

So now whoopee! We've got Gangster Bill popping in with a bunch of flowers! Then he delivers the message, not on a get-well note but in so many words: 'The Twins just want to know what are you gonna do.' I said, 'Well, what are they going to do?' He said, 'Well, they'll be satisfied if you're going to leave it alone. They'll probably give you some money later on.'

Money? I thought. Money! For shooting me in the leg? What a nerve! So I told Ackerman, 'Piss off! I'll come and see them when I come out.'

Let him take that message back, I said to myself. I wasn't going to beg, 'Please tell them not to hit me any more.' I wasn't going to show them any fear. In fact I had it in mind to buy a grenade and lob it through the window at Vallance Road. When you're in this position, these things go through your head – until you weigh up everything that would happen as a result: If I did that I probably wouldn't kill the Twins, I'd kill their mum and dad by mistake. Even if I only blew the house to bits, I'd still have to leave Bow. So would Mum and all the brothers. No. It'd all be too much.

A few weeks later I was lying in hospital when my wife sent a telegram saying, 'What you warned me about has happened.' The foot was still wrapped up, and I was limping about, but I discharged myself as soon I'd checked the hepatitis was not infectious and no danger to my kids. I went right home, and she told me how Ackerman had shown up again, in a car, with two Irish girls. They worked for him, but they also knew my wife. He didn't come to the door himself but sent in the girls with some money. The sweetener worked. My wife accepted the money, probably because I hadn't brought in a decent wage since I'd left prison.

With my leg still in plaster, there was no chance of any active work, so I started going down the Wentworth, a dockers' club in Wentworth Mews at the back of Mile End station. This was run by Joe Abrahams, the father of Harry Abrahams who had been my partner on the payroll team, so I felt comfortable sitting there playing cards. One day I went in, and I was told that about half a dozen of the Kray Firm had been there looking for me. Then Bill Ackerman finally caught up with me there. He said, 'The Firm's looking for you: Big Tommy Brown, Johnny Squibb.' So I said, 'Well, you best take me round the house.'

Now he started trembling, 'You can't go round the house!' I said, 'Look! I got my leg in plaster, they know where I live, I can't run, so I might as well go round and see them.' A couple of other guys offered to go there with me but I refused, because if I went in mob-handed, that would look like a declaration of war.

Ackerman was still protesting, but I insisted he take me there straightaway. So he drove round, we got out, he knocked, and Reggie opened the door. Now Ackerman couldn't talk. He was gurgling, 'Oaargh, oaargh!' choking on whatever he was trying to say. Then he scuttled away. He was terrified of violence. He'd browbeat people, slag them off in front of other people, and they would back off. But if a fellow stood up and walked towards him he'd disappear. That's one reason why he was never close to the action.

'Come in,' said Reggie, looking me up and down. He could see I was dressed casually, in a cardigan and an old pair of trousers split to allow for the plaster. I had no overcoat so, clearly, I wasn't hiding a tool this time. He took me in the front room, where we had what, in the circumstances, was a very pleasant chat. I had come mentally prepared for trouble of some sort, because I thought it was going to be 'off' again, but there was no threats. It was an entirely different climate. All three boys were there, Charlie as well as Ronnie and Reggie. The rest of the family were in the back room. Then Ronnie said, 'What do you think about it?' and I said, 'Well, I know the game you're in. If I'd have been in your shoes, I'd have probably done the same.' That was to show there was no animosity on my side. Nothing personal.

Don't get me wrong. There had to be animosity on my side. Under my calm exterior I was furious, hobbling round, my leg still in plaster, and who knows whether Reggie, who was so useless with guns, really did mean to shoot me in the foot. For all I knew, he really might have meant to kill me, but I was prepared to hear him out because, since the shooting, I'd found out how misleading a story they'd been given about my remarks to Lennie Hamilton over two years before. The Twins had been told that when I saw him with the poker marks on his cheeks I'd vowed to blow their heads off, but at that stage he'd never mentioned the Twins so neither had I. At first he'd refused to tell me anything, but the way my remarks had been blown up to them later, they probably thought I'd been sitting in the nick festering for two years, and that I'd walked in the Crown and Anchor, probably with a driver outside, to shoot *them* as I'd vowed. They'd got to think like this. That was their world. So their idea – sensible enough – was to do me first.

It seems Lennie Hamilton had been pokered because he'd had a fight with the son of a strong man called Henry Buller Ward who was on the Kray Firm at the time. Lennie was worried that this would upset the Twins so he phoned them up to square it. He was right. Ronnie was so upset that he wouldn't speak to him, but late that night Ronnie suckered a relative of Hamilton's, an ex-wrestler called Andy Paul who was with the Krays, into bringing Hamilton to Esmeralda's Barn, the Krays' casino. When Hamilton arrived he saw Ronnie waiting for him. He tried to escape, but he was taken into the kitchen and tied up in a chair while Ronnie applied the red hot steel to his cheeks, burnt off part of his hair and almost burnt one of his eyes out. Then they dumped him back home where we had found him late that Sunday night.

There's no point in trying to understand the justice in this punishment. There was no justice, just as poor old Lennie had committed no crime. It was simply the Twins' way of asserting their authority over everyone who heard of this branding. Discipline by example. Burn one, frighten a thousand. Kill one admiral to encourage the others.

The same lesson would have been learnt by all the bystanders at my shooting, but now as we sat in their parlour, the Krays could see I was what the Yanks call a 'stand-up guy'. I'd swallowed the shooting, I hadn't gone to the police, and now I'd walked right and fronted them. According to their logic, I'd shown I was a man. Seeing as I'd behaved myself Ronnie said to me, 'No good worrying about this now. It's over. How would you like to come and get your money with us? Forget the robbery game, no more bank jobs, that's for jailbirds. When your leg's out of plaster, we'll put you on a pension. In the meantime, just get fit.'

That's it. I'm now on the Firm. It was all smiles, and Charlie shook hands with me. For me I could see a lot of benefits ahead: money, high status in the underworld and far less risk of getting nicked. I knew that much of the Twins' money came from protection, which, in some circumstances, is scarcely crime at all. Otherwise I really didn't know how they made their bread. I only found that out later.

I could see why the Twins wanted me on board, but how could they be sure of my loyalty? Reggie had only just shot me, and most people – bent as well as straight – would think that shooting someone is a crazy way to recruit him to your gang. What's to stop that person biding his time and doing the same to you, or betraying you some day to the police?

Such thoughts never seemed to cross the Twins' minds. Strange as it seems, this was their normal method of initiation. I know half a dozen people who were recruited in a similar way, including my brother-in-law Bill. The same thing happened to him, only worse: he was cut to pieces and nearly lost an eye. There was Lennie Hamilton himself. Despite his branding, even he signed on with the Twins. Nine times out of ten, people on the real, inner Firm – not fringe folk like the Lambrianou brothers – had first had a ruck with the Twins, they'd come unstuck but had stood up to the punishment. Only then were they made full members of the Firm.

Any logical reading of human nature will tell you that, in the long run, this is a mad way to hire thugs. But, of course, the Twins were mad. And, in some respects, there was method in their madness. Most of the time they were looking for good all-round hoodlums, not weak-willed hangers-on. When they were on a recruitment drive, the first thing they wanted to know was, were you good with your fists? If you could fight, this was a good sign that you might be some use to their criminal organization.

They'd also go for people with a reputation in one of the local manors. You could be from Hackney, Bethnal Green, Poplar, Bow or wherever, but once the Twins knew you were the main man, if it suited them, they would take you to pieces in your local pub or club, to see how you reacted. If they heard you wanted to call the police, they would not even try to recruit you. You'd just be done over a few more times until you were no threat.

Once you were done, you were theirs for life. That was their idea. Like breaking in a horse. The beating or shooting was their way of giving a message. Then you had the choice: go to the police, or do something about it – come at them! – but if you chose to do neither, OK! That's it! Forget it. End of! They're thinking, you hadn't gone to the police despite a serious injury – and you haven't tried to shoot their heads off – so you must be a staunch fellow.

When my leg was out of plaster, and I had fully recovered, I took my place among the 'chaps'. I soon got to know the Firm's exact strength. At the top, of course, were the three Krays. There was the Twins' older brother, Charlie, who was more on the business side. He had a good appearance, and he could talk. He wasn't spivvy, and he had a bit of charm so he would meet respectable types. He could handle all that side. When he was among us Eastenders, at the day club in the Regency, he had a bit of a gangster's swagger, but when he was sent to meet half-straight business types in West End hotels, then he would put on his educated style. I think he was a lot brighter than the Twins. He took little part in the day-to-day running of the Firm, but he knew what was going on.

Then there were the Twins. Reggie was five foot nine, well-built but slighter than Ronnie, who was two stone heavier and carried himself to suit the weight. Reggie was more agile, fit and athletic. He'd march with you, and when we'd go for a breath of fresh air in Victoria Park, he would break into a boxer's training run and start sparring. Ronnie used to amble along, but if he had to step out and get a move-on, he would strut. He was bordering on fat and was getting a bit soft and jowly, whereas Reggie remained tight and hard throughout my time with them.

On the Firm I soon became known as Reggie's man, 'Big Albert'. Whenever he wanted a henchman, bodyguard or just company, I'd go with him. Then there was 'Scotch' Ian Barrie. He was known as Ronnie's man. Then both Ian and I were partnered off again. My partner was Ronnie Hart, a distant cousin of the Twins. Ian's partner was Scotch Jack Dickson. Then we had a few loose muscle guys like Ronnie Bender and Big Tommy Brown. If we had to put on a show of strength – go in plenty-handed – these were some of the people we could call on, but they weren't actually members of the Firm.

We were all thugs with scarcely any education, and only some of us had any common sense. Consequently there had to be an executive side to the organization, consisting of Little Tommy Cowley and above all a very bright, educated and funny man called Leslie Payne who, to my regret, fell out of favour at the court of the Twins not long after I joined.

The Firm was run a bit like a conventional business. Every morning at nine o'clock we used to have a meeting at Vallance Road to discuss what we were going to do for the rest of the day: who to visit, who to use, who to take, who was going to drive. And then we would pick up all these friends and put them to work. At the meeting we would also discuss any information we'd got from the night before.

This was where the Twins got a hefty return on all the little pay-offs they had made to people when they were in jail or when they came out. Just as I had told Ronnie I had come to the Crown and Anchor to get a few quid off them, most of London's professional criminals knew that, whoever you were, you could come straight out of the nick, and the Twins would help you with a small 'casher'. This wasn't charity. All these guys were required to pay the money back in kind – with information.

The Twins would just say to each one, 'Where are you?' and the guy would say, 'I'm in Paddington,' or 'I'm in Fulham,' or wherever. So they would say, 'Well, if you hear anything in Paddington, let us know.' For Ronnie and Reggie the return on all these hand-outs over the years was a vast network of informers. Anywhere in London, anything that went off, we knew more or less within an hour who was involved, how much they'd got and where they lived. Everything.

So at the morning meeting the discussion might start with the Other Two saying, 'We heard that so-and-so went off last night. It's a little team out of Hackney, it's got about that they're selling the stuff today, and they're going to get five or six grand for their whack. Running this team is "Charlie Brown". Now this Charlie owes us a favour, so pop round and see him. Tell him to come and see us, or get a bit of dough off him.' So we'd ask the Twins, 'What sort of dough you talking?' and they would say they'd want a 'monkey' – £500 – or a thousand off this Charlie.

That would be a one-off payment. We're not going to go back next week for more. That's it: you just go and collect the money. Or, if you don't collect, you report back. If he says, 'I'm not going to give you any money,' you don't jump all over him there and then. You come back to the Twins and you say, 'He's not going to pay.'

THE ENFORCER

'Ah!' Now that'll be the start of a different mission. You get three or four guys, and you go and sit on his house or the pub or club where he drinks, and you give him a talking-to. You send him to hospital for a couple of days and then you talk to him again.

This was the everyday work of the Firm. Most of the people who've written and spoken about the Firm discuss the three known murders – Cornell, Jack 'the Hat' and Mitchell – but the Firm's main work was hustling day-to-day, night after night.

Usually there was a big agenda to get through at the nine o'clock meets – who had heard what, who'd done this – but if it was a thin day, and there was nothing on, then the Twins would have a bet between themselves. 'All right,' Reggie would say, 'we'll go out, me and Albert, and so will Ronnie and Ian, and I bet you a tenner we get more dough than you.' 'Right, OK.' And off we'd go, and we'd blag whoever we could think of. Then we'd come back and compare what kind of money we'd come up with.

It was easy to pick up £1000. £500, that was normal. We'd be blagging off people like budding promoters, crooked bookmakers, geezers who had spiels, people who had clubs. You always got the money under the guise of a loan that was going to come back later – 'Guaranteed,' we'd say – but they would never see it again, and in their hearts they knew it.

Soon it became clear to me that the Twins operated within a series of circles, each trusted with a different degree of confidence. The regular inner crowd would meet at nine, but anyone else would be invited in only to discuss the specific business the Twins had in mind for them. After the meeting most people would drift away. There might be just one or two of us left, and that's when you would get some nitty-gritty. The Twins would say, 'We don't trust this one,' or 'Keep an eye on so-and-so.' They'd tell us who to pay, who not to pay, who was 'in' at the time, who was in favour and who was out and in deep, deep trouble with the Brothers Kray.

Fairly early on I realized they would discuss certain things with me that they wouldn't discuss with others. This may not prove I was a special confidant – it was partly 'divide and rule' – but certainly Reggie did a lot of his confidential business with only me present. I was always with him, alone, when he went on his business meets. I looked the part – big, fit and menacing – but I was always far more than a bodyguard. It's clear that the Twins instantly felt able to trust me with big sums of money. Within days of joining the Firm, I was their main collector of protection pay-offs, not just in the East End but in the rich pastures of the West End too.

One Friday early in 1965 Ronnie Kray and Big Tommy Brown – 'Brownie the Bear' – took me on a taxi tour of the West End. We went to all the different clubs where the Twins were getting paid off, and in each place I was introduced to the characters who did the paying. First he introduced me to Frannie Daniels at the Mount Club in Mount Street, a good upper-class spieler. Ronnie told Frannie, 'This is Albert. He'll be coming round to see you from now on.' He memorized my face, and every Friday after I used to go up West alone at dinner time – or lunch time, as they called it in these places – and see a woman called Bette. Funny how things stick in your mind: I remember she had a poodle dog. She'd give me an envelope with £40 in it.

Then Ronnie introduced me to Joe Dagle, Pauline Wallace's partner at the New Casanova. He told Joe I was now the collector. After that I called on Joe every Friday to pick up £50. The exchanges weren't menacing. It would be, 'Morning! Happy Day! Raining out!' There was no money counted out, I'd just collect the envelope, nobody begrudging it because this was already a recognized routine. All I did was take over the existing round. Joe Dagle was a white-haired man in his sixties. He had a little flat at the top of the club. I'd go up there, have a coffee with him; he'd be having his toast and marmalade, reading the *Sporting Life*. We'd discuss the weather. And there's the envelope, just like that. When we'd finished talking, I'd say, 'Right, see you later! Back next week.' Gone. I'd be off to collect from another place, the Grosvenor.

I never made any threats. I just picked up the money. Any heavy business had been done well before I arrived on the scene, but even then it would not have involved direct violence. You never threatened people or smashed the place up. You'd say, 'Look, you're opening the gaff, and we're looking after it. So where do we come in?' Then the club owner would offer, say, £50, and there'd be a bit of haggling until an agreement was struck. In a lot of cases club owners would have come to a nine o'clock meet to ask the Twins to look after the places, so there had always been prior negotiation before I turned up for the envelope.

Making all these collections became my regular Friday job. We used to call it the 'Milk Round'. I would get up, skip the nine o'clock meet and get to the West End, often by public transport. First I'd do one casino, where I would go upstairs, drink a cup of coffee with the old boy there and have a friendly chat. There was no ''Ere, give us the dough!' – none of that business. I would just collect an envelope from him, then pop on to the Mount Club. I'd do two or three other places, then it would be back down the East End, to do all the 'little piss-holes' as I called the gambling clubs under the Twins' protection. From each spieler I'd collect tens or twenties.

I used to go to the Little Dragon, up an alleyway off Whitechapel Road, to collect a tenner from Dutchy Sam. Then I'd go to Dodger's. His real name was Silvers, and he owned the Twentieth Century Club in Brick Lane on the corner of Fashion Street. Either Dodger or his runner Boris would give me £15. Then I'd go to Benny the Cabdriver's. His club was above a women's dress shop, pretentiously called a 'costumier', in Commercial Road. Benny gave me just £15. This was a good deal for him, because most of his patrons were his old mates from his days as a black taxi driver. These guys were compulsive gamblers who would do a few hours' work, lose all their takings playing kalooki, then they'd go out and drive for a few more hours, and come back and gamble it all away again.

I would always do the Milk Round on my own. In his book Tony Lambrianou says he accompanied me on a round and watched me pick up forty envelopes. I would have looked like a bloody postman with forty envelopes in my pocket, but that never happened! I never took anyone with me, certainly not Lambrianou.

The idea of one man doing it was so that you didn't expose the Twins' business. If I'd have taken anyone on the Milk Round, we'd have shown out. When I had to go to the West End, either I went by public transport, or I took a separate cab to each location. I couldn't even take one of our own drivers along because they would learn my rounds. Then they could inform on me and the Twins, either to other criminal gangs or to the police. That was a risk we just couldn't take.

None of the people who were paying us would go to the police themselves, partly because we were giving them a genuine service. If they hadn't paid us – so we would be on call with instant muscle if ever they had trouble – they would surely have had trouble from some other mob. The mere fact that they could spread the word that we were protecting them was enough to frighten off every other mob in town.

I know this because sometimes people would come directly to me to get other people who were demanding money off their backs. I would tell a victim to tell each troublemaker, 'Albert says, "If you don't behave yourself, then I'm to pop round and see him".' This way there was no threat of violence, yet the troublemaker knows he must lay off the guy. But now this victim is indebted to me for the service I've performed, so he's got to come up with money for me instead. He knew he would have to do this – that was understood right from the start – only he's doing it willingly. Such a man would now become my private business, nothing to do with the Twins.

We never touched totally straight pubs or bookmakers, because publicans and bookies have to hold a licence so they're usually pretty clean. If you go into them for dough, all they've got to do is to call the police. You've got no chance. When we did have an arrangement with a bookmaker it was a side deal, away from his shop, for something the Twins had done in the past. We only collected off crooked people, or off people who were dealing with crooked people. That left us with plenty of opportunities, because right through the 1960s there were dozens of pubs and bookies all over London with clean licensees as front-men, but where the true owners were convicted villains. These people fully understood the language the Krays were speaking.

Today the sums I was collecting may not sound large, and they weren't colossal even then, but a tenner in the 1960s would be worth, say, £150 today. So as my total weekly collection was around £200, it's as if today I'm walking round with £3000 cash in my pocket every Friday.

Being trusted to hold that amount of cash soon led to the Twins giving me the job of handing out the wages to the rest of the Firm. I would bring all the money back to Ronnie, and he would say, 'Right, give so-and-so 15 quid, give so-and-so a tenner, give so-and-so a score.' That was the wages, the 'pensions'. Nobody else got anything, only those individuals the Twins told me to pay.

There weren't many of us on the payroll: myself, Ronnie Hart, Ian Barrie, Scotch Jack Dickson, a stocky torpedo called Cornelius 'Connie' Whitehead and Ronnie Bender sometimes. We were the 'pensioners'. If somebody else did anything requiring payment or expenses, they dealt with Ronnie or Reggie direct. Tony Lambrianou would only get paid occasionally, if, say, he was sent up West on a job. He was not on a pension because he was not on the Firm. I know. I paid out the wages.

My own 'pension' was £25 a week, but Reggie would give me 10 per cent of any other business we put together, so that would bring me in another £50. So I was picking up £75 a week in all from the Firm in those days. That's around £1200 today – tax-free of course. All this only a year after coming out of jail. And the figure doesn't include various private deals I was building up on the side.

On the Firm nobody trusted anybody, but I was the person the Twins trusted most. I could be relied on both to collect the money and to steer clear of betting shops, where others might lose it all. I wouldn't play a game of cards with it. I would do whatever job the money was for, and the Twins got everything that was left. Another good reason for making me the Firm's paymaster was because I could count. There were some real thickos among us who just couldn't add up. Some had more severe disabilities. Once Ronnie Kray bought a Christmas Tree and a set of fairylights, and I watched as Ronnie Bender tried to set up the lights circuit. It was so simple, basic school-science stuff, but he couldn't manage it. I thought he was going to electrocute himself.

The Twins would try each person on various jobs, then if they wanted someone to perform a particular task, they'd say, 'Oh, Albert's capable of doing it.' I did anything I was asked to do, so they came to rely on me. On that basis I got a lot of additional work. They would loan me out, on contract you might say, to friends or allies who were a bit short-handed or who genuinely needed protection.

One such man was my old bookmaking boss, George Mizel, under whose board I had worked, years before, at the point-to-points. He had a 24-hour spieler called the Green Dragon, in the same alleyway as the Little Dragon, off Whitechapel Road. Now, when I was having time off from the Firm, I used to go there privately to play cards and relax. One night I was in there with Georgie and his wife – a real Jewish mama who also liked a good game – when in came this guy, effing and blinding. He was a docker, a Saturday-night drunk, who'd come straight out of a pub into the Dragon. So I said to him, 'Listen! We're having a quiet game of cards. Stop swearing, there's a lady present.'

Everybody laughed at this, but it pleased Mama Mizel and Georgie too. It didn't please the docker who kept on swearing, so I wound up throwing him out. Georgie was so pleased with this, that he asked Ronnie for regular benign protection. After that I was sent to the Dragon to collect £40 a week, a call that I added to the Milk Round. Then one day in 1965 Ronnie called me up and said, 'Mizel's had a bit more trouble up the Dragon, and he wants to know, can he have you working there?' That suited me fine because I was going to get another £25 wages on top of my other earnings. And the Twins didn't mind because I was still collecting £40 from the house every week for them.

The job at the Green Dragon, where I was part doorman and part storeman, led to me looking after another spieler, the Silver Spinner in Stoke Newington, Harry Cashman's place. He was known as 'Boot' Cashman because he had a boot-shaped nose that had been broken a few times. The Spinner opened early in 1965, and the Twins had a piece of it right from the start. I was there at the opening, when there was a row between Jack 'the Hat' McVitie and a Greek. The Greek pulled out a gun, and Jack pulled out a knife. I jumped on Jack's back and pushed him away and took the knife off him. Then I faced the Greek who was still waving his gun about. I realised the guy was trapped. All he wanted to do was get round the room to the door. These people in the club were all fussed, so I said to them, 'Just back off! Leave it,' and I went towards him as he sidled his way round.

I could see he didn't want to shoot anyone. He just wanted to get away, so I got him outside and let him go. I didn't even try to disarm him, but when I walked back inside these people thought I had done a very heroic thing, a Gary Cooper, facing the Greek down in a *High Noon* job. After this Boot Cashman asked the Twins if I could work there on a regular basis. I became the Spinner's houseman and doorman in return for another £20 a week, but again the Twins were copping on the side. That money was collected by Billy Exley, an old lightweight boxer, and I don't know how much.

These kind of incidents – exaggerated in the retelling, no doubt – kept boosting my reputation leading to more work. There were some Americans who rented part of the Spinner to run blackjack games. They also had tables at the Starlight, a spieler in Stratford Place off Oxford Street. One night these Yanks were held up there by a little firm who lined up the dice and blackjack croupiers and forced them to remove their trousers, then walked off with about £400. I was at the Spinner that night when the Yanks ran back and told us. They needed somebody to protect the place so they wanted me there, all because I'd faced down this Greek with a shooter.

The Yanks had to come to a deal with Boot Cashman who agreed to have me transferred to the Starlight as security officer. My wages went up to £25 a week, for which I worked several overnights a week. I'd dish out the cards, collect the house tax money and explain the rules to newcomers – but there were a lot of bits and pieces on top. Whenever I sorted out any trouble the croupiers would give me gambling chips. Winning punters would give me good tips. Even the Ladbroke Grove tearaways, whom I would have to deprive of their axes and bayonets as they came in, would tip me as I handed the items back on their way out. From all these sources I would pick up an extra tenner every night – £150 at today's prices.

I think the Twins had a third share in the Starlight, and they also took a protection pay-off of £40 or £50 a week, which again I think Billy Exley used to collect. After the stick-up the Yanks never recovered their confidence so they left town. For a while the tables were taken by Micky Regan, the business partner of Ronnie Knight, Barbara Windsor's ex-husband, but eventually the Starlight closed down. These clubs used to come and go, but there were always some in business, and any time a shooter was mentioned, I was called in because people thought I could handle armed robbers. In a way I could because I knew their psychology. I could tell what was running through their minds because I'd been there myself. It takes one to know one.

Not every protection pay-off was collected by me and Billy Exley. Other people used to do specialist runs, and some 'clients' paid their dues directly to the Kray family. When an associate of the Firm, Fat Wally Garelick, opened up a cab business, he paid the Twins a score – £20 – a week. He would deliver the money to their Aunt May who lived at 176 Vallance Road, right next door to the Kray household. She knew nothing. As far as she was concerned, it was just an envelope for her lovely nephews Ronnie and Reggie.

THE ENFORCER

If only the entire operation had been as cosy a family business as that arrangement makes it sound. Instead Ronnie's idea of family was plotting to use his own mother's caravan to kill poor Fat Wally. Despite joining the Firm with my eyes wide open – knowing only too painfully about Lennie's branding and my own shooting – I had seen nothing yet.

4: THIEVES' PONCES

Getting as much money as I now was every week, but without running any of the risks involved in armed robbery, had a lot to recommend it. Of course, the Twins had realized this years before I did. They seem always to have understood that, 'crime doesn't pay,' but for them that only ruled out 'straight crime' – good honest-to-God thieving – which certainly is a mug's game. Far better to let other people risk going to jail. Then if they're lucky, and they get away with a big wad, that's the moment you steam in and levy your underworld tax on them. Looking back, I wondered why I didn't get into this game sooner.

Ronnie and Reggie Kray never did any skilled theft, burglary or robbery themselves. They would never go on an organized blagging – they said that was strictly for 'jailbirds' but as soon as they heard someone else had 'had it off', their first concern was, did they know anyone on the team? If they did, then they would go in for their share, their 'whack'.

They were just parasites. Thieves' ponces. It was common knowledge that the entire Firm were thieves' ponces. We'd wait for someone to have a blag off, and, if we knew someone on the team, we'd go after them for our corner. That's how we operated day-to-day. We'd find out who's just had a tickle and go in. It's a despicable form of crime, nothing to be proud of, but we didn't even pretend to have pride in our craft. We weren't top-notch master criminals. We were just bloody thugs, simple as that. Leeches.

Look what we did with a bunch of brothers, a second-generation

THE ENFORCER

Irish family called the Barrys – no relation incidentally to my stepfather. Two of them ran a club in Stoke Newington, the Regency, which the Krays once had a share in, but which we still used as kind of a club-house, especially the downstairs after-hours drinker. We heard one day that some of the Barrys had got involved in dodgy fivers. They were supposed to have a printing press set up and were running off counterfeit £5 notes, which were pretty good, so we said we wanted a 'joey' off them, a parcel. Like good little boys, they sent us a parcel containing £10,000, but there was a problem with them. As the first ones came off the press the ink was heavy, which was OK, but as the print run continued, the ink became too light, which meant the later forgeries weren't any good. Because of this, the Twins weren't happy with their parcel. No, they wanted a parcel that only had good ones. So we just went round and took a couple more parcels off them. We didn't buy them from the Barrys. We just demanded them, because we knew the business, and they knew they couldn't refuse. Who could they complain to? The police?

If we went to a team with the intention of profiting from their hard graft, we wouldn't necessarily tell them we knew they had 'had it off' yesterday. We might say, 'The word is that you've been a bit active lately.' Then we'd say, 'The Other Two need a bit of dough, and they've asked us to pop round and see you 'cos they done you a few favours in the past.' We didn't say 'the Twins'. Calling them 'the Other Two' was enough: 'The Other Two need a bit of dough, and they want a monkey,' or 'They want a thousand pound.'

No one I went to see for the Kray Firm ever rebuffed me, because, as Don Corleone used to say, I was making them an offer they couldn't refuse. Not even the old Chainsaw Gang, who were supposed to be the top fliers at the game. Their leader, Big Splinter Woodruff, had put up a bit of resistance one night and come to grief.

The incident happened, like so much else in this saga, in the

Regency, where my colleague on the Firm, Scotch Jack Dickson, came up to me one night and complained, 'This bloke Woodruff is getting on my tits,' so I said to Jack, 'Well, do him.' He said, 'Leave off, Albert. He's 17 stone, and he keeps having a prod at me.'

Scotch Jack couldn't fight to save his life, but he used to whip people up into doing his fighting for him. This evening I decided I'd help out. I was with a girl at the time, so when Woodruff went to the toilet, I timed my attack. On his return he had to walk 20 feet to get to the bar, so I got hold of the girl and pretended to dance with her, just to get moving. She didn't know what was happening. I spun her this way, then that way, as though I was in mid-dance, and when I knew where he was, I spun round on him and wham! I hit him on the chin, and he went down. Then he rocked on his shoulders and started getting up. I thought, Ooh no! because I knew I'd hit him good. So I went back over, gave him another one, and he went down again. Then everybody seemed to steam into him, hitting him with bottles, until Parky Barry (who was both a counterfeiter and a robber) dragged him into a store-room, then took him away. I had broken his jaw.

The next time we should have met, we missed him. Apparently he was going down Whitechapel Road in a cab, when he saw me and Reggie Kray walking along. Suddenly he dived on the floor saying, 'They'll kill me! Don't let them see me!' Now, you can imagine what the rest of his team thought of all this! He's supposed to be a big bandido, and there he is, grovelling on the floor.

Our information had come through a middleman acting for the Chainsaw Gang who wanted to know why their esteemed leader had suffered the belting that gave him a wired-up jaw. The fellow also wanted to know whether this was the first strike in a Kray gang war. Was this going to carry on? I said, 'No,' but now I knew the way Woodruff was behaving, I decided we should take some money off him, so I continued, 'Apart from the fact that he's ruined Parky Barry's suit and my suit too. Tell him to give me a fifty and that's the end of it.' So a few days later, we had a meet in another of our pubs, the Carpenters' Arms in Cheshire Street. In came our middleman with a guy from the Chainsaw Gang itself. He asked, 'Is this a one-off or a regular bite?' 'No,' I said, 'just expenses. Not a blag.' So we got the fifty, we had a drink with the guy, and he tailed it back to Woodruff.

That encounter in the Regency, and especially the news that it had blown his nerve, destroyed his gangland status for ever. But we only got that news because the Twins had a spy, in the shape of the middleman. It's not much of an exaggeration to say the Krays had a thousand spies. Certainly hundreds had been carefully cultivated over many years by means of the Twins' activities on behalf of the same 'jailbirds' they had such contempt for: the Aways.

In the name of the Brothers Kray the entire East End criminal fraternity would be drafted into fund-raising for the Aways. Any reluctance displayed by these donors wasn't caused by a lack of sympathy for their less fortunate comrades. It was down to their irritation that any gratitude would flow in the direction of the Other Two and nobody else.

Of course, I'd run into 'Aways' collections years before, at those point-to-points, but I don't believe any of the money collected by the Brown twins ever reached any jailbirds or their families. All money raised by the Krays would certainly have reached the right people – because it served the Twins' interests that it should.

The Aways fund-raising was conducted once a fortnight, according to a complicated ritual. We drank in quite a few pubs, and we gave each pub its own number. This was because the Twins were convinced that all the phones they used were tapped. I don't suppose they were far wrong. Anyway, if I was out somewhere and I phoned the Twins, I might say, 'Everything's all right. Where shall I see you tonight?' Then Ronnie or Reggie would say, 'Number four.' Right. Now number four might be the Merry Widow's in Bethnal Green or it might be the Grave Maurice in Whitechapel. And in the evening you would go to that pub and either hand over that day's money or report on whatever you had found out.

Once that business was done, people would be sent out to other pubs to gather up the rest of the clan. That was because the Twins had already arranged meets with other people at some totally different pub. They'd have said, 'Go to the Red Crown, and we'll see you there at eight o'clock,' but now somebody else would have to go there at eight and say, 'Listen, the Other Two are round at the Merry Widow's,' or wherever, and they'd take them there. If you think this is unnecessarily complicated, you must always remember that the Twins were paranoid people who had every reason to believe the police had almost as many spies as they did!

So as the chosen place was filling up, and it might look promising if there were a few obviously rich guys there, the Twins would wink at you and say, 'Do the Aways list.' So now you would go round with a piece of paper and say, 'We're collecting for the Aways,' and we'd get whatever we could get. Then some guy would say, 'Well, who's away?'

'Well,' we'd say, 'Harry's doing two, and then there's his missus, and he's got two kids.' 'All right. Here's 25 quid. Send that round to them!' And on we'd go to the next guy. Until we'd bagged up a pretty good sum, only part coming from the Twins themselves.

But the Twins would get all the credit, because when we went round to see the man's wife, we'd say, 'The Brothers sent you round this, to help out with the electric or the gas.' And the woman would say, 'Oh, aren't they lovely boys?' You still hear that today – 'lovely boys' – but they were getting the glory for money that they had just nicked off other people.

Mind, even when you were doing this apparent act of kindness, you had to handle yourself carefully, in case the jailbird read things the wrong way. That's why we always went in pairs to an Away's house because, you can imagine, the guy is sitting in the nick while someone's going to his house, dealing with his wife and handing her money. That's why we *had* to be two-handed.

I can think of only one occasion when somebody said, 'Sod it,' in effect, to the Aways. It was Lennie Hamilton, the man who'd been pokered by Ronnie and whom I'd stuck up for, only to get shot by Reggie. Well, the next time I saw Hamilton after my shooting, he came in the pub when I was doing the Aways list, and he tried to give me just a fiver. So I said, 'You're not getting away with that, you little rat, I want some more!' I managed to get 25 quid out of him, which upset him because he couldn't buy a drink after that. I just wanted to get my own back. It was revenge for me, but I can understand why he didn't want to give generously to a Kray fund-raiser.

People rarely had to be forced to hand over a decent sum – this Hamilton incident was exceptional – because it would have been dangerous for anyone to spurn a collection for the Aways. The news that you hadn't forked out would rapidly be reported to Ronnie and Reggie who wouldn't like to hear it.

The bigger point is that when the Aways came home, they were beholden to the Krays. As soon as they came out of jail they were expected to go and see the Twins to say thank you. Then they'd get a few instructions. But sometimes guys didn't do this, and then there'd be trouble.

You'd get a report that 'Pete' is out. Maybe he's been out a week. Then Ronnie might say, 'And he ain't been to see us yet? Bastard! We sent him round some money!' Now they're after getting the needle with him. So, somebody would see Pete and say, 'Listen you'd better get round and see the Other Two, 'cos they're getting a little bit shirty.'

But Pete may have screwed up his courage and resolved not to see them for all sorts of reasons. He might not have liked the idea of their henchmen coming to his home and handing unsolicited cash to his wife while he was locked up. Or he might have had a row with her because she's banned him from seeing them: 'I don't want you to go round there. I took the money because we needed it but I still don't want you to go.' He himself may resent the idea of grovelling to them in grateful homage. He might fear he could get involved in the scene again and wind up getting nicked, so he just wants to keep a low profile. Anything like this would have to be explained to Ronnie, because he couldn't understand why anyone would want to go straight. But in the end Pete would have to come in to clear the air, to explain directly to the Twins why he hadn't come earlier. There must also have been times when wives didn't even tell their husbands the Krays had given any money, which would have provoked rows all round.

Not all the Aways' money came from fund-raising nights. Under the Twins' instructions I'd often pay out from what I had collected on the Milk Round. 'Go over and see Freddie's wife. He's in the nick – one of the Aways – I think she's in a bit of trouble. Someone's rung up and says she can't pay her electric bill.' So I might give her a fiver or a tenner, then the Twins would get whatever was left from the round. I'd have to account for the rest. I'd tell them, 'She got a tenner, he got a fiver, this one got a score, and this is what's left.' I had to keep a note of it all, so the Twins didn't think I was tucking a lot, pocketing a slice of the action. I never had to do that because I had enough action that was entirely mine.

If you were known to be 'on the Firm' there was a lot of money to be picked up on the side. I had a lot of separate earners. This was Albert Donoghue's private enterprise. My own work. It was nothing to do with the Twins. I was still freelance in that sense, but, obviously, the fact that I was known to be on the Kray Firm gave me a leg up in getting all this outside business.

The Twins didn't quarrel with that. They knew you couldn't exist on what they were paying you. Let's say you went out, and you nicked £1000 from people on behalf of the Twins: all you got out of it was a score or 25 quid. You only got expenses, drinking, beer vouchers. Other people say I was getting £100 a week with the Twins but that would only have been if we'd had an exceptional hit. If the Twins knew somebody on the Firm was getting a regular

£100 a week off them, they would have gone potty. They were getting scarcely £100 each themselves. But I could certainly pick up a lot more than £100 with all my own private 'nips' added in.

A 'for instance'. While I was minding the Starlight I always needed a cab to get there. It was up in the West End, off Oxford Street, and it didn't open till eleven o'clock at night. So I'm waiting for a cab one night, and the manager of the cab firm says, 'Could we have a talk? We're in a bit of trouble.' I said, 'We'll leave it till later, yeah? I got to go to work. I'll see you down the Regency when I get back.'

So I get back there about three in the morning. By this time I've had a few drinks, and he says, 'We're getting a bit of trouble with scrub calls. People are phoning for cabs, but when they get to the address there's nobody there, so it's a waste of time.' Also, in those days there weren't any radio cabs. The drivers had to carry a pile of sixpences with them and call back on the phone, so getting a scrub call was a big aggravation.

So I said, 'Well, why don't you stop it?' He said, 'Well, how? Who? Er . . .' The guy was lost. So I said, 'Well, I ain't going to do it for a pension. Bring me in on the firm.' So he said, 'All right, all right,' very quickly. I said, 'Sixty-forty.' He said, 'All right.' And for a joke I continued, '*My* way.' And to my surprise he said, 'All right.' So suddenly I've got 60 per cent of the Advance Cab Company!

But now I've got to solve the problem. I just looked at the map, and I tried to work out, who can affect him? Where will his competitors be located? He was in Bow Road so I looked at the map and thought, Mile End . . . Stepney . . . going towards Hackney, Victoria Park, that way. . . Poplar that way . . . Stratford . . . then I picked out all the cab firms and phoned them. I said, 'Listen,' and I introduced myself, 'I've heard that some of your drivers is sending us scrub calls. Now if this don't stop, I'm going to come round your gaff. If we get one more scrub call, we're going to come round your gaff and disconnect your wiring.'

So, it stopped. Straightaway. Now up to that time my man had five owner-drivers, but from there we went up to ten owner-drivers, and we were running a nice little business. So that's what he should have done from the start, only he didn't have any weight behind him to back it up.

Sure, now he was giving me 60 per cent, but his turnover was so much increased that he was probably getting twice as much money himself. I did the man a favour. I did myself a favour, but I saved his business. Look at it that way. Today, when they bring these big guys in to big companies – management consultants – they do the same thing. They nick a bit, don't they? Far more than we thugs ever did. So, business consultant I was, already.

Another little earner was a fellow called Bosher. I never knew his real name but he had a little scrap-yard off Queensbridge Road in Bethnal Green. George Dixon, who had his own family firm based in Poplar, had been round threatening Bosher for money, so he'd come to the Twins for help. Ronnie told him, 'Albert will look after it,' so my scheme was to phone George and tell him to leave Bosher alone. We weren't going to do this for nothing, so I went to see Bosher and made it sound more involved than it really was. I asked him for £100 down, and he dragged up £85. Then I told him, 'Well, knowing George, he's not going to let it go with just one meet, so I'll have to keep a regular eye on the place.' Bosher said, 'Don't worry, I'll pay you every week.'

So I said, 'Fair enough. That'll be a tenner,' but he could only afford £5, so I would collect a tenner fortnightly. Silly money but it all added up, and, anyway, I didn't have to do any more for it because it was all sorted in one little chat with George. I arranged a meet, we went through a jokey routine, rubbing each other down as if we were likely to be tooled up, and then I said, 'You're messing about with a very good friend of mine.' And he said, 'Well, in that case, I'll leave it out.' It was done with a smile and a joke because we weren't enemies at all. We were all in the same game.

George Dixon was a flash guy. When he came into a place he

was always shouting and hollering. He'd shout just for a drink, and if anybody so much as glanced at him it would be, 'Who you looking at, Sunshine?' Once he went too far and said something that upset Ronnie Kray. The next time he was in the Regency, Ronnie stuck an automatic in his face and pulled the trigger, but the gun didn't fire. He pulled it again, and it still didn't work, so Ronnie gave up and presented George with the bullet. The Colonel must have been in a pretty good mood to let him off that lightly.

Our relationship with the Dixon gang had other ups and downs. Once the Twins called me at three in the morning to go to the Regency where George's brother, Alan, was terrifying people. When I arrived, I told him to behave himself, and that he owed me a score for getting me out of bed, for my cab fares and for the aggravation. He said, 'Albert, I've only got a tenner on me, but if you come round the house in the morning you can get the other ten.' I thought, No. It'll be an ambush, so I said, 'Just give the tenner, and we'll call it a night.' I think he believed he was playing with somebody new to the game. Three years after the Krays went down, the Dixons found themselves playing against Commander Bert Wickstead who accused them of trying to take over where the Twins had been stopped. Alan got a nine-year jail sentence, George a twelve.

A lot of what we did was opportunistic. We'd see how far we could go and get away with it. I was astonished at what even other villains would put up with. Not everything took the form of a weekly payment, but there was something else we called 'the nip'. This was used on pubs and clubs where we couldn't get a regular pension, so we would nip them about once a month by putting up some story to justify a special payment.

We did this to the Barry brothers. Not only did we do them over the forged fivers but we were always thinking up excuses to clip them for a few quid. We nipped them so often that we decided what they really needed was a protection deal – from us! Late one night the Twins sent me, Ronnie Hart and Dickie Morgan, their old mate from military prison days, down the Regency to tell Johnny Barry what we wanted. We knew people were in there but they wouldn't open the door, so we went through the cab entrance at the back. Johnny wasn't there so the doorman gave him a ring, and he came down. I told him, 'The Twins want £50 a week.' He wasn't too pleased, but he agreed on the understanding that the nipping would stop. So from then I or young Ronnie Hart would pick up the Regency fifty.

Later the Barrys wanted it down to twenty, and somehow the Twins agreed. Then Johnny Barry tried to get away with not paying anything, so me and Ronnie Hart went in and boosted it back up to fifty. We didn't tell the Twins till later, when we explained how Johnny had tried to wriggle out of the deal so he needed to be taught a lesson. The 'moral' to this story is that protection is a circular racket. Any trouble in the Regency, we were causing it. Then we were paid to stop it. When the Barrys dared to appeal, we made it clear the trouble would start again. The Twins went and spoke to them – and it was all put back as it was. If the Firm had its claws into you, there was no way you could get free.

Some nips were done more for a laugh than because we needed the money. Sometimes the *Evening Standard* or *Evening News* would have a sensational front-page report headed, say, PAYROLL ROBBERY IN SHOREDITCH or WAGES SNATCH IN BISHOPSGATE. So a pair of us would go in a pub or club, where we were known as villains, and where the landlord was a bit iffy too, and we'd go up to the bar and drop the paper on the counter so the governor could see the headlines. We'd have our ties undone and our hair messed up, and we'd whisper to each other over a couple of light ales. The governor would pick this up. He'd see us carrying on in a very furtive way, then he'd see the paper, we'd have another whisper, and he'd go, 'Oh, shit,' as it dawned on him that we must have been on the robbery. We'd say, 'Look, Harry, we're in a bit of shtook. How about forty or fifty shots? Just some running-round money till we get our share.' He'd put two and two together, and he'd hand over the dough, no questions. He can't really refuse. He could call the police, but it's all aggro. He'd rather give us the money. And all along we'd never been on the robbery or had anything to do with it!

Sometimes people would offer us money to apply our brutality as mercenaries, on guys we had no personal quarrel with. These propositions were too much trouble to carry out but could still be good one-off earners. One day when I was working for George Mizel at the Green Dragon, I was approaching the place, and a Jewish guy says, 'Do you want a bit of work that Billy Maguire used to handle?' I knew this Maguire. He'd been in the Crown when Reggie shot me. He was a hoodlum who claimed he'd been fitted up over a robbery. He got 14 years in jail, came back out, shot a cop, was jailed again and then disappeared.

So I agree to consider the proposition. We go to a garage in Hackney Road, this guy gets on the phone and then gives me a name and an address. He says, 'You do this guy – hurt him, hospitalize him – and you get £250. Then you get another address. That's how Maguire used to do it. That's how it goes.' I say, 'No. That's not how it goes. First of all, it's £300, and I get the first lot of money up front.'

So I get paid up front. Then I go and watch this guy, who turns out to be a milkman up West Ham way. And I start asking around, and I find out that when the Nazi party used to walk round Epping Forest in uniform, he was one of them. So this is a Jewish firm that wants these guys done. They've infiltrated this Nazi group and got their names and addresses.

Maguire had been making his living by putting these guys in hospital one after the other, but I cut it short there and then. I took the first £300, but I didn't touch the milkman. It was mug's work. If I'd been interested, I'd have subcontracted it. I would have got hold of a couple of young tearaways, given them a hundred each to go out and do it, and I'd keep a hundred myself. But I didn't want it. At that time I had been used to going out, doing a pay-roll job, and getting four or five grand for my whack – not a £200 or £300 piss-up. Also I probably thought this mercenary stuff was beneath me.

There was no danger in reneging on a job like that and keeping the money. Who was going to report me to the cops for not fulfilling the contract? Also I sussed that the man behind the scheme was George Mizel himself. He was superficially legitimate – a licensed bookmaker, as I've said earlier – but he was also London's biggest receiver of stolen jewels. He had a Hatton Garden jewellery repair business, through which he bought and sold bent precious metals in league with another receiver, big Matty Constantino. George was into everything, he even owned this garage in Hackney Road where I was asked to take over the Maguire contract. That's how I knew all this was to do with the Jews. I didn't say I knew. I wasn't supposed to know where the job came from. So either the £300-a-hit money was George's or he was middling for rich respectable Jews who had turned to the underworld to do this work.

Mizel was also in with bent cops. Once I had to collect our Green Dragon protection money from his Hatton Garden premises. I walked into George's room, where he was sitting at his desk, talking to a police detective who could not have been there legitimately because he was on his own. No straight copper would have been allowed to see notorious characters like George and Fat Matty by himself because anything could be alleged against him, especially on this occasion when a guy called Dennis Stafford was also in the room. Stafford was a colourful, independent villain who was later convicted of a murder in Durham that he always denied committing. When George saw me he said, 'Oh, hello,' and Fat Matty handed me an envelope. I said, 'Ah, so that old horse won, then?' and Matty said 'Yeah.' We did this because, even if the copper was bent, he didn't need to know this business. And he certainly would have wanted to know that the Kray Firm was protecting the godfather of the 'Garden.'

Back in 1960, before I was on the Firm, Mizel and Constantino really needed protection – not from anyone else but from me and the boys from Bow. We'd heard they had bought the stash of jewellery stolen from Sophia Loren when she was staying north of London while filming at Elstree. One night a good source told us that Constantino had only just finished taking all the stones out of their settings, and he now had a whisky bottle full of rubies, emeralds and diamonds. Our source also said we should get straight down to the Green Dragon, where he would be going later this night. So we drove down and sat in Whitechapel Road opposite the alleyway leading into the Dragon. Sure enough, we saw him arrive in his Mercedes, go into the Dragon, where he spoke with Mizel, and get back into his car. Now our job was to tail him and mug him for Sophia Loren's stones but, after all this, we lost him in traffic. It's never easy to tail someone, and it wasn't easy even 35 years ago when there were fewer cars about.

Being philosophical, I can console myself by saying that even if we had lifted the jewels, we would have had a job getting rid of them, because Mizel was the main man in this business. He had the trade connections not just in London but in Antwerp and New York as well, whereas we didn't know anybody. We would have had to get someone else to take the stuff abroad, and we would have wound up with peanuts. But there you are. When the stakes were big enough – and Sophia's jewels were worth so much, a dozen villains could have retired on the proceeds – I was prepared to deprive even dear old George Mizel of his dishonest earnings. He never knew we'd got that close, but he would have forgiven me. After all, every thug in London would have done the same.

Looking back, I'm amazed I stuck it out so long with the Firm. I must have been mad in those days. I just seemed to get involved. It was a stupid way of carrying on, but a lot of the attraction of being on the Firm and a leading player in it was the fear and respect that other people showed me, the glamour of being with the top team in town. On the other hand, if I had never got involved with the Twins, I could have had a good life running my own painting and decorating business. Even after I'd joined them, I could have quit and gone forward with the Advance Cab Company. Other people had eased themselves away from Ronnie and Reggie in the past and were still walking around.

Instead I stuck with them and endured the other side of the Firm: the sheer tedium. A lot of it was just sitting in pubs and clubs, trying to keep awake. Right from nine o'clock in the morning you were at the Twins' beck and call. OK, some weeks you could see nothing much was coming up, so you might say to them, 'You don't need me till Thursday, I'll take the kids to the zoo.' But Fridays I always had to be on duty to do the collections and the pay-outs, so I had to wait till these employees' came in for their wages.

I'd tell them, 'I'll be at the Dragon tonight,' or, 'I'll be round the Beggars or the Widows' or at one of half a dozen other places. If you had to give them money, they'd always show up, but when? Or it might be around five in the afternoon, and you're thinking, Thank God. Everything's done. I can have a quiet night home, until the Other Two would say, 'See you around the Grave Maurice tonight. We've got a couple of people coming round.' Then something unexpected might occur, and there'd be a bit of a scurry. Someone might have been arrested, or the Twins had realized someone they'd hurt had complained to the police Then I'd have to get on the phone and call the solicitor down, and we'd be running round in circles all night, till we sorted out the problem.

This kind of life didn't do much for my marriage, especially when my wife had our third child, our younger son, after I joined the Firm. Inevitably she and I would argue about what little she knew of my work, especially the hours I kept. Even so, considering the hours my stepfather worked at the foundry, my wife probably saw more of me than my mother did of him – provided I stayed out of jail, which I was more likely to achieve with the Krays than without them. So I just went about my business. My wife never said, 'You'd better come away from the Twins or I'm leaving.' Nothing like that. It never got to that stage. It's partly the East End upbringing. That's the way women thought in those days: you went along with whatever the husband was doing. Women would, more or less, put up with anything the man was doing.

My wife only came out with the Firm once, and she didn't like the experience. I took her to the Society Club in Jermyn Street, where we had a party. Barney Ross was there that night, and it was great to see this scruffy little pug-nosed ex-fighter, drug addict and alcoholic, playing all that Beethoven stuff on the piano. People loved it but, later on, the missus said she didn't like the crowd. She wouldn't come out again, except occasionally to pubs to meet a couple of the boys and their wives. She ruled out attending a full-blown Firm meet with all the hangers-on, in-laws and outlaws. She didn't want that. She was a straight girl from a straight family, and she just wasn't into that scene.

She met Ronnie and Reggie, but she didn't trust them. She never got over the fact that it was Reggie who had shot me. Then there was all that business with the flowers and Ackerman knocking at the house. She was worried about how I was going to take it – would I go round their house and start shooting? – until I told her, 'It's calmed down now, forget about it.' Life on the Firm never calmed down. It just got crazier and crazier.

I hardly ever took my work home. I think a couple of times people had been to my place and been patched up, if they'd had a cut, but I never laid stuff on her, I never got her involved. She wouldn't have it but she knew I was 'at it'. She knew I was a hooligan, but I think people turn a little blind, as long as they don't know the details.

There were other issues between us. It's been said that I was the womanizer of the Firm. It's true I met a couple of ladies, but I was a young man, still only twenty-nine when I joined. So, if I didn't look at a lady what was I going to look at? It was better than meeting boys. I was never a saint. You meet a girl, and she looks at you and you look at her, and you ain't going to live like a monk, are you? You go, 'Yeah, OK.' I can't see anything wrong in that, apart from the 'unfaithful' bit.

Some women were attracted by the air of power and danger surrounding the Firm. There were other fringe benefits. You could always get tailor-made clothes half-price. You might take your own material to the tailor, but he was still well pleased because he could say he was making suits for the Firm: sharp, well-made, always on view wherever you were on parade. People would see these expensive 'whistles', and the tailor could trade off that. But if he fell out of favour, and you felt like a change of style, there was always someone else happy to get the work.

Women, clothes and money. Some compensation for what was a highly stressful and nerve-wracking occupation. We worked hard and played hard, but boy! Anywhere in London it was impossible ever to drop your guard and completely relax.

My only fuse box was Tuesday. Unless there was something special on, Tuesday was always a slack day. I'd got over all the weekend's business, and next weekend's was a long way off, so every Tuesday I'd go and get drunk at the Regency, where I had my own little corner. I used to stand there, and everybody stayed out of my reach because they knew I was getting drunk. I'd have a good night, relax and probably talk to one of the waitresses. But early Wednesday morning I was back on duty, sober and ready to face whatever lunatic tasks the Other Two might throw at me.

Sober or drunk, I wasn't someone to tangle with, even though I was rarely armed. I only carried a gun on special assignments, and I didn't carry a knife, because at any time you could be stopped and searched by the police. I could never see why you would carry a tool unless you were going on a mission where you were likely to use it. So if ever I found a knife on someone, I would use it on him. Indeed, on the Firm I made a point of it. We would grab these people, dip them, get hold of their knife and slice them with their own weapon.

Once I found out that a Birmingham guy, who was a casual friend of ours, was plotting behind our backs against the interests of the Firm. Then I was told he always carried a knife and where he kept it. A few days later he was with Ronnie Hart and me in a pub. When he went to the toilet we waited for 15 seconds, then followed him in. As he was coming away from the sluice, we started talking to him. Then Ronnie grabbed him, I took his knife out and stuck it in his arse. It was a classic gangland move. We did it to teach him a lesson. Later the Twins approved, they told his bosses, and when he staggered back to their territory they gave him another belting.

The underworld is a different world with its own codes, and you work within those codes. When someone gets out of line, it's normal to give them a slash. Most people in the 'overworld' would say, 'Oh, disgusting! Call the police!' We'd just go, 'He was out of order. He was getting trappy. Pack him off for some stitches! Send him home!' No one would call an ambulance. The most we'd do is call a cab.

In the East End the underworld and the overworld perpetually intertwined. We villains operated almost with impunity, breaking the law every hour of the day. Yet most of us had homes where our wives and kids, or mums and dads, lived straight and law-abiding lives. Wondering how much Ronnie and Reggie's parents connived in their criminal activities, or if they knew what an evil pair of brats they had reared, was like trying to solve the riddle of the Sphinx.

5: THE PRIVATE LIVES OF PUBLIC ENEMIES

If you were on the Firm, you couldn't help getting to know the Twins' mum and dad, Violet and Charlie, because the morning meets used to be held in the family home, 178 Vallance Road, Bethnal Green, otherwise known as Fort Vallance. It was a tiny, rented, terraced house, and there's no point in going on a tourist trip to see it nowadays because it's long been demolished. There were three rooms on the ground-floor. The front room was used as the main office. That's where you said or did your bit, before you were sent off, not necessarily out of the house, but usually to one of the other rooms where it would be 'tea and biscuits served' all day, and you would do any other business that didn't need the Twins being present.

If you had said to Violet Kray, 'What's going on?' she would have replied, with all honesty, 'Well, my boys have got a crowd of their friends in, and they're sitting in the front room talking. What they're talking about, nobody knows.' Half the time we didn't know, so I'm sure she knew nothing in any detail. She made sure she didn't know, but she probably had a good idea. In *The Krays* movie, Violet was portrayed as a very formidable woman, with a ferocious tongue. I must say I was never on the wrong end of her tongue, but then I was never with her when anybody ran her boys down. All that stuff took place when the Twins were growing up and neighbours were reporting them to the police for any mischief. Then she might have ripped into any 'interfering busybodies', but I've never known an occasion when she did it in the 1960s. By then, if somebody was mouthing off about the Twins and running them down, she wouldn't have had to lift a finger. One of us would have gone and sorted it. After that, there wouldn't be a peep out of the offender!

Of course, she must have known the Twins were 'at it' in pretty spectacular ways. The record shows they were tearaways right from the start, but, thinking of my own start in life, that didn't make you an exception among East End kids, and it didn't make you socially unacceptable. On the contrary, in many households it was a passport to social acceptability. Your anti-social behaviour made you a welcome guest. This was the world turned upside down, so it took a lot of Eastenders a long time to realize that the Twins weren't just extremely successful tearaways but dangerous psychopaths masquerading as traditional thugs.

Their dad, old Charlie Kray, certainly knew there was a lot of heavy stuff going on. If somebody on the Firm was involved in any violence, he was an expert in getting bloodstains out of clothes. You could just hand a suit or a coat to him, and he would clean it up by the next morning. There'd be no forensics left. But as long as he didn't ask, and nobody spelt it out to him, he could claim he knew nothing. It's like the Germans didn't know about concentration camps. OK. You believe it, if you like. Don't believe it, if you don't like.

It was easy to underestimate both Twins because they were educationally sub-normal in the extreme. They couldn't read, and they couldn't write, beyond a normal six-year-old's ability. You know the kind of joke, 'I read a book once. It was a green one.' In the case of the Twins, that was literally true because they'd once been given a book, *How Green was My Valley*, and for some reason they'd both been forced to read it. So whenever anyone mentioned a book – in our circles, I admit, this wasn't very often – that was the only one the Twins could come up with.

When people are bending over backwards to say nice things about the Twins they say, 'Ah, but they never gambled.' That's true but that was only because they couldn't understand betting odds. They could not count or calculate. Yes, they could count money like a fairground gypsy can, but no basic education had sunk into them at all. One time Reggie went to see Doc Blasker, the Firm's tame GP, about a bit of an infection. He came back and asked us what was on the prescription. We read, 'Urethritis', except of course that when we Cockneys spoke, it came out as 'youthritis'. So Reggie said, 'Is that anything to do with youths?'

Mechanically, too, the Twins were a complete catastrophe. Reggie was a terrible driver. He had a licence, and now and again if they bought a nice new car he would want to drive it. Until he hit something, and he usually did. Then we'd have to get one of the boys to drive it. Ronnie didn't drive at all. They were completely helpless without someone else to prop them up. They had just three things going for them: considerable physical strength, a ruthless capacity to direct it and instinctive animal cunning. Oh, and they had one other thing: each other. They were like two hunting dogs. If there'd been only one, you could have whacked it out with no trouble, but the two of them together could come at you in any way at any time. A lethal combination.

I don't think Violet Kray 'created' the Twins. It wasn't her fault that they turned out like they did. I often wonder how they evolved, what turned them into what they were. Ronnie once told me that he had a cousin two or three years older than they were. When they were seven or so, this kid used to take them on to the bomb sites, which, after the Blitz, made marvellous play areas for children all over the East End. Boys in particular would make little dens and camps among the rubble.

So this older cousin would get the Twins into one of his dens and torture them. Well, in the middle of one of these deserted sites, you could scream, shout and cry for hours, and no one would hear you, or come to your rescue.

Did this torture have any effect on the Twins? Well, I suppose it must have done. They never told their parents about it, but obviously it had to be stuck deep in Ronnie's memory for him to tell me about it. I don't know what happened to the cousin later on, probably something drastic, but I'm sure it wasn't Mrs Kray who made these boys villains. It was just the way you grew up in those days. If you were a little bit handy with the fists, you got into the fight game, and from there you could go into protection or robbery. If you weren't any good at fighting, you'd go to work in a factory or on a building site. Anything, just to get your bread and butter, but the Twins had something else in their make-up. They weren't just desperadoes, they were mad.

I can't claim to know how Ronnie Kray came to be queer either, but he certainly was queer throughout the time I knew him. He didn't hide the fact that he was a homosexual. He liked the young boys – I mean young men not children – and they were known as his 'prospects'. There were a lot of scouts who used to go out hunting for good-looking, susceptible youths. They would come back and say, 'Ronnie, I've got a terrific boy you've got to meet,' and then this kid would be brought to the pub. Some of these kids would be fit young fighters, and I used to think, Christ how can that lad get involved in this sort of stuff? But, they did. It surprised me.

Ronnie wasn't the only gangster I knew who preferred men to women. There's half a dozen villains I can name who were queer, and they weren't shy about letting anybody know about it. Even in the sixties this wasn't anything unusual. It was just something you didn't mention. I mean, if this guy likes tying women up, then that's his business; if this one likes them wearing black stockings, that's his business. You don't ask these silly questions. It's none of your business. So some guy likes a young man, and that guy likes a granny: it's just how they get it on. Nothing to do with me – as long as they don't start tampering with my trousers.

There was a thing within the Firm. Supposing Ronnie might fancy a showbiz star – male, of course – he used to put out what they called a 'W': W for 'Warrant'. Anybody who can service the warrant, by getting that star back to meet Ronnie, would get some sort of cash reward. There were other Ws. One was put out later on the detective Nipper Read. Nipper wasn't gay, of course, but by that time he was hot on the trail of the Krays. When he heard about the 'W', he took it seriously enough to take steps to protect himself. But mostly the Ws were for pretty young men in the entertainment fraternity.

We were all up the West End one night in this well-known Chinese place, the Oasis Restaurant, a perfectly straight establishment, and we saw this guy sitting on his own. He was sitting there with shades on, at a deserted table. Ronnie spotted him and said, 'Who's that then?' and somebody said, 'That's Cliff Richard, an up-and-coming singing star.' Ooh!' said Ronnie. 'I'd like to meet him. If you can get him for me, there's a tenner in it for you.' So straight away there's a W out on him. If anyone can get him in to a meet, that's all he's got to do. Can't guarantee that he'd fancy Ronnie's company. God! Cliff's not even gay! But that's what the W was, to bring him in. It certainly wasn't to kill him, like the one for Nipper Read. It was so Ronnie could have his evil way.

Now obviously Mr Richard never had anything to do with Ronnie Kray. Nobody ever got hold of him to serve the W. It would have been bad, if it ever had happened. Lots of straight people have suffered damaging publicity just for appearing in one photo with the Colonel. I mean old Cliff, I don't particularly like his singing, but he don't seem a bad guy, and I would've hated to see him involved with that sort of person.

Most of Ronnie's successful Ws involved less elevated folk. But with Ronnie, where there was sodomy, sadism wasn't far behind. Years before I joined the Firm, they had the club in the Bow Road called the Double R: that's R for Reggie and R for Ronnie. One of the barmen there was gay. Barry was his Christian name. For some reason this guy topped himself, hanged himself. We heard it was a lover's quarrel or something, so the Twins dug around and found out that Barry had been involved with a Greek guy. So they captured this Bubble – 'bubble and squeak' equals Greek in Cockney rhyming slang – and they kept him locked up in a cupboard in the Regal billiard hall in Mile End for three days. No clothes, nothing. And they just used to whack him now and again, and put a hose over him and throw bits of bread at him, and stuff like that. And then they just let him go.

They didn't kill him. Even so, none of this could've been much fun for him. I dare say his tormentors got a weird kick out of it, which is probably what the torture was all about, because, whether this Greek had really had any responsibility for Barry's death, or if he was just a boyfriend, I don't know, and I'm sure the Twins didn't either.

Then there was Boxer Billy. He was a good little fighter who was one of Ronnie's prospects. But he upset Ronnie, and so Ronnie just did him. Billy called into the pub one night, and Ronnie didn't talk to him. He just pulled out this Gurkha knife and did him with it. Billy was paralysed with fear, he couldn't move, and Ronnie just cut the kid to pieces. Billy was still alive, but we just had to wrap the guy up, dump him on the steps of London Hospital and go away.

That 'affair' was obviously over. Ronnie used to get through boys like hot cakes. You'd see them come in, but at the end of the night you'd go your way, and he'd go his. You never saw what was going on but, for sure, Ronnie worked himself into a fearful passion over these kids. People who were on the Firm before I joined told the story of what happened once when they were in some pub with Ronnie and his latest swain. Apparently Ronnie broke down while he was telling this kid how much he loved him. Ronnie was crying as he took a knife out and ran it through his own hand to show this boy, 'Look! That's how much I love you!' The cut left a permanent scar in his left hand. That shows how much he thought he loved the boy. It shows even better how potty the man was too.

At the same time Ronnie was socializing with high-class queers. He got involved with a lot of well-connected males. There were writers, budding stars and famous politicians like Lord Boothby, Tom Driberg and a few others. There were also several solicitors. These were all known homosexuals, and it was nothing unusual to see them in Ronnie's company.

You might think it odd that there should ever have been a relationship between Ronnie and Lord Boothby, especially when, as we know, there are agencies who try and keep our 'Great and Good' on the 'straight and narrow' away from scum like Ronnie. But boys will be boys, especially Tory politicians with a taste for rough trade. That big business about the *Sunday Mirror* having a photo of the peer and the gangster was just about over by the time I joined the Firm. Boothby sued and got a fortune from the *Mirror*: £40,000. All Ronnie got was an apology, but even this meant that Fleet Street didn't dare do any more exposés of the Twins for years. I'm sure there was something more to the affair. Ronnie didn't spend all that time with Boothby just for the pleasure of his company, and certainly not for some lunatic development scheme in Nigeria. They were sharing low-class boy lovers.

Ronnie's preoccupation with violence was weird. Not only did he enjoy inflicting it but he also used to love hearing stories about other people's violence. If someone was telling him about a real incident in which violence had occurred, Ronnie would get them to sit down and give that stuff to him again and again, detail by detail. He got something out of it. He was definitely a Freddie Kruger type.

Ronnie would get a deep pleasure out of smashing somebody. He would literally smash a person with whatever he had in his hand. It didn't matter if it were a hammer, a bayonet or an axe, he would just slice somebody for the wrong word. And enjoy it and say, 'Hold that!' and walk away.

That's different from what we might have had to do from time to time in the course of our normal activities as a gangster. Quite often you can be sent to give someone a slap. You've got no personal problem with him, you might not have even met the guy before, but the Twins just say, 'Listen. Go over to so-and-so's warehouse. We've asked him for this money, he ain't come out with it, give him a slap.' So you go and give him a slap. There's no personal anger in it, you're getting paid for it, that's professional violence. But for you to react with violence of Ronnie's ferocity, you've got to feel someone has insulted you to your very core – or, of course, they've just whacked you.

With some people, this kind of thing can get to a stage where they do it purely as a way of life. Lay the man down, break his leg, when you'd never met him before, and you're not even angry with him, and he has never done you any bad turn. But to do what Ronnie did on a regular basis, that was something beyond belief.

Dickie Morgan, who had joined the Firm before me, used to tell me a story about when he was locked up with the Twins in the army nick around 1953, waiting to go to military prison for repeated assault and desertion during national service. He said they kidded the corporal on guard into the communal cell and beat the shit out of him. Then they all held him down, while Ronnie masturbated him. So that is weird, yeah? So he obviously got something out of that. And, in a heterosexual encounter, that would be the equivalent of violent rape. And how bizarre that a man who was incapable of accepting any military discipline should rejoice in a nickname 'The Colonel'.

When I was on the Firm we all knew Ronnie was a certifiable case. He was mad by any reckoning, according to any school or theory of psychiatry, and he ought to have been locked up years beforehand, for his own safety as well as other people's. If you went to Fort Vallance, you would see him sitting in the armchair, and he'd be chain-smoking and popping these heavy pills, and he'd be scowling. He used to scowl a lot.

Ronnie's favourite pills were downers called Stematol. They were really high-powered tranquillizers, and his main supplier was this Doc Blasker. I think Ronnie latched on to him because he was Ronnie Bender's local doctor over Millwall way, on the Isle of Dogs. If he looked like running out, or if he was going to go away for the weekend, he would tell Bender, 'Nip over to see Blasker, give him a tenner, take him a bottle of whisky and get my prescription!' I think it was Blasker who first came up with the idea that Stematol was just what the Colonel needed.

Alcohol was just what the doctor needed. Blasker was an alcoholic and a compulsive gambler. He would give you a prescription for anything, he'd sew you up, and he'd come whenever the Firm gave him a call. Then he'd be given a bottle of whisky and a tenner, and he'd be quite happy, placing a bet or having a game of rummy or kalooki. He was a chubby little man, with a rosy-faced but scruffy appearance, like a character out of Dickens. He had the bluffness of a real Colonel – 'Oh, yes, my boy. Yes, yes, very well.' I used to have to drag him out of the Green Dragon, where he'd be gambling with George Mizel and One-armed Lou. I'd say, 'Finish your hand, Doc! We need you.' He was lucky if he could keep his hand still long enough to identify the cards. And this was the man treating our beloved Fuhrer! No wonder Ronnie's behaviour was so dangerously unpredictable.

If there was a general conversation going on, but Ronnie wanted to listen to one particular person, he'd say, 'Shut up you!' and then you knew it was time to shut up. Everything depended on his moods. If you were close, as I was, you could say to him one day, 'Time to go down the caravan, Ronnie. You look like you're putting on a bit of weight.' Now that would be OK. But you could say exactly the same thing tomorrow, and you would have to fight for your life. He would attack you with whatever was handy. That was what happened to an old friend who jokingly told Ron he was looking fatter. Ron cut him up so badly, the guy needed 70 stitches just in his face. We called him 'Tramlines' after that. That was a regular thing for Ronnie. It was just whatever shape his head was in. The man was a psycho walking round with deadly weapons in his pockets. Reactionary social commentators might say we should have all been put down. According to a straight person's way of thinking, we probably should have been. But, for sure, he had to be first in line for the stun gun.

Ronnie also used to have manifestations. He would take on

religions. He would become a Buddhist for about three weeks, till he found out how awkward it was to live life as a Buddhist, then he'd turn that in. And then he would become Jewish, and then he'd hear something about a visionary Christian thinker, like Dietrich Bonhoeffer, and adopt him as a role model for five minutes. There was always stuff like that going down.

A good sign that he was 'going into one', as we called it – going into a depression – was when he started playing his Winston Churchill records. He had an LP of Churchill's speeches, which, for me, has got to be the most boring thing I've ever heard. I thought so then, but I think so even more now, especially now it's been shown that it's not Churchill's voice on half the speeches but some actor pretending to be him. Ronnie used to sit and listen to every word of this, so you knew he was 'going into one'. The guy was just on his own planet.

Ronnie also used to hear 'voices' – I'm sure this much was genuine – but, when he knew that other people knew he used to hear voices, he would often fake it to intimidate people. He could say to someone, 'You went to so and so, didn't you?' and the bloke would go, 'How did you know?' 'I know these things, I hear these little things,' and the person would go, 'Oh.' And he might go away believing that Ronnie had picked the information up through some psychic power. So he was a bit clever, he had an instinctive cunning, a natural guile. If he'd had some education, he could have been one of the great dictators.

Ronnie must have inherited his preoccupation with the mystic and supernatural because the whole Kray family was into this psychic thing. I think they half took a shine to me because I was Scorpio, same as the Twins. To them that was important. Now I had heard something once where there was supposed to be a ghost of a long dead uncle in the Vallance Road house. Well, for some reason I was sleeping there one night, and when I woke up in the morning, I came down, and Mrs Kray said something like, 'Here's your breakfast, have your cup of tea.'

Aunt May was in from next door – she was the main clairvoyant – so, they're all sitting there, and I said, hesitating, 'Did, er . . . Did anyone come in last night?' and they said, 'No, what?' So I said, 'Well, there's this little old boy, with a shirt on with no collar' – I was describing the old collarless shirts to which you can attach clean collars instead of washing the entire shirt – 'he had braces and baggy trousers, I saw him.' And everybody stopped and looked at me, because I've just described what's supposed to be the resident ghost. Except I've made up the entire story as a joke.

Then I realized that I've gone a bit too far now. I've got to carry on with it. I can't laugh, because they might all have jumped up and hit me, but I had to carry it through now, so I say, 'Yeah, I saw him, I just saw the guy.' And they all looked at each other, and they looked at me, and they were all firmly convinced it had actually happened. Ronnie believed it too.

It's said that, when he went into Broadmoor, he was diagnosed as a schizophrenic, which is what they do with someone who hears people giving him instructions. Well, I don't know what instructions Ronnie had when I was working for him, but in the long run they didn't do him a lot of good.

If any of us members of the Firm might have been tempted to follow Ron as a visionary religious leader, complete with voices, we'd all have been put off by another side of his wonky personality. He'd often behave like a little boy and sit round giggling. Somebody might fart – 'Hee, hee, hee' – you'd hear Ronnie giggling. And he'd giggle for the next half hour. Over a fart. OK, there are times when anyone might make a crack about someone farting, but you wouldn't go on giggling uncontrollably. There was one occasion, while Ronnie was in hiding, when he and Big Pat Connolly held a farting competition. Can you imagine it? There's this top hoodlum – a friend of peers and MPs – and this huge, fat, scar-faced, guttural Glaswegian who weighs 20 stone, sitting there giggling over a farting competition!

People often ask me, which Twin was the more dominant one.

THE ENFORCER

That depended on moods. Sometimes they would scream and fight and slag each other off. They would get into proper fist fights. But sometimes Reggie would blaze back at Ronnie, and Ronnie would sit there and take it. Sometimes it was the other way round. Piggy-in-the-middle was Charlie. He always got a slagging from the pair of them.

When the Twins had fights together, they would be screaming, rolling round on the floor. But although they were capable guys – they'd both been professional boxers – there was always a certain restraint. You know how it is: two brothers can be really angry with each other, but somehow they instinctively hold off, they don't go the full way. Well, these two would hold their punches, but they'd still make each other bleed and give each other black eyes.

When these guys narked each other up we wouldn't interfere. You didn't interfere with them two. That would be like trying to separate a couple of Dobermanns: they'd both turn on you. So you waited till they were flagging out, then you would interrupt and say, 'Somebody's coming up the stairs,' something like that, and break it up that way. We had to stop them once because Ronnie was showing some serious marks, and he had a big meeting with some Yanks the following week. These were serious people – representatives of the Mafia – and the only way we could part the Twins was by saying, 'You don't want to meet the Yanks looking like that!'

Normally we wouldn't interfere. We'd let them carry on. These brawls usually took place in a pub where we had control over the landlord. It was usually after closing time, and we'd be upstairs or in a backroom. But the fights would also break out in a house or a flat. They were always at it. We just let them knock it out of each other. If they don't take it out on each other, they're going to take it out on one of the team, so, just stand back and watch the show. Sell peanuts.

Apart from these fraternal rumpuses, Reggie's violence was different from Ronnie's. It was also unhinged, but when Reggie lashed out it was nearly always over some perceived slight on his gangland status. So we might be in a bar or at a party, and Reggie might say something, then somebody else might say, 'Oh, shut up, I don't believe that!' Well, that cheeky fellow would get a smack in the chin, because no one could be allowed to talk to a boss of the underworld like that.

It was just this unpredictable mix – Ronnie's nutty kind of violence and Reggie's controlled brutality – which made them so dangerous. This is what had got them to the top of the underworld and what made it so difficult to depose them. As Twins they balanced each other out. Reggie was a lot more logical, but probably more dangerous because of that. He would do the same things as Ronnie – hack people down or shoot them – but he would do it with an end in mind. Not in a wild rage but for a purpose.

I never had straight violence with either one of them. I could have handled Ronnie, I wouldn't have worried about him. You could just say, 'You're a poof', and he'd go into such a frenzy that you could pick him off easy. But Reggie was a good, calm fighter. I wouldn't have been able to box him. I wasn't worried about Charlie. In his younger days he'd been a good fighter too, but now he was too soft – and too nice.

So this fine pair were our leaders. Hardly inspirational -nothing like Robin Hood, Napoleon or Nelson – not the kind of people you would go 'over the top' and die for. Except that, rather like those poor sods who did die for mad generals in World War I, few of us had any choice. If we refused to do what they wanted, we could have been shot. We could try and ease our way out discreetly – as a few people did – or we could run off and disappear, or we could just submit, which was by far the easiest option. Also, to our shame, we saw the Twins as our meal ticket. They were the best payers. In fact, where we came from, they were the only game in town. A good family business.

6: NAUGHTIES

Somehow the Twins had come to understand that, to get away with running a criminal enterprise in the middle of a moderately law-abiding community, you had to carry local opinion with you. The locals didn't have to approve of your rackets – your average Eastender would normally turn a blind eye whatever you were up to – but if you wanted to win general goodwill and discourage straight folk from shopping you when police came snooping, you had to be seen doing good works in public.

That's why the Twins consciously created their charitable image. This started as a myth – they weren't charitable at all – and became a legend – the gullible, the religious and the just plain dumb spread it around the East End as if it was not only true but also uplifting.

The legend was this crude: people really did believe the Krays were good to dogs, old ladies and nuns. Well, you'd have to be some kind of psycho not to have some kindness in you, say, for an old girl down on her luck. Of course, you'd give her a fiver if you had it, or a couple of quid. But the Twins were very conscious of their image, and they worked a lot on it, thanks to Leslie Payne, their main business schemer, who had impressed on them the 'Public Relations'side of organized crime.

And so they would hire a pub or club, or use one of their own premises, and they'd let it be known that they were organizing a charity night. A regular good cause was the Bancroft Hospital in Mile End. They would invite a ward sister and probably a matron from the maternity unit, as well as the mayor, the local priest and, most important, a few people off the local weekly paper, the *East*

THE ENFORCER

London Advertiser. Then they would go to a couple of local florists and ask them to make up one of those big floral display baskets. They'd do the same with the local fruiterer. Then they would hold these baskets up for auction, and they would start off the bidding at a tenner, £20, £25 and up and up. But what people didn't realize was that, instead of just the last bid being collected, all the smaller intermediate bids were also being extracted! Then when the proud winner was presented with his basket, one of us would be standing near by and embarrassing him by shouting, 'Offer it up! Offer it up!' – forcing him to put the basket back into the auction all over again, but still obliging him to pay over what he'd already bid to win.

For this the poor guy would get a clap. People would say, 'What a wonderful chap he is!' And then the prize item would go again, and all the proceeds would be collected up for some good cause. Often it would be the kiddies' unit – a good one for tugging at the emotional heart-strings. Sure, it got some dough, but in next week's *East London Advertiser*, it was the Twins who got the glory. An article would appear saying, 'Local sporting gentlemen donated a sizeable sum of money to the maternity unit,' complete with a big blazing photograph. To guarantee the story would get a decent spread, the Twins would make sure a few well-known sporting names, like the boxer Terry Spinks, would turn up in all innocence to back the good cause.

There were other ways we used to raise money for charity. We would visit local businesses like the florist's, and somebody who half knew them would say, 'Listen, the Other Two are doing a charity night and would you like to do us a flower arrangement? The MC will say, "This arrangement is by Mary Jones, the Florist's Shop," so you'll get a bit of advertising.' And so the shop would produce the goods, but we never paid for them. We just got them to do it for us – with a smile! The net result was that the credit didn't go to dear Mary Jones. All she got out of it was the mention of her shop. In contrast the Krays appeared to be very generous, which, I suppose, they were – with other people's money!

They also practised their own brand of community policing. Sometimes people would come to the Twins and say they'd been 'tucked up', or somebody had jumped all over them. If Ronnie or Reggie already knew the plaintiff, they would listen to find out who had done the foul deed. If they had a previous reason to dislike the offender, they were more likely to do something to him. Any action would now appear to be a favour to the guy who'd come for help, whereas they were just settling their own long-term feud. Only the guy would think they'd done him a favour, so he would now owe them a favour. But that was the exception. Nine times out of ten, all they'd do is tell a lieutenant like me, 'This man's boy got a slap round the Regency – so tell the guy who did it to piss off.'

Otherwise, the Krays weren't in the business of settling other people's problems. For instance, if a girl claimed she'd been assaulted or raped by some toe-rag, that wouldn't have troubled the Twins at all. They would have thought, 'She's probably an old slag anyway,' and that would be the end of it. On the other hand, if they were trying to court the girl's father or brother, they might say, 'Leave it to us, George, we'll sort it out.' Then they might well say, 'Right, we'll go give him a slap.'

Not many legitimate people ever asked such favours. The Twins would think it must be a get-up if ever a straight person did come to Fort Vallance and say, 'Listen, could you help us out over so-and-so?' They'd say to themselves, 'Who is this stranger?' and they'd go in the other room and keep asking all of us, 'Who is he?' Then they'd send someone else in to talk to him, because by now they were thinking there's some sort of wind-up here. Perhaps the police were behind this guy and trying to entrap them.

The Twins' paranoia about spies and infiltrators was partly a reflection of their own mass exploitation of spies and infiltrators into other gangs. Most of their own 'thousand spies' contributed information only occasionally, but there were several full-time professionals. One was called Joe Schaffer. He was just like someone out of *Fiddler on the Roof*: a typical old Jewish gentleman. He would creep around all the places frequented by other mobs. He knew everybody. And anything we needed to hear, he would tell us. Or you could send him on special trips, specific missions: 'Have a look round so-and-so,' or 'See what you can find out about this person.' Then he'd go out and discover if this target was using a particular club, or how the individual or group was moving around the West End.

I could not stand spies like old Joe Schaffer, even though they were meant to be working for us. Those people were creepy but they all had a use. The Twins could get them to do anything for a fiver. That pair had a talent for finding just the right bloke for any job but they had no training for this. Nowadays you go to college to learn business management, even industrial espionage, but Ronnie and Reggie knew it instinctively – just as they knew how to terrorize people better than any terrorist. They knew how to question folk and how to kid them. It was just basic instinct. And you could see it working, you could see it unfold, from one day to the next. You'd get an idea one day and discuss it with the Twins, they'd go silent for a while, then they'd say, 'Oh, yeah, get hold of so-and-so.' They'd know exactly who to put into a scheme to make it work. And work it would.

I'm not thinking only of grand scams, but of all sorts of little rip-offs too. Say we want a decent car because we've got to pick up a top American boxer like Barney Ross, so we decide it's an American Galaxy we need. So the Twins send a family friend called Nobby Clark to get hold of that. He's packed off to see Horace, the car-dealer over south London, who deals in Yankee motors. 'Go and get hold of Horace,' the Twins would say, and they'll pick out Nobby for the job because they know that, if one of us guys on the Firm goes over, Horace would immediately realize it's a straightforward blag. So it would be, 'Send Nobby over to see Horace. Tell him, "The boys want to borrow a car, they've got to meet someone." Then invite Horace to the party.'

That's why, when you see those posed photos that the Krays were so fond of taking, you'll often see a lot of funny unfamiliar faces. That was usually the only reason they'd been invited – 'Have your photo done with the ex-world champion' – as part of the perks. The poor dupes didn't realize that the invite and the photo were all they'd be getting. They certainly weren't getting paid for the loan of the limo or supplying the booze. That was just the soft part of the business. There'd be no explicit coercion, not a whiff of violence, although even a straight man like Horace would have known not to mess with Reggie and Ronnie.

Some people might never have had anything to do with the Twins, might never have met them or known they exist, but these innocents could still be gunned down on Ronnie's orders. One day Ronnie got a message from a man he'd met in jail who was still locked up. This guy was complaining that his wife was having it off with a carpet salesman who worked in Romford Market, and he was asking Ronnie if he could get the salesman seen to. So the Colonel told Ronnie Hart and Connie Whitehead to go and shoot him. We had his car number, and a dealer got us his address from hire-purchase documents, because he was buying the car by instalments. So Hart and Whitehead drove off to Romford and came back telling how Hart had gone up to this carpet guy in the market and shot him in the hip, while Whitehead stayed in the driving seat for a quick getaway. Then they described how the impact of the .38 bullet had made the victim do a somersault. As soon as I heard this, I knew it was baloney. I could tell it had never happened, but I wasn't going to say this to Ronnie Kray, because the fellow should not have been shot anyway.

Even though I bit my tongue, I could see Ronnie wasn't sure about their story either because he said, 'Be in the paper, won't it?' 'Yeah,' said Connie and Ronnie Hart in a faltering way, as if they didn't believe it themselves. 'Let's get the local Romford and Dagenham papers,' said the Colonel, as by now both the Twins wanted proof that the guy had been hurt. So someone was sent out to get all the papers, but there was nothing in them.

So, to defuse the situation, I said, 'Well, if the bullet has gone right through the guy, he's not going to report it. He's going to go home and patch it up, so it won't be in the papers, will it?' I didn't have to say this was what I had tried to do when Reggie shot me, but Ronnie got the message. 'Oh, yeah,' he said, and he stood for it. He was convinced. So I looked at Hart and Whitehead, and I could see the relief on their faces. I should have gone into them for barrister's fees. Ronnie Hart told me later he had no intention of doing the guy: 'Nothing to do with us.'

So we weren't blindly obedient to the Colonel when he was in one of his silly moods. We just worked our way round it because we knew that in a few days' time he would have totally changed his mind. Then he'd probably say, 'Oh, sorry about him. He wasn't a bad fellow really,' but by then it would have been too late. He'd have been gone.

With these shoot-to-kill orders being issued for no good reason, even us members of the Firm took precautions in case Ronnie condemned us to death. This was no paranoid fantasy. Most of us had been recruited through violence, and we could all see that it wouldn't be long before Ronnie took his violence to the ultimate degree and killed somebody. I'm not being wise after seeing what happened later. It was happening within the Firm as soon as 1965, when he was already operating what he called his 'list'.

It didn't take much to get 'on the list'. It must have been in early summer 1965 when Ronnie had called a meet one afternoon at a house in Ilford off the Eastern Avenue near a big roundabout. A Jewish girl named Sandra lived up there, though she wasn't around when Ronnie unveiled his deadly intention against one of our own colleagues on the Firm: suddenly he announced he wanted to see Connie Whitehead. Then out came the tools: it was a hammer stuck under this cushion, a Gurkha knife under that one, an iron bar over there – all so that when Connie came in the room, wherever he sat, a tool would be handy, and he was going to get done. Now, there we all are, stuck in the house, nobody can leave, and nobody can use the phone, in case they warn him.

But of course somebody still had to tell Connie to come to this house, so Ronnie ordered Fat Wally Garelick to phone Connie up and kid him into coming. Meantime Ronnie, me, and somebody else I can't remember, were all going to be ready to ambush him and send him to his maker. Well, Wally went out to phone Connie, but, instead of kidding him into showing up, he warned him not to come. He just said to Whitehead, 'Don't show, they're going to do you.' And so he didn't show.

Meantime Wally came back in the room. While we were all waiting for Connie, who should show up instead but the police, who'd been called by suspicious neighbours curious about why so many obvious thugs were padding around Sandra's flat. These coppers came in and took our names and addresses, but they didn't bother to search the place or look under the cushions. Anyway, they went away, and Connie never showed up. He owed his life to Fat Wally.

Now Wally had warned Connie partly because he felt, on past form, that the delay would give Ronnie time to wear off his mood and calm down. And, very likely, tomorrow he would see whatever Connie had done to upset him in an entirely different light. Well, all that was fine for Connie, but, by tipping him off, Wally had now put himself on the line, because he was the only person who could possibly have given the warning.

For a couple of months Ronnie seemed to forget entirely about doing Connie. Instead he brooded on Fat Wally Garelick, first by dropping him out from the fringes of the Firm and then by suckering him down to where he was due to meet a fate even worse than Ronnie had planned to inflict on Connie.

It was now high summer, when the Twins often stayed at Steeple Bay, near Colchester, where their mum and dad had a caravan. At weekends Fat Wally Garelick used to ferry people down there in a big old Rover with plenty of room for huge hoodlums. This particular weekend down Wally came to join half a dozen other folk. But Ronnie was in one of his moods, some kind of depression, and as soon as he saw Wally he called him into the van. He was going to kill him there and then. He was going to kill the man himself. Now, Wally was a big man. He was only twenty-two years of age, but he weighed twenty-two stone. He was vast yet harmless, but Ronnie was going to do him with a kitchen knife! In his mother's caravan! Until somebody managed to get Wally out of earshot and told Ronnie that, because of Wally's size, he would have to stab him at least ten times, and this would make a terrible mess of his mother's caravan. That stopped it. Ronnie decided not to proceed, but only because he didn't want to upset his mum. It was as close as that. So very easy, whether that guy lives or dies.

Of course, the reason why the Colonel had picked on Wally was because it could only have been Wally who had disobeyed him and warned Connie Whitehead. Here were two clear conspiracies to murder, the year before Ronnie finally managed to 'make his bones' and kill someone. If Connie had turned up, he would surely have been killed. And if Wally had been lighter, we would have had to wrap him in the carpet, take him out from the caravan and dump him somewhere. He would have gone. So that summer several of us led charmed lives. Not just Connie and Wally, but me and the rest of the Firm too, because we could all have been done for murder along with Colonel Ron.

It still wasn't over, because Ronnie hated Connie and was still looking for a way to get him done. He saw his chance at the Starlight one night, while I was working there as the security man. Connie was being a bit flash and had upset our colleague on the Firm, Scotch Jack Dickson. Ronnie picked up on this and stirred Scotch Jack up into a Scotch broth. He was stamping around and complaining to Ronnie, 'That Connie Whitehead! I don't know what he's being so flash about.' This suited Ronnie just fine so he said to Jack, 'Well, go and do him.' As I've said, Jack wasn't the toughest of men, and he didn't think he could come off best in a head-to-head with Connie, so he told Ronnie, 'No, I don't fancy it.' But Ronnie urged him on: 'Wait till he's getting a drink, then do him in the back.' And Ronnie meant, do him with a knife.

I couldn't interfere directly, but I could see that at this moment Connie was at the counter with his back to Jack, just as Jack was psyching himself up to do him. Then Connie came away from the counter, so Jack wouldn't be able to do it for a while at least. Then Connie came past me through a little lobby where I was standing, on his way to the toilet, so I said, 'Get out! Just get out!' He didn't need any more telling. He walked right on past the toilet and out. He could have been killed that night, as a follow-on to the Ilford business, only this time Ronnie was trying to get someone else to do the murder for him.

In this homicidal climate it wasn't surprising that we all began to take serious precautions against Ronnie's mad and murderous moods. Even one of the Twins' own relatives didn't trust his own life in their hands.

Young Ronnie Hart was one of thousands of Eastenders who claimed to be cousins of the Twins, but he really was a cousin by blood. He and I partnered off together. This is something you quickly pick up: being partners. If you get on with a guy, if you feel you can trust him, it's chemistry. It's like all those cop buddy movies you see. Professional criminals are just like cops in all sorts of ways. We both can live or die through our partner's common sense or stupidity, loyalty or treachery, his split-second reactions or his loss of nerve.

So Ronnie Hart and I came to trust each other as partners. If I was going somewhere and I needed a driver, it would be Ronnie Hart, rather than, say, Ronnie Bender that I wanted with me. This is how we were paired off and became a working team. So Ronnie and I might be sent to a drinker to see so-and-so. And we'd go in there, and if we saw any opportunities to 'nip', if we could frighten the manager and take some dough, that was our money. We didn't take it back to the Twins. We'd got it by our own efforts. But in those circumstances you couldn't afford to trust anybody but your partner because the Twins were shrewd. They weren't what you'd call intelligent, but they were naturally shrewd. They would slip in a spy who would then criticize Ronnie Kray in front of you, saying something like, 'He's a fat bastard.' Now, they're standing there at a bar wanting your reaction. So, if you say, 'Yeah, you're right, he is a fat bastard,' this *agent provocateur* would go straight back and report what you'd said to the Twins.

To avoid this, what you had to do was discipline the *agent provocateur* for daring to come up to you: you give him a roasting for having called Ronnie a fat bastard. Then he would tail it back to the Twins and report that you were OK: you'd passed the loyalty test. So all the time you had to be on your toes. You had to be more wary of your own criminal kind than of the police.

For safety's sake me and Ronnie Hart developed a little code, because, if the Twins wanted you for what they called 'Naughties' – to do you over – they would never send a stranger to your house, because you wouldn't come out. Or, if you did come out, you were going to be tooled up, ready for the maniacs. So we knew that if the Twins were going to send somebody to get you for 'Naughties', they would send your own partner, because that's the only person you trust. So me and Ronnie worked out that if we were ever told to get each other, he would call me 'Jake', which was a nickname I got from somewhere. Then if he said Jake, I knew it meant danger. I had another special name for him, so we would both know if something was wrong, and we had to be on our 'dancers'.

You could be up for 'Naughties' on the slightest pretext. 'Naughties' meant you were to be reprimanded and disciplined for something they felt you had done wrong. That's why we needed this little code, to forewarn each other. Then, if during the next few hours or days you were asked out for a drink by the Twins, you knew it wouldn't be a drink but a beating. Because you'd been a naughty boy.

Suppose, within the Firm, you had done something that upset the Twins, or you might have overtrodden your limits and nicked a bit of their business, then they would decide, 'We want to have a word with him.' Then they'd tell someone else to 'go and get' you. If that happens, you're in for 'Naughties', the severity of your punishment depending on what you'd done. Or, on Ronnie's mood, because he was a lunatic, there's no two ways about that. He would pop these very strong tranquillizers like smarties. Whether a man lived or died would depend entirely on his mood. Or on whether he'd got in a running supply of Stematol from Doc Blasker.

We knew that whatever Ronnie and Reggie were ready to do to us henchmen, they were bursting to do even worse to their enemies. But what about the police? Weren't they going to step in and impose law and order on gangland? Well, no, we all thought. Neither the local Old Bill nor Scotland Yard's finest were much of a factor in our calculations. No one on the Firm believed the law would step in to avenge any of the Krays' victims. We felt that in a large part of east London the Twins had become the law. They were the police force. If there was any justice going, it was in the gift of Ronnie and Reggie.

We never thought that the real cops would come at the Twins again. The *Mirror* libel settlement had made the entire Kray Firm immune from investigation by the newspapers. And then we had a whisper that a Scotland Yard investigation, which had been running since the summer of 1964, had failed to persuade credible victims of our protection rackets to give hard evidence. Nor would any of the front men arrested over the Twins' long-firm frauds name their ultimate bosses. Everyone was scared stiff to come out against Ronnie and Reggie because of the Boothby fiasco and the general feeling that they would always be free to kick your door down, and your head in, and put a bullet in you on the way out.

OK, in January 1965 they were charged with demanding money with menaces from Hew McCowan, a poof aristocrat, soon to inherit a baronetcy, who ran a club called the Hideaway in Soho. He had the courage to testify against them, but he had an embarrassing past. The supporting witness fell apart, and in March Ronnie, Reggie and their co-defendant, Mad Teddy Smith, walked out of the Old Bailey in triumph and celebration. That taught Eastenders and even Westenders a lot, above all that they should 'Watch the wall, my darling, while the Gentlemen go by!' The Twins themselves spread the message far and wide. How often did I hear them say, 'They can never nick us now. People just won't stand for it again.' For the next three years they acted as if they were immune from prosecution. And they almost were, because surely no witnesses in their right minds would come forward again and risk getting murdered by these gangland Untouchables.

There's no doubt the detectives on the McCowan job had done their damnedest to put the Twins away. We knew that Inspector Nipper Read almost pulled it off, and now he had a bee in his bonnet over their acquittal. Then we heard his squad had been disbanded. I can imagine the guffaws of all those bent cops who'd connived in the rise of the Twins and other firms across London, as they saw this straight Johnny humiliated. He'd have the last laugh, but in 1965 that never looked remotely possible.

Even if all Scotland Yard's detectives had been straight, they would have had a tough job nailing the Krays, but we knew a lot of coppers were bent, and the Firm had plenty of dough to hand out in their direction. It was the only time, I think, the Firm did anything sensible with its income. We drank most of it away. It was far more constructive to give some to the police, to Old Bill. So as well as paying underworld spies for information, the Twins paid cops for information from the other side: who they were targeting, who was going to get nicked, who'd had a good tickle and was sitting on a fat wad, but also – and most important – which of our underworld cronies might be informing on the Twins themselves.

This may come as a surprise, because the tradition is that the Krays so intimidated the locals, they didn't need to pay police.

Nonsense! In our day gangsters always needed to pay police, and the Twins paid on a regular basis. We didn't all sit round a table and say, 'OK, Sergeant, here's £300, what can you tell us?' It was done more discreetly.

The Firm used to go to a pub in Walthamstow in Hoe Street, but often me and Reggie would talk to the 'enemy' before we went in. We'd peel off separately. We would walk down a row of parked cars, then suddenly he'd say, 'All right, walk on a bit.' Then he would jump in a car, and I would walk up and down while he'd be sitting with a copper, doing the business. As the meet was so clandestine, and the copper was all alone, he could not have been talking to Reggie for any legitimate reason. When it was all over Reggie would get out, and the copper would drive away. I hadn't overheard anything, but we'd go back to the pub, and Reggie would have a private discussion with Ronnie. Then they would both feed out what they wanted us to know. We knew it had all come from the copper, because it was like a weekly news bulletin straight from Scotland Yard, hot off the press.

The trade went both ways. That's common sense. People say, 'Oh in the good old days nobody grassed,' but that's rubbish because a CID man cannot exist without his informants. So if you give every CID man in the Metropolitan Police at least two informants, you've got a lot of informants buzzing round. For instance, we knew that anybody who got bail at that time had to be an informer. How else would they have got bail? They got bail for bodies – for shopping people to the cops. So you wouldn't have anything to do with them because the police would be expecting them to deliver a return favour, which might just be your body.

As for Ronnie and Reggie, they have this image of being staunch, of never informing to the police, but this was a false image they created for themselves. There were several cases where people who had upset the Twins for some reason, such as refusing to give them a share in a club, would suddenly be arrested. Now these were people who we couldn't just walk in on and slap, because they wouldn't stand for it, but within a couple of weeks of spurning the Krays, they'd be busted by the police. There was no way you could prove a connection between the two events, but it only had to happen two or three times, and you knew it was going on.

I personally never paid police officers. I didn't have to. As a member of the Firm, I was safe under the blanket of whatever protection had been arranged by others. I couldn't stand in court and say, 'They paid this particular copper money,' because I didn't see the money change hands. It was just common knowledge that this was what we were in Walthamstow for. It would happen once a week, and as soon as we came away from that meet, Reggie would have fresh knowledge he couldn't have got anywhere else.

Outwardly, of course, the Twins kept up a fierce hostility towards the police. One night we all went up to the Gallipoli restaurant and night-club, a Turkish gaff in the City of London. We'd finished our meal, and Ronnie and Ian Barrie were already out sitting in the motor. I was still inside with Reggie, waiting while he was collecting his coat, when a guy came up the stairs, swearing and shouting at Reggie, whom he obviously recognized. I thought there was going to be the most awful punch-up, maybe even a manslaughter or two, because this man was showing dreadful disrespect. He was drunk out of his skull, and then his mate came up from behind and grabbed him and said, 'We're Old Bill, he's off duty, leave him alone.' It just must have got up this guy's nose to see us parading around, splashing out money, gained by criminal means, on good living. 'We don't want to know,' said the sober cop, and we all just backed off.

The encounter was symbolic. The myth of the Krays – Krayology as it was later called in court – made even tough coppers think twice about ripping into the Twins. The entire police force of London was backing off, and there'd be dead bodies all over the place, before they got back on our case.

7: A WAR IS DECLARED

'Executive stress' is what they call it nowadays. All we knew then was that Ronnie and Reggie kept on saying they'd had enough. So much decision-making every day: who to rip off, who to extort, who to slap, who to 'do', put 'on the list' and plot to kill. Life's tough at the top in any field, but for the Twins to retire? At just thirty-two? We couldn't believe it. We didn't believe it, because it wasn't true. They didn't really mean it, though by Christ we wished they did.

Of the two people we were working for, one was a certifiable lunatic, and the other wasn't much better. So when they talked about going to live in a mansion in Suffolk, we did everything to encourage them. They had a friend called Jeff Allen who specialized in buying country houses, doing them up and selling them off at a fat profit. He had a beautiful place called Lavenham Hall, where, while they were in this retirement mood, we met some people from the American publishers McGraw-Hill to discuss a deal for their 'official' biography, which didn't come off.

Later Jeff Allen was nicked for setting fire to some properties that he couldn't shift, but at this time he helped the Twins buy a beautiful pile called The Brooks in Bildeston, near Lavenham. There was also a lodge cottage and eight acres of land with a little stream running through it, all theirs for a mere £12,500. They had to spend a bit more doing the place up, but they said it was the kind of home they had dreamed of owning ever since they had been evacuated near by. Their idea was to live down at The Brooks while we carried on in the East End. They would still head the Firm, but we were to run the business and just report to them at weekends. This sounded great except I could never see the Twins settling down in a dear little village like Bildeston, where the only nightspot for miles was the local pub.

Even so, we wanted this retirement scheme to go through because they were ruining a lot of activities from which we could all have made huge profits, if only they had left us to run them. A for instance. They knew casinos could make a lot of money so they 'bought' Esmeralda's Barn. Then they ruined the place, partly because they couldn't understand the odds in any form of gambling, partly because they had no patience. To get the best return from a casino you have to hire straight front-men: efficient croupiers and managers who are reasonably honest, who won't steal from the house (provided they're under strict scrutiny), but who also know the technicalities of the casino game.

Little Tommy Cowley, who was on the brains side of the Firm, understood the gaming racket perfectly and could have run the entire operation. If we had hired the right people to set up American dice tables at Esmeralda's Barn, it would have been like printing money. But the Twins could never work with straight people, because their own greed would undo them. They would see a lump of money, and they'd pull it out. They'd spoil a whole operation for a quick buck, rather than leave it ticking over nicely, making a steady and legitimate profit.

They had acquired the Barn for a mere £1000 after their business brain, Leslie Payne, had intimidated the previous owner with veiled threats of Krayland violence if he refused to sell. Its smart Knightsbridge location, in Wilton Place, was perfect for the high-class punters who had been going there before the Twins moved in. If only Ron and Reg had stayed away, it would have earned them a fortune, but instead, they behaved just like they did in Bethnal Green and the Mile End Road. They frightened the very people who were busting to gamble fortunes away. Big casino punters were perhaps the first people the Twins had ever come across who would, in effect, throw huge sums at them, just for pleasure, without a beating or even the threat of it.

At first the Twins took plenty from the Barn, because it had not yet lost its reputation. They could have pocketed £40,000 a year each if they had just left everything as it was, but within a year the place was losing money, because all the rich punters had de-camped with the manager, Tony Mancini, to another casino that he set up in Mayfair. This Mancini was a very smooth army-officer type, an absolute charmer, who knew the casino business backwards and all the really good customers. He was his own man and wouldn't put up with any of Ronnie's nonsense.

At the Barn Ronnie would act the generous host and just give the profits away. If he wanted to favour a punter – and this punter did not have to be homosexual – Ronnie would give him unlimited credit. It didn't matter if this guy lost £20,000, Ronnie would still be saying, 'Give him some credit. It's down to me.' When the guy ended the evening still a long way down and wrote out a cheque to settle his debts, it would only be days before that cheque bounced. Ronnie hadn't grasped that you should only give credit to people you know have the money to settle their debts. That way he ran Esmeralda's into the ground. The place crashed when it failed to pay its taxes. It went into liquidation, owing a vast sum of money. The Twins had managed to turn a straight business, which was making a fortune, into a financial disaster. In our terms this was one of the most 'criminal' things they ever did.

Another classic was the way Ronnie and Reggie blew the gaming machine business. In 1960 one-armed bandits had been made legal so suddenly that most of them had to be bought in from America through firms with Mafia connections. Now if, as the Krays always fancied, they were well stuck in with the Mafia you might reasonably believe they could have had this one-armed bandit business to themselves – at least in the East End, where a lot of pubs and clubs would have found a Kray offer to install and service these machines impossible to refuse.

THE ENFORCER

But oh no! For the Twins this business didn't bring in a fast enough return. They were incapable of grasping that machines could have brought them a steady income over a long period. The tax was just £75 a year for one machine, but the take could be thousands. I found this out by accident when I walked up to the guy who emptied the machine at the Starlight. I just asked him, 'You all right, mate? How's it going? How's the machine doing?' He looked at me a bit nervously and then he gave me a big bag of sixpences. I must have given the impression that I'd sussed he was up to something, so this was my pay-off. I didn't ask, 'What's this for?' I just went, 'Oh, all right, yeah, that'll do.' Every time he came in after that, he gave me another big bag. That was a bonus for me, but he must have been stealing fortunes from all the machines on his round. Now if the Kray Firm had owned the machines, he wouldn't have dared steal because he would have got his head broken.

At bottom, the Twins' mentality was no better than this collector's. They only wanted quick money. Instead of operating a lucrative machine rental business within the law, they preferred to sell the machines and then frighten the new owners into making pay-offs. They couldn't see that doing it near enough legitimately would earn you far more money than using criminal methods, and without any risk, aggro or stress.

They weren't capable of seeing that all we needed was a team of straight machine engineers to make this business a lasting success. They should have got hold of at least a half-straight person, and said, 'Right, we're going to put you in charge of the machines. You'll be given so much a week, you'll be responsible for organizing a couple of mechanics, we'll get you a van and some tools, you'll collect the takings and return them to us, and we don't want any messing about.' Suitably frighten him so he knows where he stands, then just leave it to him. If there's any trouble – any publican or club-owner who says he doesn't want the machines any more – then our man is to come straight back and report to Head Office! Now the diplomats of the Firm should go and have a quiet word with the client and convince him how good a deal he's getting – without any express threats or violence. All that's left unsaid, though it is implied, because people still know it's the Kray Firm they're trading with.

This is the ideal criminal enterprise: a crooked business run straight. We could have done the same with minicabs. We could have smothered the East End with cab companies, but the Twins couldn't cope with that idea because it meant running a business, as opposed to going in and demanding money off someone else's business. They had no way of grasping the difference. They had no concentration either.

At one point they were so impressed with the way the Mafia had taken over the wealthy Teamsters' Union in America that they thought of getting hold of the dockers over here. They got talking to a convenor in the docks who, they thought, could act as their Jimmy Hoffa-type front. That idea fell apart so they switched to the other side, scheming how to operate a gang of strike-breakers against the Transport and General Workers' Union whose members always seemed to be walking out and bringing the Port of London to a standstill. It was all talk. Nothing came of it, because this kind of thing needs brains, strategy and application to pull it off either way, and the Twins had none of these.

They didn't even have the patience to run what was then the easiest rip-off fraud of all: the long-firm. In a long-firm all you do is set yourself up as a company in some rented premises, a suite of offices or a warehouse. You get a front-man with no criminal record to speak of, but with a plausible educated manner. On your instructions he sets up a few bank accounts and acquires bogus credit references, preferably from other companies that you have set up specially to write them. Now your man starts ordering lots of gear that you know you can flog off quick at knock-down prices. Drink, cigarettes, electrical goods, stuff like that, which everybody wants. You settle the first few invoices on the dot, until you've established yourselves as good solid customers. Now you get extended credit, and the manufacturers and wholesalers are bursting to supply you with more and more goods, worth many thousands of pounds. Then suddenly, after three months or so, you shift everything out of all your traceable premises within a day, selling the gear off as fast as you can.

When the suppliers suss you've disappeared without paying them, it's too late. If the police or trade officials bother to investigate, it will be months later, and they won't find any of the goods. The only person they may arrest – if he's still in this country – will be that plausible front-man. But he's known all along what he was there for, and you've paid him handsomely in cash, which he'll have stashed away in some secret account abroad. So usually he'll plead guilty, take all the blame and do a year in an open prison without bitterness. And as he knows you've got a lot of gorillas on your firm, and he's concerned for his wife and kids, he'll keep stumm.

I have never run a long-firm, and I don't like the idea of using front-men as fall-guys. But there's no doubt that, in those days, long-firms were a very easy way to make a fortune. Through Leslie Payne, the Twins were behind a number of long-firms and made quite a lot of money from them, but even in these safe bust-out jobs they didn't have the patience to let them run long enough. They'd wait only until a fair sum had been run up, then they'd grab it. Once again, their greed was self-defeating.

As the Krays were considered to be at the pinnacle of organized crime in Britain, it's a pity they couldn't organize. They certainly couldn't delegate responsibility when it came to serious financial matters. I don't think they trusted anybody enough to let them get on with it. They didn't like to see other people getting rich. They didn't see that money could make more money for everyone. They thought of it as a one-off commodity: you nipped it off other folk, then you spent it. You didn't invest it. You blew it.

Right. If they retired, we could diversify, we could get into all sorts of fresh business. We wouldn't have Ronnie and Reggie walking into pubs and frightening the shit out of everybody. We could talk to folk who we couldn't talk to in front of them. They'd always chip in, 'What are you talking to that slag for?' when we were on the verge of getting hold of real money through quality people. On the other hand, if they disappeared to Suffolk, we could step forward as reasonably respectable types. We'd still be Ronnie and Reggie's men but we'd cut out all their silly, unpredictable violence. I'm sure Charlie Kray felt the same way. Their shenanigans didn't help him in his efforts to cultivate legitimate people. So all of us were waiting for them to go, but they didn't. They clung on.

This was self-defeating because, the longer they clung on, the more jealous they became of firms ruling other parts of London who were making fortunes out of a wide range of enterprises. The Twins became obsessed by the versatility of the Richardsons in south-east London. Led by Charlie Richardson and his brother Eddie, this gang were into everything because they were a well-organized business team.

We knew a lot about them because another south London boss, Freddie Foreman, was a long-time friend of the Twins, and his firm had a spy in their crowd. This source was telling us how the Richardsons were getting £1000 a week from just one bit of business: the London Airport carparks. Charlie Richardson also had his scrap-yards, his long-firms, his South African stuff, plus all his regular protection rackets on the other side of the water.

The idea that Charlie Richardson was becoming stinking rich drove Ronnie into blind jealousy – blind because he should have seen we should copy the Richardsons. But no. Just because he couldn't match them, all he wanted to do was smash them and take over their empire. He believed that if the Firm didn't soon crush the Richardsons, they would quickly crush the Firm.

For once Ronnie may have been right. They were certainly trying to get in the West End, which the Twins felt was mainly their territory. Far worse, they were invading the East End as well. They were getting money out of a local minicab firm, and one of their outfit, Brian Mottram, had a long-firm fraud running in Hackney Road, so we began to feel they were nicking all the sweets out of the East End. They'd got as far east as Southend where we traced another Richardson long-firm, involving Billy Stayton. Once we went to look for him there but we couldn't find out where he was living. Someone on the Firm found his girlfriend and tried to get to him that way but nothing happened. So Ronnie was feeling powerless while his arch-enemies were popping up all over our own manor.

To try to cool things there was a meeting – not a boardroom meeting, more like a gangland summit – between Freddie Foreman's firm, from inner south London, the Nashes, north London, the Twins, east London, and the Richardsons, south-east London. The idea was that they were getting together to cut London up, and to make sure they didn't interfere with each other's business. But the Richardsons were already getting too much money. What they said amounted to, 'Piss off, we don't need you,' and this upset the Twins.

I wasn't at the meeting. Afterwards Ronnie said, 'The flash bastards. We spoke to them, but they didn't want to know.' He had to tell us this much because the Twins were now telling us to get ready to go to war.

And so a war was declared. The Firm had a meet at Vallance Road: there were the three Krays, of course, then me, Connie Whitehead, Scotch Jack Dickson and Ian Barrie and a few others. And all of a sudden we were told we were officially at war with the Richardsons because of a big row over their man Billy Stayton's operations on our turf – not just the long-firm in Southend but some club he was running with Ginger Dennis, who wasn't strictly on the Richardson firm but was connected to it. We were told that both Stayton and Dennis were 'going to go': they were on the Twins' list and had to die. But they were only on the fringes. A lot of other people were 'going to go' too.

The Twins cut a list up. We were each given the name of a member of the Richardson firm, so that when it really came off, our job was to take this one particular person out to kill him. So me and Connie Whitehead were given Brian Mottram, one of the Richardsons' long-firm men. 'Take Mottram out' was the command. Once we'd done him, we would probably be given another one. Scotch Jack and Ian Barrie were given Frankie Fraser; Ronnie Kray and Nobby Clark were going to have Charles Richardson, though, if it had actually come to it, Ronnie would have wanted to do Fraser too. Reggie was going to have Eddie Richardson. George Cornell was also mentioned, but he wasn't top of the list.

We were also told where our various targets lived, what pubs and clubs they used, if they had a girlfriend, what place of business they used. In Mottram's case we were given the address of his bolt-hole in Hackney. Most important of all, we were each given access to a gun. This was true for every pair on the Firm. All we had to do now was wait for the off – the order to move into action.

The scenario would have gone something like this. As soon as Ronnie went into one of his depressions, or something upset him, he would have said, 'That's it! Go!' Now it would have been make or break. We either go and do the guy, or we take off and go somewhere else. Split from the East End. Disappear. Vamoose. You either do it or you don't, and then you go from there.

What would have happened at that point, you can only guess at. I imagine the police may have known about the whole business all the time. They probably knew what was occurring, but can't you imagine a couple of old superintendents sitting there saying, 'Why don't we let them do it? They can blow each other away!' That would have saved the police and the public a lot of trouble and money.

There was one serious difficulty. None of us knew the faces. Most of us had no idea what our target looked like! We were going to have to assassinate people we weren't even able to recognize. Sure, we knew what Frankie Fraser looked like. He was the main man on their firm, their torpedo. He wasn't on the business side, that was Charlie Richardson's area, but if you wanted to speak to them, you spoke to Fraser first. He's only a little guy, about five foot seven, but he had the guts to come right into our territory to talk with the Twins. The three of them would go into a huddle and talk business, but nothing came of it because the Twins never announced a truce with the Richardsons, and we certainly never joined forces.

Whenever Fraser came over, back-up muscle wasn't far away. This got our nerves jangling, because we never knew if the war itself was just going to start. Once Fraser came to the Black Lion and was talking to Reggie on his own. Then one of our Firm came in and whispered, 'There's a motor parked up the road, and they're sitting in it four-handed.' Naturally we assumed this was Fraser's crowd so, if anything had happened in that pub or if he hadn't come out by a certain time, these guys would have come in. Later we were told that they had all been tooled up with shooters. This made us jumpy. As we had all their names and addresses, we assumed they had the same on us. As we had a spy in their camp, it was possible they had a spy in ours. This was one reason why the Twins were always worrying about who they could trust among us. When they suspected someone, they'd feed him misinformation to see what would happen with it.

Once Reggie came to me and said, 'I've been told to look out for a guy called Barry.' So I said, 'Well, my name's Barry' (because, to fox the police, I wasn't generally using Donoghue). 'No. It's not you,' he said, which meant they had already done some checking. So I said, 'Well, it can't be Ian Barrie, surely?' 'No. I don't know.' And that was the last of it.

Up the West End we also used to see a lot more of Fraser, along with Charlie and Eddie Richardson at various clubs, like the Astor, the Pigalle or the Society. We'd bump into them sitting with the likes of Jimmy Moody who was another name 'on the list'. The West End was neutral territory. You'd measure each other up, and make sure nothing was going on. But, if there was going to be war, we wouldn't fight it out in a locale where one hundred uniformed coppers and the entire West End Central CID would be on us in no time.

Meantime Connie Whitehead and I still had no idea what Mottram looked like, though we did get some help. I went to see Freddie Foreman at his pub in the Borough, and he gave me a photo of a football team: the Soho Rangers. This was basically the Richardson mob in shorts, including Eddie Richardson, Fraser and Billy Stayton, with Stanley Baker the film star in support. The photo was useful for the rest of our Firm, but no use to me because Brian Mottram wasn't in the team.

I can't say my heart was in this assignment. This Mottram we were assigned to kill wasn't a man of violence, he was just involved in the long-firms. Also I had no personal animosity towards the Richardsons. As long as they stayed away from me I stayed away from them. I wasn't at all sure then – and I still can't say now – whether I would have done this killing or deserted the Firm and risked facing a firing squad. I just hoped something would happen to stop the war starting, as we had no idea where it might end.

We all knew these south London guys were no pushovers. They were thugs just like us, though when it came to violence, even nastier. We already had a good idea of the tortures used by Fraser and the Richardsons. Gruesome stories would dribble through. There was Harry 'Boot' Cashman, the guy who had the Silver Spinner spieler over Stoke Newington, where I worked for a while. After I'd talked that Greek guy with the gun out of the Spinner, Boot told me, 'I liked the way you did that. I've met all these so-called gunmen. I'm sick of them, specially that other mob over the water. They done me.' He went on to explain that somehow he had upset them, so he was called into their scrap-yard in Peckham. It was common practice to get a general beating, have your toes broken or your teeth pulled, but he had the real treatment from them. He told me how they had charged him up with the electric generator. They wired victims up to this generator and gave them a couple of turns. They called this the 'Crank Up'.

So in revenge Boot sat in the Astor Club up the West End every night for two weeks with a gun in his pocket waiting for them to come in. Only they didn't show. Not that I think they would have been afraid to show, they just had business elsewhere. After that Boot gave up. He said they crippled some people, mentally as well as physically. When a person's had such a going-over, with all the jeering and laughing that goes on while he screams, he gets done in the head. Psychologically he's wasted. I can't think of anyone, other than Boot Cashman, who ever went on a vengeance trail. The guy had guts.

We were told that the Richardsons even tortured their own people, especially the men who fronted their long-firms. As I've explained, when gangsters shut a long-firm down and run off with all the goods, the front-men are always the fall guys. They get nicked because their names are on all the paperwork. Most front-men regard jail as an occupational hazard, but a few – particularly those who don't come from a criminal background – may get upset when they realize they're really going to jail. Now sometimes these guys want to start screaming. But if a Richardson fall-guy went to complain to them, or if the Richardsons heard they were getting pally with a copper, they would be taken in, cranked up and given the 'electric'.

We were told all this stuff about the Richardsons and how they nailed people to the floor. Some of this has filtered out and been used in films like *Villain* with Richard Burton, where they hung a guy out the window, cut his arse with a razor and left him hanging there. The Richardsons did something similar. It seems they went to some guy's premises and had some argument with him, but he wouldn't let them walk out. He kept going, 'Let me explain! Let me explain!' but they just wanted to get away. So they gave him a right-hander, held him down and just put a nail through his hand into the floor so they could walk out in peace. They just left him there. Like tying a dog to a lamp-post.

We heard another story where there was a guy who was forced to sit on the floor and was then whacked over the head with a bayonet. You haven't got a lot of flesh on your skull so the blow left a gaping wound. Then one of the Richardson crowd remarked how much the wound looked like a mouth. So another gangster who was eating a pie at the time, said, 'Yeah, well, let's give it something to eat!' and ground the pie into the gash. Meantime the victim was just sitting there moaning and screaming.

Well, whether these stories were true or false, when Ronnie heard them he used to say that anyone who tortured somebody must be a coward. That was rich coming from him! What's the difference between torturing someone and having him paralysed with fear while you whack him with a Gurkha knife or brand him with a poker? There's no difference to me.

A lot more torture stuff came out when Fraser and the Richardsons went on trial in 1967, how their victims had their toes smashed and their teeth pulled with pliers. Of course, the Richardsons say it was all a get-up, they never did any of this, but there's people walking or limping around today who'll tell you different. Some were brave enough to give evidence against them in court.

This torture was still going on while we were getting ready for war. So if we were ever sent south of the water, we always went in a hired car, and we always had a shooter in the door pocket. This way, if the police stopped us and found the gun, we could protest, 'We didn't know it was there, Guv'nor, it's not our car!' That was our legal 'out'. But we had to have a gun because everything on the other side of the Thames was Injun Country. If the Richardsons could have got hold of any one of us, we'd have been 'cranked up', so we didn't take the risk. The only communication between the two firms was now strictly ambassadorial. If the Twins spoke directly to the Richardsons, it would be only to settle demarcation disputes, to tell them to get off our manor and to test each other's resolve to go the whole way.

There came a moment when communications had completely broken down, and the Twins were ready to go the whole way. We were all set to make the Thames foam with blood when suddenly, on Monday, 7 March 1966, almost the entire Richardson mob were caught up in the battle of Mr Smith's, a gambling club in Catford, south of the river. Frankie Fraser and Eddie Richardson were shot, and a guy in the opposition called Dickie Hart was murdered. This Hart was no relation of Ronnie Hart's, and he wasn't on our Firm. He was with another south London mob led by Billy and Harry Haward, who had decided to block the Richardsons from moving in on this club. If we work on the principle that 'my enemy's enemy is my friend', then these young Hawards were on our side. I knew Harry Haward because I'd been in jail with him, and we got on OK.

Both sides lost the battle of Mr Smith's. Victory went to Catford CID who, with a gangster's corpse on their turf, went straight in and wiped up as many Haward and Richardson soldiers as they could find. They even charged invalids like Fraser and Eddie Richardson and put them out of action. We heard about this shoot-out on the Tuesday morning, and it was top of the agenda at our regular nine o'clock meeting.

The mood was buoyant, though not triumphant. We all felt able to relax and move around London more freely. Most of our serious opposition was off the streets, so it seemed our war had ended before it began. No contest. But how long were these guys really off the streets for? Neither Fraser nor Eddie were at death's door, they might be bailed and back at work any day, a prospect likely to frighten off all witnesses against them. Anyway, their boss, Charlie Richardson, wasn't even there that night. We didn't know he was in South Africa, but, wherever he was, we knew he wouldn't let this trouble interfere with his imperial ambitions, and he'd quickly regroup his forces. Many members of his firm were still at liberty, including my target Brian Mottram and a man called George Cornell. They weren't at Mr Smith's that night, they couldn't be implicated and were still walking about.

So we'd have had to be completely stupid to stand down, beat our swords into ploughshares and our guns into wrought-iron railings. The command from Colonel Ron was eternal vigilance. This was just the moment the enemy would be expecting us to drop our guard, so this was just the moment they might strike.

On the same Tuesday we were warned that the remaining Richardsons were already planning a strike. The coming Saturday they were going to lay up for us outside the Lion pub in Tapp Street, Bethnal Green. Naturally this intelligence made us all a bit edgy. There were a lot of guns about, we were ready for the 'off', fingers on the trigger.

The very next evening, Wednesday, 9 March, we are all sitting in this same Lion. We called it the Widow's – sometimes the Merry Widow's – because it was run by a widow. With death and guns both regular topics of our conversations, this may have been unconscious black humour. We had no idea that another woman was about to become a widow.

At a quarter past eight one of our spies came in the Widow's and walked up to Ronnie Kray. I found out later that he told him, 'George Cornell is sitting round the Beggar's drinking.' To Ronnie this was a diabolical liberty – a provocation, an act of war – because he regarded Cornell as one of the Richardsons' men, and here he was in our midst, drinking right on our manor. He was just round the corner because Tapp Street is only a quarter of a mile from Whitechapel Road, where you find the Blind Beggar pub.

All of a sudden Ronnie strutted off out the Widow's with Scotch Jack Dickson and Ian Barrie in tow. At this point we had no idea what Ronnie was going to do. To us it was just movement. Then Reggie told me, 'Cornell's round the Beggar's, and he's going round there. I hope he doesn't do anything stupid.'

THE ENFORCER

A quarter of an hour later Reggie asked me to phone somebody. The phone was in the living-room behind the bar, but I'd only just got there when Reggie put his head round the door and said, 'Scrub the call. Get off the manor. We're moving.' By now the other three had come back, we all went outside and jumped into whatever car there was room in. As always, they were all pointing in different directions, to fox any police who might have been about. They wouldn't know which cars to follow.

I was in a car driven by Scotch Jack, with Ronnie Kray beside him in the passenger seat. We drove to the Stowe Club, a little spieler in Hoe Street in Walthamstow, and went straight up to the old poker room on the top floor. Then Ian Barrie came in, and Charlie Clark was brought up. Charlie was an old cat burglar, who'd had to retire after falling off a drainpipe, so he was given a little bit of work up at the Stowe. Then I saw Ronnie give him two guns – a Luger, which looked new, and a small black automatic. Ronnie told old Charlie to get rid of them, dump them in a canal, so they'd never be seen again. Then we all left the Stowe and went over to the Chequers, where, as it happened, the landlord was an ex-cop.

We walked into the back bar, which wasn't normally used, and someone was sent off to get Ronnie, Jack and Ian all a change of clothes. By now Ian was telling me what had happened. Scotch Jack had driven them round to the Beggar's, then Ronnie and Ian, with a shooter each, walked into the pub and saw George Cornell sitting at the end of the bar with another south Londoner, Albert Woods, a feller called Dale and somebody else. Ian said he let one go in the ceiling near the door, just to get people's heads down. Ronnie Kray walked straight up to Cornell and fired off two shots into his head. They walked out and zipped back to the Widow's. Then Ronnie Kray walked up to Reggie and said, 'Well, I've done mine now. You'd better get on with your lot.' Then Reggie said to Ronnie, 'What? You've shot Cornell! You've fucking done it now. You've got to get off the manor!' which is why we'd all sped down to Walthamstow.

Later that night we were all standing round drinking when we heard a report on the news that Cornell was in the London Hospital. He had to be there because it was only 100 yards from the Blind Beggar. One of the crowd knew a nurse in the London who was phoning us hourly updates until the early hours of the morning, when he was transferred to another hospital with a neurological unit for a brain operation. It was between two and three o'clock when we heard he'd died, and a little cheer went up. Ronnie started cheering, and all the little wets joined in so they wouldn't stand out as dissenters.

You may think I'm being wise after the event, but even at this highly emotional time, I thought this whole scene was disgusting, because we never really had anything against George Cornell. He was only equivalent to what we were. He was a soldier for the Richardsons, just like we were for the Krays. He did the same things we did, for them. Nowadays all the Kray supporters say Cornell and all the Twins' other victims were vermin and scum, and they deserved to die. Well, if that's true for George Cornell, it's true for all the rest of us especially Ronnie and Reggie. None of us was any better than George, and certainly it wasn't up to Ronnie to decide whether he lived or died.

Anyway Ronnie was totally wrong in branding George as some alien from south London who had no right on our manor. He may have been running from Old Bill, perhaps he had to get away from south London because of the hue and cry after Mr Smith's, but he was an Eastender, a one-time member of the Watney Street Gang. This was an old team of dockers from Watney Street in Stepney, so George was entitled to sit in the East End if anyone was. I knew him, and he wasn't a bad guy, a dapper, short, fit, well-made typical cockney. He was really one of us. But Ronnie considered he was just taking the piss by sitting drinking in one of our locals, so without consulting Reggie, he just sent for a shooter, and then Pow! he just did him.

THE ENFORCER

It was nothing to do with Cornell calling Ronnie a 'fat poof'. He may have called him a fat poof, but that certainly was not the motive for Ronnie killing him. There was no real motive. It was just a whim.

But it got worse. Ronnie wanted us to go straight out and kill Cornell's brother, Eddie, who was also known as Eddie Myers. We heard that Eddie was shouting a bit in his drink that he was going to 'get the Twins'. So Ronnie called up Ronnie Hart, Connie Whitehead and me, and suddenly announced, 'There's far too much shooting going on in the East End.'

What? we thought, as we couldn't believe what he was saying. Has killing George Cornell driven him through some overnight conversion? Is this the new pacifist Ronnie? But, no, we realized, as Ronnie went on, 'So we're going to change the pattern a bit.' Then he produced a whole load of axes that he'd bought, just little firewood axes, and he continued, 'Now that slag Cornell's brother is spouting his mouth down Watney Street. I want you to dig him out and do him with the axes.'

So we said, 'Oh, all right,' and we went out with these silly axes. Of course, we had no intention of using them. We had no grumble with Eddie at all. We just made a public point of looking for him and left a thick trail. We'd go in a pub and say with a bit of menace, 'Where's Eddie Cornell?' Of course, they would say they hadn't seen him, so we'd say, 'Well, when you do see him, you tell him we're looking for him!' We let it be known we'd been there, but we had no intention of catching the man. Our aggressive manner was all part of the act. It would ensure that Eddie kept out of sight so we couldn't kill him, and for sure it would be reported back to Ronnie that we'd been doing our job.

We knew we could get away with not killing Eddie because it was all a question of Ronnie's mood. Give it a couple of days and he'd have gone off the idea or forgotten he'd ever issued the order. And that was the tragedy about George Cornell. If Ronnie had been in a good mood that day, Cornell wouldn't have died. Ronnie would have said, 'Cheeky bastard,' and left it at that.

Anyway, the morning after Cornell dies, when we stir ourselves, it's like D-Day. Everybody's looking for us, and we're thinking even the Home Secretary is bound to step in and say, 'Look, just clean the place up. Get rid of this mob!' Then we start hearing little stories that Nipper Read is disguising himself as a milkman or a priest and seeing people who know things about the Firm. Every hour Scotland Yard was blustering about taking the East End apart to find the killers. Even their top detective, Tommy Butler, came to the scene of the crime. This all may have been public relations, an effort to appease politicians and honest local citizens, but we knew for sure that the police would be gathering some intelligence, so we expected to be jumped on and whipped off a bit lively. Quite simply we thought, you can't just go round killing people without getting nicked. But we were wrong.

For years the police couldn't get any hard information about the murderers, and, if the Twins had never killed anyone else, no one would ever have been charged over Cornell. Ronnie and Reggie's ten-year campaign of intimidation all over the East End was paying dividends. At this time there wasn't a single witness to any event surrounding Cornell's death who was prepared to tell all to the police.

Even if people who saw the shooting had been asleep for the previous decade and knew nothing of Ronnie's reputation, the mere sight of Ian Barrie waving a gun would have terrified them into silence. He deliberately cultivated a gangster image, which leant heavily on a ghastly scar on one side of his face, the result of severe burns suffered while he was in the army. He rarely smiled, and his stern expression was matched by a stiff, upright walk, which gave him a mechanical gait, like Frankenstein's monster. To compound this, he would focus on people with a fixed glare. The overall effect appealed to Ronnie. It was Ian's appearance, not his limited strength or courage, that made him so valuable to the Colonel. If you ever saw this guy staring at you in the half light of a drinking club, with his wrinkled scar gleaming as if lit up from within, it would make your pants rattle. His soft-spoken Edinburgh accent only enhanced the nightmare.

Everyone on the Firm played their part in imposing the silence surrounding Cornell's murder. We all had bits of business to do. We had got to get going on Patsy and Jimmy Quill, the brothers who owned the Blind Beggar. They weren't in the bar at the time, so they couldn't be severely pressured by the police, but someone from the Firm would have to question them straightaway about what they knew, and what they were going to do about it. They were well known to us, ever since the days when they ran a car business, and they certainly weren't going to betray Ronnie Kray.

A week or so after the killing I had a meet with Patsy Quill at the Rose and Punchbowl, Jubilee Street. This had to be done carefully because we knew the police were following Patsy about. I met him upstairs, and we talked about the barmaid on duty that night. Apparently she'd seen it, and Ronnie wanted to find out what she was like, whether she would talk to the law or not. I think we gave Patsy £100 for her, though I don't think he ever found her to hand it over. He seemed to think she was pretty reliable, so the Twins asked me to set up a meet with her. I don't know why they picked on me. Maybe they thought she'd trust me. I arranged a meet at another of the Quills' pubs, the Three Swedish Crowns over Wapping, but it fell through because the girl was too frightened to show up. Anyway, when the cops spoke to her, she said she couldn't remember the gunmen's faces.

At the same time feelers were put out to Albie Woods, the man who was drinking with Cornell when he was shot. He was given a talking-to, though apparently he never saw who did the shooting. The Twins were also worried about the kid Dale who ran out of the pub when it happened, but then they found out he was going to be no trouble.

These approaches quickly paid off, because soon the police

raided a place where the Twins were staying in Lea Bridge Road. It was a well-organized, ladders-through-windows job but they didn't find any guns. They arrested the Colonel on the basis of an anonymous tip-off and put him on identification parades. No one picked Ron out, certainly not Albie Woods, so he walked out free, like a hero. And as the months went by without him getting charged, he really believed he was untouchable. He thought he had got away with one murder, so, in his twisted mind, there was nothing to stop him doing a few more. His 'list' got longer and longer, in his dreams the bodies must have been piling on top of each other, but the police could do nothing because of the wall of silence the Twins had built up around themselves – thanks partly to the menace of people like me.

If Ronnie and maybe Reggie thought they were untouchable, some of us could see things would fall apart fairly soon. When we thought about the killing of Cornell – and we thought about it every day – we wished they had already retired to their mansion, then none of this would have happened, George would have still been around, and we could have sorted things out with him in a calm and reasonable fashion. He certainly wouldn't have got killed. In the meantime the party rolled on; the Krays had become part of show business, and everybody wanted to get in on the act.

8: THE GANGSTER COMPLEX

Everybody loves a gangster. Not everybody maybe, but a lot of people love to see them in films, read about them in books, even visit the places where they did their wickedest deeds. Kray camp-followers still go in the Blind Beggar and order a 'Luger and Lime'. The bigger the crook, the bigger his fan club. But when you're on the inside with these people, they don't look so glamorous. They're nearly all creeps. There's nothing to admire about them. Straight folk should be glad they never meet them in the flesh.

There's one group of people who can't resist tangling with gangsters, and that's the rich and famous. It's a weird chemistry, but there's something irresistible that attracts show-business people to gangsters and gangsters to showbiz people. The thugs are star-struck, and the stars are mob-crazy. When we saw this at work around the Kray Firm we called it the 'Gangster Complex'.

Many showbiz people were sucked into our world. A lot were raging poofs. This may just have reflected Ronnie's own taste in company but, gay or straight, I couldn't understand why they hung around our clubs. Maybe they liked thinking that any moment there was going to be violence – a fist fight, a knifing, even a shooting – and the sense that any minute it's going to be 'off'. They used to love it, dozens of them, especially the Yanks. Judy Garland, Sophie Tucker, George Raft, all paid homage at the court of Ron and Reg. They were told these Twins were prominent businessmen but, coming from America, where mobsters and stars also feed off each other, they'd know exactly what that meant, especially Raft who spent most of his career playing gangsters. Another Hollywood guy who used to show up was the British star, Edmund Purdom. I was astonished that these people wanted to be seen with men they must have realized were thugs. But that's the Gangster Complex. Reflected Glory.

A lot of stars were chaperoned and shepherded round town by Little Sammy Lederman who used to have an agency up the West End. Singers and dancers were his speciality. He had the tap-dancing Clark Brothers and the ballad singer Lita Rosa on his books. Sammy was a frail old boy, about five feet two. Once he might have been big in show business but now he was just another Kray gofer. They used him to show visiting American celebrities the sights. He might even get them a few extra dates by introducing them to bigger agents, a service for which they'd be grateful to the Twins. But Sam was a bit trappy. He'd take liberties, because he knew the Twins were behind him. He'd wind people up and provoke them until they snapped at him. Then he'd run to the Twins for protection.

Sam was always toting round one person in particular, the American singer, Billy Daniels, who'd made a hit out of 'That Old Black Magic' many years earlier. He was a regular at the Krays' clubs. He was well past his best and a severe pain, a crawler, a Uriah Heep. We fell out the first time we met. It was one night at the Regency when Sam introduced me: 'Billy, this is Albert.' Daniels said, 'Albert? Not Albert Dimes!' 'No,' replied Sam, 'Dimes couldn't clean his shoes.' Suddenly Daniels started strutting round in circles, doing a cockerel impression and staring at me. I thought he was taking the piss – he probably was – so I said, 'Just go away or I'll give you a smack.' He could see he'd gone too far but before anything could happen, Reggie came up and stopped it all. The Twins came to despise Daniels. He'd get on their nerves too. They'd push him to one side, but if they were going to the West End they'd take him along as a celebrity because it would add to the buzz of admiration that went round wherever they walked in.

Another face was the British film star Stanley Baker, of *Zulu* fame. He was another celebrity with a strange weakness for hoodlums. He was a big pal of Albert Dimes, and they were both in the Soho

Rangers team photo along with the Richardson mob. But the weirdest friendship was between Judy Garland and the Twins. They didn't just throw parties for her in the West End, they would tote her down to Bethnal Green, to see your genuine Eastender. They even took her in the Crown and Anchor, where Reggie had shot me.

Esmeralda's Barn was where the Twins entertained most of the stars. Top American boxers were always on hand. Again this echoed the scene in New York where the Mafia had controlled the fight game for years. That's why ex-world champions like Joe Louis, Rocky Marciano and Rocky Graziano wouldn't have blinked an eyelid at the Krays. After spending so much time with the mob, they may have thought all humanity were wiseguys, and everyone looked like fridges on casters.

Two other American boxing legends, Homicide Hank Armstrong and Barney Ross, were in London at the same time, but they had been brought over by two old promoters, Harry Levene and Jack Solomons, who hated each other. They weren't supposed to meet, but when Ronnie realized this he thought he'd stir up mischief by making sure they did so. So we brought Hank and Barney together at the Cumberland Hotel and tipped off a publicity photographer to be there to snap them. Upsetting Solomons and Levene was just the kind of thing that appealed to Ronnie.

Both twins loved to be photographed with celebrities. They loved to be photographed anyway, but they always welcomed a few stars to boost their own status. They wallowed in this glamour stuff, but I felt it was a dangerous distraction from our real business: making money, not splashing it around. As the years have gone by, the photos have boosted the Kray legend, not that anyone could have foreseen how the legend would build.

Locked up in jug, the Twins recycled these photos in their books because the reflected glory still reflected. When the photos were taken the gangster glitter boosted the stars. Now the star glitter boosted these sad old thugs. After thirty years inside all Reggie had left were a few hundred snaps of snatched moments with people who mostly had only five minutes of fame themselves. But canny gangsters – the survivors who make real money from crime, who keep hold of it, and who die free men in their own beds – they don't go round getting their photos in the papers. They don't seek publicity, they shun it. It's partly because the Twins wanted to be famous that they were locked up for so long. Sure they were famous. They're infamous. Their names will live for ever in the Hall of Infamy, but that's a fat lot of good when you've spent half your life in jail and then you're dead.

Sometimes the stars added more than glitter to the Krays' circle. In the case of the Clark brothers, the black tap-dancers from America, it was business too. They had a dance studio in Tottenham Court Road, and I went in there a couple of times with Reggie. In one of his own books Reggie says he used to go there to 'improve his social graces'. I suppose that means he went there to learn to dance, but I never saw Reggie dance. When he spoke to the brothers, I'd sit a few feet away, and I'm pretty sure he was getting money from them. He didn't go there to socialize or learn Fred Astaire's routine for 'Top Hat, White Tie and Tails'.

A few Eastenders who'd made it in show business were genuine friends of the Krays. I can't fault Barbara Windsor for standing by such people, even when the association may not have served her reputation too well. While she was filming *Sparrows Can't Sing*, a cockney musical, she used to go to the Kentucky, which the Twins had set up after the Double R had folded. When the film had its première in the Empire cinema in the Mile End Road almost opposite the club, the Twins held a big party for the stars. All this was before I joined the Firm, but I remember her coming in years later, with her good pal, Limehouse Willey. He'd been a member of the Firm until he reached an age when he wasn't so handy. Then he was put in charge of the spieler at the Stowe Club in Walthamstow.

Then there was the West End mob, as we used to call them, people who'd be snared into coming down by one of the Twins' sharks. The head shark was Dickie Morgan who had been in the glass-house with the Twins during their squalid national service days. Later he was jailed for hi-jacking a lorry full of meat. I called him a shark because he was always swimming round the West End. He would be sent to other people's clubs like the Latin Quarter, where he had an 'in' and knew the managers. He was a 'face'. Everybody knew him because he was unforgettable. He was quite the oddest member of the entire Kray fraternity. He was like one of the Dead End Kids, the tallest of the Bowery Boys who was always getting swiped with a cap. He had a manic giggle – 'Hee! Hee! Hee!' – and he would stand with his shoulders up and his head forward, just like a vulture. And he would giggle. He was very slippery, but he gave the impression of being a crank. If you didn't know him, you'd take him for an out-and-out idiot.

This, then, was the Twins' ambassador up West. When he caught up with a group of well-known people, he would go up and say, 'Why don't you come on to the Twins' place?' – the Double R or the Kentucky, depending on the year – and they'd say, 'Yeah, what a wonderful idea!' Then off they'd go slumming down the East End to see the hooligans. When they trooped in, everybody would be going, 'Oi! Keep it down, stop swearing, no dirty jokes!' and they'd lay on a little bit of jazz for them.

When you hear the word 'club', you might imagine somewhere with real style, but these clubs were just shop premises or large houses that the Twins had taken over and then decorated in obvious club style: plenty of red-flock wallpaper, carpets and bright or dim lights, according to the mood. The bar used to be installed and stocked by the brewery, on credit, and there'd be a juke box. Then Ronnie and Reggie would hold a grand opening, using a well-known name to get publicity. When they opened the gym at the Double R, they brought down the British heavyweight champ, Henry Cooper, to open it.

He's such a decent guy, I don't think he wanted anything to do with it. He came, of course, probably out of politeness, because he'd been invited, but once the photos were done he just went down the stairs and whoosh! he was out, gone. He didn't stay for drinks or any socializing. But that didn't matter to the Twins because now it would all be done by word of mouth: 'The Twins have got a new club,' 'Ronnie and Reggie have set up a new place.' The word would spread and then any celebrities Morgan or Lederman could find up West would be dragged back there to have their photos taken. Their clubs came and went. The Double R kept losing money and collapsed when it lost its drink licence. No worry. They rapidly set up the Kentucky around 1962 and entertained all their show-biz buddies there. Ronnie would entertain us all with his favourite novelty acts: dwarfs, midgets and Humpback Hank, a guitar-playing, cowboy-style singer who would ride around the Kentucky on a donkey.

Another venue was the Old Horns pub, off Hackney Road and Bethnal Green Road, where the landlord was Teddy Berry. Years before Teddy had driven for the Twins until a south London firm shotgunned him from a car in Hackney Road. Then they got out of the car, stood over him and gave him the other barrel, severing his leg. The Twins had nothing to do with this, so they helped him buy the Old Horns as a living. This generosity provoked one little guy called Webb, in the 'crazy mob' out of Tottenham, to ask the Colonel, 'Is that what you do to them, Ron? Blow their legs off and then buy them a pub?' He got off light for that: Ronnie only gave him a smack in the mouth. We called this Tottenham mob crazy because they suffered from an acute form of the Gangster Complex: they used to burn themselves with pokers to give themselves scars.

Teddy's brother, Checker, was a boyhood friend of Ronnie's as well as an ex-con. Somehow he had got to know the American singer Tony Bennett, and one day he took a party of Kray familiars to see him doing his show in the West End. Tony Bennett was one guy who did not suffer from the Gangster Complex. He didn't know Checker's East End connections, and I'm sure he didn't leave his heart in Bethnal Green.

We used to meet other stars who weren't sucked in by the Gangster Complex either, but whose reactions on meeting the Twins were just as weird. One night me and Reggie went up to the Arethusa Club in Chelsea. It was the first discotheque I'd ever been in. Pow! Three floors of noise and lights. We were sitting at a table with David Bailey, another top photographer called Brian Duffy and his Australian girlfriend. No business done, just a social talk. At other tables Michael Caine and Richard Harris were hopping around, calling each other 'Darling' and 'Love'.

Of course, at that time, coming from the East End was almost like coming from Eton and Oxford. It had a strange inverted cachet about it because this was the Swinging Sixties, when so many top stars had come out of the East End. So some toff, who must have lived out in the Essex stockbroker belt, came up to our table and said to me in awestruck tones, 'Every morning I go through Mile End Station.' Well? What was I supposed to say to that? That was his claim to be connected to the East End. People were sick for it. And then Duffy's girlfriend started talking to me. She asked what did I do for a living, and I said, 'I'm a gambler.' Then she said, 'Oh, my father's a gambler in Australia.' I suppose in some circles this is what they call small talk, but I couldn't see the point of it.

Anyway, we finish our meal and come out of the restaurant on the top floor, we go down the stairs, and we're standing round in the main area. Then suddenly I hear, 'David! David! Are you all right?' And I look round, and it's Richard Harris bounding down these stairs to catch up with David Bailey and, presumably, save him from a fate worse than death. I just burst out laughing. I mean if we're going to do anything to David Bailey, we're not going to do it there and then. Harris must have believed his own press cuttings about being a 'hellraiser'. Was this great 'I am' really game to take on Reggie Kray and his heavy? I often wonder what he would have done if Bailey had said, 'No, I'm not all right. These beasts are going to do me over.'

But Bailey said, 'Yeah, yeah, it's all right,' and Harris said, 'Are you sure?' And I looked at his face, and I just burst out laughing again because Bailey was never in any danger. He wasn't my bosom buddy, but Reggie would never have laid a finger on him, because he was almost one of their family. He came from the East End himself, from East Ham. It was Bailey who took Reggie's wedding photos, and, looking back, it was Bailey's photos of all the brothers that, more than any other images, have crystallized the legend. What's more, those images – along with the headlines and the muscle – helped intimidate other villains at the time. They definitely traded off it. They were pretty cute.

* * *

On the Firm we were always bumping into other celebrities. Over at the Pigalle Casino, which Tommy Cowley used to collect from every week, we'd meet Joe Louis, the former world heavyweight champion. He was employed there as the big-name greeter, but he was a very sad sight because the punches must have gone to his head. He'd gone mental. He'd shamble round, eating peanuts, grunting at people. Obviously he'd been hired for his name, not his manner. If you said to him, 'Hello Joe,' he'd just go 'Murgh,' and carry on eating his nuts.

We patronized a lot of other clubs that the Twins weren't protecting, and we didn't even attempt to nip. There was the Society in Jermyn Street, which we reached through an underground route from the Pigalle – the places were in parallel streets. Sometimes we'd go there showing people around, sometimes we were just bored with sitting in some East End piss-hole, and we'd say, 'Ah, let's go up West.' Although we never protected the Society – we didn't take a monthly pay-off – we never paid for anything either. Food, drink, everything was on the house, just like the Pigalle, so we used both places whenever we felt in need of a good night out or we wanted to pull a bird.

That's another funny thing about the Gangster Complex. Women are attracted to you because you're a gangster. Of course, you're dressed well, you're a bit flash, and you've obviously got money (even if you're not spending it at the Pigalle!), but that's not why women are drawn to you. It's the aura of danger, violence and evil that captivates even very attractive, high-class women – especially if you're with the Firm. They'd come on strong, and you wouldn't refuse it.

Not everybody who hung around the Firm was so decorative, but even the deadbeats had their uses. At the Double R there was always a retired drunk solicitor. He was perpetually crying or on the verge of it. You could go in and get free advice off this guy, just like Doc Blasker. Then there were toffs like Lord Howard of Effingham who joined the Twins on the board of Esmeralda's Barn. He was an earl who had no hereditary wealth whatever. He was so hard up he was prepared to work for Ron and Reg at £15 a week. His title would have looked good on the letterhead and the company records, which is obviously why Ronnie was so keen to have Effingham on hand. Many top companies have lords on the board today for much the same reason, so perhaps the Twins were ahead of their time.

Then we always had a couple of priests out of Bethnal Green: one Catholic, one Anglican, both queer. And there was a mayor who used to show up wearing his silly chain alongside the Twins whenever the local newspaper photographers were flashing. What on earth got into these people, that they should want to hang around punks? This mayor didn't need their votes. Labour had run the town halls for generations round our way, so his lot were bound to get elected.

But the weirdest group of people snuggling up to the Twins were businessmen, who seemed to volunteer for the bloodsucking treatment. There was one guy called Lennie Martin who rode himself into the Krays. First he sent them each a gold watch, but kind of anonymously. For months Tommy Cowley was the only person on the Firm who knew who he was. He wasn't supposed to tell anyone else the guy's name – not even the Twins – he just called him the 'Mystery Man'. But if they were ever short of money, Cowley would go to him and he would come up with £500 or £1000. This was totally down to Martin. There was no pressure or extortion from the Twins, because they didn't know who he was. It was the Gangster Complex again, working its magic power to delude sane people into acts of extraordinary stupidity.

Then somehow his name came out, and the Twins got hold of him properly. It now came out that he ran a firm called Hi-Heat, which installed central heating systems. Outwardly he was straight but, if that was so, I can't see why he would ever have wanted to get involved. He never got anything out of them, but now they were into him; they put one of their distant relatives into Hi-Heat as a senior salesman. Then they stuck a girl into his office, so now they knew everything about his business. Silly Boy.

Then I was put on the payroll, and I got to know Lennie Martin pretty well. He came to the pub one night, and Tommy Cowley introduced him. He said he thought I looked like Henry Cooper – which I did – and he asked if I could do a bit of work for him: just acting, walking round, pretending I was his bodyguard. Apparently he'd been telling people he had heavy connections, and I was just the guy to prove it. He wanted someone big enough and ugly enough to frighten people, so I became his minder, not just in his business. I used to escort him to big fights too.

At this time central heating was a comparatively new thing, and Hi-Heat used to sell it door-to-door, like the double-glazing guys did a few years later. Obviously the Twins were nailing Martin for payments every week. He was happy to pay because he knew this gave him a bolt-hole. Even if he got done legally, or legitimate people were howling for his blood, he had somewhere to go. He had protection. And he needed it! Irate customers were always complaining that their central-heating system wasn't working. They'd come in the office demanding that if he didn't put things right, he must give them their money back. They had every reason to be mad, and they'd start shouting, but, emboldened by me standing behind him, he would just shout back. I would growl at them too. Now that was a respectable businessman!

The Krays weren't the only mob with a piece of his company. In 1970, after I broke with the Krays, and they were all locked up, I went back and saw him. The office was still there, and I took some money off him, even though he knew I no longer had the Firm behind me. He must have thought it was wonderful to hang around gangsters. I don't know why the guy did it. There's got to be some psychiatrist who will tell you.

There were lots of people like that. One day they got hold of a car site owner called Johnny Hutton. They brought him to the house in Vallance Road and sat him on a chair in the middle of the room, whilst three of us were ready in the other room, dressed in identical macks and wearing stocking-masks. The Twins gave him a terrible dressing-down and told him how much money they wanted off him. Then Ronnie said, 'Now, we want this money every week and if anybody in this room gets nicked, this is what will happen.' Then we three were marched in. We didn't have to say a word. We just walked in a circle round the chair, staring at him. And then we walked out again. Then the Twins said to this guy, 'Now, them people have got your face, but you don't know who they are, so if anybody gets nicked, they'll come and see you.' That was another respectable businessman scared out of his wits. The Twins performed this ritual because back in the late 1950s Hutton had been shot, and he'd had the nerve to call the police. No one was nicked, but he had to be frightened into not going to the law again.

Then there was the battle of the rival boxing promoters. These two young guys were both on the way up, but they were getting in each other's way. One of them decided to sabotage a show that the other was promoting, so he approached the Twins and put up some money for us to fuse the lights during the main bout. He also supplied us with ringside tickets, so we had cover for being there. Well, we took the money, and some of us sat in the ringside seats, but, far from one of our guys fusing the lights, we made sure nobody touched them. This was a good venue, and nobody wanted to see it ruined for up-and-coming local fighters, so we protected the fuse box and all the cables. And we kept the money! But the rising star of the boxing game never dared protest. Who could he complain to? What would he tell the cops?

All this was pretty small stuff. The Twins wanted to get into the real big time, so their role models, Ronnie's especially, had to be the mob bosses of America, the Mafiosi of the American syndicate. This was another aspect of the Twins' own Gangster Complex. They wanted to be up there with the superstars of crime, Al Capone, Lucky Luciano and Meyer Lansky.

The biggest New York crime family got a spectacular foothold in London in 1964 when the Colony Casino Club opened up in Berkeley Square. It's pretty clear now that Meyer Lansky and Lucky Luciano were tied in with this place. Two of its directors – Dino Cellini and the front-man George Raft – were nominees of the Genovese crime family in New York, which Luciano had headed before he got deported to Italy. Lansky had been the family's financial brains and its main casino strategist, from Las Vegas to Havana to the Bahamas and now London. He didn't need to come here personally. The whole operation could be handled by Cellini and other capable mechanics.

When the Twins realized how big these guys were, they felt their own status as London's biggest crime family should be respected. They wanted to be given percentage points in the Colony, a share of the profits. The Americans didn't see things the same way. They refused them a piece of the action, but they did agree to pay the Twins a fixed sum on a regular basis.

By our standards it was a lot of money: £500 a week, or £3500 paid every quarter. I know it was over three grand because I had ideas of putting the Colony on my Milk Round, collecting the money and whipping my family off to Ireland. In Dublin in the 1960s you could start a good little business with three and a half grand. But I was never allowed to collect from the Colony. That was Little Tommy Cowley's job. He used to collect it from the club manager, Alf Salkin, who was an Englishman on the Colony board. At the time Cowley was trying to tie up a casino junket scheme with the Yanks. The idea would have been to fly planeloads of American gamblers to London, take them into Esmeralda's Barn as well as the Colony and fleece them over 48 hours. This would have been done repeatedly, and both joints would have made millions. But, as with so many of the Twins' great schemes, it never came off. After all, why should the guys behind the Colony share such a lucrative racket with the Twins, when they could handle the entire operation themselves?

The whole scheme shows yet again that the Twins were suffering from delusions of grandeur. The Mafia just did not consider the Twins fit to be their partners. The Mafia despised the Twins. Ronnie and Reggie weren't paid to look after the Colony. They were paid to stay away! The Colony guys knew from what had happened over at Esmeralda's Barn, that if the Twins visited a club three times on the trot, they would ruin it. When rich people go out for an evening, they don't want to have to look at thugs like the Twins, grunting in a corner. They don't want to be glared at and insulted by them. That would ruin anyone's pleasure.

There was a particular incident that provoked the £500-a-week pay-off. One evening the Twins went into the Colony's restaurant and did their usual takeover act; lounging around to make sure everybody knew 'the boys' were in town. But there were a couple of visiting Mafiosi sitting in another corner. They were disgusted by this act, and they wanted to know who these punks were. When they were told, 'This is the Krays,' that's when they ordered, 'Pay these guys to stay out. They're bad for business.' In their eyes, the Krays were like Capone's people back in the 1920s: too rough and too obviously crooks to be allowed into any establishment trying to pass itself off as respectable.

They were embarrassing to be around. Even with their fake good manners, they were rough and ready. None of us on the Firm was any better, except for Charlie Kray. Sure, we all wore three-piece suits and expensive jewellery, and we weren't totally repellent, but we were still low life compared to Sir So-and-So sitting in the corner with Lady Blah-di-Blah. So, of course, the people who ran the Colony didn't want us in there! They didn't want men sitting around with scars and broken noses, especially as we hadn't come to gamble and lose. The Colony was forking up all that money – £14,000 a year then would be worth around £200,000 a year today – just so the entire Firm would stay away.

You might be thinking that this sum was so large it couldn't have been just stayaway money, but the Colony was making millions. It was making far more in a night than it was paying the Firm in an entire year. The Twins only had to create a big scene on just one night, and the Colony would lose far more than fourteen grand. It would also have made sense for the Mafia to pay off London's worst thugs because it stopped the Twins running to their police friends to get the place shut down.

Even so, it was hard for the Twins to swallow the ban on visiting the Colony. It was so much of a humiliation that Ronnie couldn't admit it to the rest of us. He just said there was some rule there about not letting the faces in. He told us all to keep away from the Colony because they took photos up there. I know they both really wanted to use the club because it was the best place for any 'sportsman' to be on show. Before the ban they made a fuss of George Raft. One night they even brought him down to the Starlight when I was looking after it. 'Take his coat, Albert,' said Reg as if I were a cloakroom attendant. Raft was only there a short while, then I gave him his coat back. They were showing him round to impress him, but it was such a sleazy little place the visit probably had the opposite effect.

In 1967 Raft was booted out of London. So was Dino Cellini and all the other known American mobsters involved in the Colony. The casino itself closed ahead of a new gambling law that tried, fairly successfully, to keep organized crime out of Britain's casinos. By then Esmeralda's Barn was long gone. Under the new set-up the Twins would never have got a casino licence. You had to be what's called a 'fit and proper person.' Crazy killers with long criminal records wouldn't qualify. And the killing had scarcely begun.

9: BIG FRANK MEETS THE BIG SLEEP

I'd been on one visit to Dartmoor to see Big Frank Mitchell. I didn't know the guy, and I didn't have anything to say to him, but I sat there alongside Ronnie Kray as he promised that the Twins would get Frank out. It was the least they could do for an old friend who felt the system wouldn't be letting him out for a long time, if ever.

Poor Frank had been in the zoo since he was seventeen. He was now thirty-seven, four years older than the Twins who had both first met him in Wandsworth, though at different times around 1960. Frank had a long record for violent crime, especially for violence against prison officers. He was mentally subnormal, and he'd been deemed insane. He'd been to Rampton, he'd been to Broadmoor, he'd been everywhere. You name it, he'd been locked up in it. He'd had the birch, the cat, the whole lot. Finally he had broken out of Broadmoor, broken into a house and terrorised an old couple by threatening to kill them with an axe. This was how he earned that terrifying nickname, 'The Mad Axeman'.

Soon he was recaptured and sentenced to life. That decision always struck me as lunatic in itself. Here is a guy who's been locked up in Broadmoor because he's criminally insane; he breaks out and commits a criminally insane act; but when he's convicted, the judge decides he was sane after all and packs him off to an ordinary jail. Now tell me who's mad.

By 1966 Frank had been in Dartmoor for nine years, which was about the stretch normally served for a life sentence, so what he wanted was a guaranteed date for his release. When you've been in the nick as long as Frank, a date is something special. He had built up a special relationship with the governor of Dartmoor who had made him a kind of promise, a verbal commitment.

According to Frank, the governor had said he would urge the Home Office to give him a date. Whether it was immediate or a couple of years ahead didn't really matter. All Frank wanted was a date to focus his mind on. But months went by, nothing was heard back from the Home Office, and so the governor had nothing to tell Frank. So Frank is raging because now he feels the governor's promise isn't worth the paper it isn't written on.

Then in flies the good fairy: Ronald Kray. Our Ronnie now makes his own promise to Frank along these lines: 'OK, we'll get you out, but you've go to stay out for six months. During this time you write to a few top people we'll give you their names – so they can get public opinion rolling on your side and bring pressure on the authorities to guarantee you a release date.' The idea behind the six-month period was that if Mitchell could stay out that long without committing violence or any other crimes, then he could morally force the Home Office into giving him his date.

Well, I'd never heard of anyone escaping from a British jail, giving himself up and then coming out sooner than if he had never escaped. Escaping is a crime in itself, which means you always get time added on, not deducted. So when I heard that Ron had fed Mitchell this story, I knew it didn't add up. Anyway, who was this R Kray esq. to make promises on behalf of the authorities that he couldn't fulfil? Not even the Home Secretary could get away with this kind of deal, so how could an East End hoodlum?

Yet, ludicrous as it sounds, that was the deal the Twins had persuaded Mitchell to believe. He didn't think it was ludicrous because to him Ronnie was God. To us in the Firm Ronnie wasn't God: he was a crazy man who thought he was God. We also knew he had a habit of changing his mind and forgetting his promises. We were usually relieved he'd forgotten them, especially when it meant we didn't have to go out and kill somebody on his 'list'. So when we heard this guff about springing Big Frank we all thought it was just talk. None of us believed it would ever happen.

Lo and behold! I went round the house one day, and the Twins were seriously discussing it. Then they announced we were really going to pick Mitchell up.

It wasn't going to be a 'great escape' – no derring-do drop over high prison walls – because most days Big Frank was let out of the prison as a most trusted member of an outside party working on a council rubbish tip. Even better, to keep him quiet the screw would allow him to go off and feed the wild ponies with bread that he had saved up in the prison. He'd walk miles from the other prisoners, but he'd always show up again, so even if he was half an hour late the screw would not think of raising the alarm. On escape day he would be picked up by car within that half-hour and whisked off to Krayland.

We had to get a move-on because it was coming up to December, when the outside working parties would soon be suspended for the rest of the winter, and Frank would be brought back inside. But for a few more days we were all right. Two of our guys went down on a final visit to make precise arrangements with Frank about the time and place for the pick-up. As he had roamed all over Dartmoor and knew it so well, he was able to give them the perfect spot.

The pick-up itself was given to me because I hadn't visited Frank for months, so I was unlikely to be identified. The driver would be a completely strange face, Mad Teddy Smith, who had never been down at all. So early on Monday, 12 December, me and Teddy headed off to Devon in a grey Humber, which Billy Exley had hired. We found the pick-up point with no difficulty. It was a phone box by a T-junction close to the Elephant's Nest public house, near Peter Tavey. We had to meet him there at midday, and at just ten past twelve he came walking round the corner. He was all on his own, and he got straight in the car.

He wasn't particularly excited or elated. He was just quiet and relieved, confused and surprised, because I don't think he believed this would ever really happen. These kind of people loved to sit and talk and plan, but they still don't think the escape will ever take place. If you've been in prison as long as Mitchell had, you can no longer separate fantasy from reality.

As we drove off we couldn't help fearing the whistle would go up almost straightaway and there would be instant roadblocks on every route off the moor. But the screw in charge of the working party must have been scurrying all over the moor trying to find Frank before he dared report him missing, because he knew he would get into terrible trouble for allowing the Mad Axeman to wander off on his own. So that would have been one delay in raising the alarm, and then the prison bosses would have squirmed with embarrassment and disbelief for a few minutes before they dared call the local police. Then the police would have taken some time to raise the manpower for the roadblocks, before doing the widening cordon routine, first five miles, then ten. And all that time we were driving on home.

We'd brought along a change of clothing for Frank: an old suit, shirt, socks, shoes and a tie. We'd got them off Big Tommy Brown, the ex-fighter, who was just about the same size. Frank changed in the car, shedding all his Dartmoor gear: an old khaki anorak, blue jeans, gum boots, scarf, prison shirt and underclothes, and a beret. He also had a long home-made knife, which he'd brought along for self-defence. He didn't want to give this to me, but I said, 'The whole reason you're out is so you do not get involved in any violence. Then you can write to various people, and they will work on your behalf to get you a release date, so the last thing you want is any tools on you, so let's get rid of them.'

Then we took the knife off him, and I told him that, even without the knife, there was to be no violence. If we were stopped at a police roadblock, we would have to split up, and then he would be on his own. This was all true, and it made common sense, but I still had to kid to him. It was like talking to a naughty boy. Then he settled down. We put all his prison clothing into his anorak, tied the neck strings and the arms so that it formed a bundle, and stuck the knife in the middle. I then slung the lot over a hedge.

Once we got through Andover, 150 miles away, we knew we were safe. No problem. We were well out of it. Throughout the journey Frank had been listening to a transistor radio he'd brought along, but nothing came up about his escape until we were already back in London. It was half-past four, and we were in Fulham when we heard the news that he'd been reported missing. While we were in Fulham I phoned Reggie over at Vallance Road. Using our usual simple code, I said, 'That horse won,' so he knew everything was all right.

We took Frank to a place in Priscilla Road at Bow, where we were going to hide him for the time being. It was the home of Nobby Clark's parents. Nobby and Scotch Jack Dickson were waiting for us but, when we knocked on the door, out came Nobby looking terrified. It turned out that this little rat had volunteered his mum and dad's flat so he could look big in Ronnie's eyes, but all the time never thinking this would ever happen. So when he saw Frank with us, he said, 'Ooh, you can't go in there. The old man's not well.' Then he said, 'It's been changed. We got a new address,' and he gave me a piece of paper with a number in Barking Road written on it. So we had to head off to this gaff near Canning Town, where a little guy named Lennie Dunn lived on his own. We called him Lennie the Books because he had a bookstall on Whitechapel Waste.

Near Bow Bridge we got tied up in a bit of traffic. As we drove slowly past a particular turning, by way of conversation I said, 'You know that one, Frank, that's Old Ford Road.' I shouldn't have done that because his parents lived there, so naturally he wanted to see them, but we had to keep him with us. He was getting excited but we quietened him down. Between half-five and six o'clock we reached Lennie's flat and took him up. We watched the six o'clock news, then me and Teddy Smith left Frank there with Scotch Jack and Lennie. We drove back to the Twins at Vallance Road and told them what had happened. Then we each went home. We had been up since six, and I was shattered after what had been a pretty tense operation, even for someone reasonably calm like myself. I was glad to have a night indoors.

I woke to find we were being treated as heroes by other members of the Firm. All I had done was babysit the guy on the drive back, but everyone was impressed because, when the papers got hold of it, they blew it up as if there was a lunatic apeman rushing round Dartmoor, and no one was safe in their beds. I think they had the Marines out for three days combing Dartmoor for him, when he was far away in London, watching it all on the box! I remember a Giles cartoon with three or four Marines crossing a bridge over a stream, and there's this big hulk underneath looking up, with his hands down to his ankles. Far from being offended, Frank was excited by the coverage. He thought that all this fuss was good for his cause.

Now I already knew from handling Big Frank that he wasn't as bad as the papers were painting him, but he was obviously nowhere near normal. In the next few days we had to handle him very carefully. Here was a man who had been locked up nearly all his life, he was totally institutionalized, he was simple, he was big, he was hugely strong, and he had been clinically diagnosed as a nutter. And now we've ended up with him in a little flat, and he starts performing. You imagine: if all the psychiatrists and screws can't control this guy, what chance have the Twins got?

To start, we had to get on with writing these letters. That was down to the driver on the Dartmoor trip, Mad Teddy Smith. He thought he was a bit of a writer – he said plays of his had been broadcast on the radio – so he spent a lot of time with Frank, composing letters in Frank's name. In the one that appeared in *The Times* Frank explained that he felt like 'a dog that had been given a bad name'. He had escaped to draw attention to his 'unhappy plight' and to win a release date: 'From the age of nine I have not been completely free, always under some act or other. Sir, I ask you, what is the fairness of this. I am not a murderer or a sex maniac, nor do I think I am a danger to the public. I think I have been more than punished for the wrongs I have done.'

This was how Frank was expressing himself to absolute strangers, but what was he saying to his dearest friends, Ronnie and Reggie? Well, nothing to Ronnie because Ronnie never came to see him. As for Reggie, I took him to Frank on the one occasion he bothered or dared to visit him. It was partly to discuss the letters and partly to discuss getting Frank a girl. He was obviously busting for one, and we thought a bit of female company would keep him occupied and calm him down. We brought Tommy Cowley in on this because he often went to Winston's night-club and knew a lot of the hostesses there. He thought one girl in particular would be just right for Frank, so Reggie and me and Tommy all went up to Winston's to see her.

She was Lisa Prescott, and she was very pretty. I remembered seeing her before when she worked at the Bagatelle. Then she was pretending to be Swedish but she was really from up north. This night she'd had a few drinks, but as the three of us sized her up and talked it over, we agreed with Tommy that she seemed a sensible girl, and she'd keep her mouth shut. Not that we told her anything except that we wanted her to take care of a good-looking friend of ours. She would have to look after him for a day or two, but she'd be paid well. Reggie and I agreed I wasn't going to tell her exactly what was going on until I'd got her into Lennie's flat. Then I'd spring it on her. She must have thought she could trust us, as she got in a cab with us. I dropped Reggie and Tommy off at Vallance Road, and Lisa carried on to the flat with me.

I knew that if she rebelled at any point after meeting Frank – or if she wanted to walk straight out – she would have to be detained. But I also knew that she'd have to know the full form on this guy once she'd met him. If she'd seen the TV or read any newspapers in the previous few days, she was bound to have known about the lunatic they'd been calling the Mad Axeman. There was no point in pussy-footing about the guy's identity. I took her straight in the room and I said, 'This is the guy we want you to look after. Meet the Mad Axeman!'

Looking back, I feel this was the Blind Date of all time, and yet, crazy as it may seem, Lisa and Frank clicked immediately. It wasn't so strange. You could easily imagine Frank being attractive to women. He wasn't revolting to look at, he was a big handsome man, and these two got on fine straightaway. They had a little laugh together, and that was it. I went off and left them to their first night of what turned out to be two weeks of almost relentless passion. She stayed there throughout, except for one chaperoned trip to her flat to collect a change of clothes. She was taken straight back to Lennie's. Otherwise she was not allowed out at all.

Nor did we ever leave the pair of them alone, just in case the police ever did find out Frank was there. At least one of us had to be present to talk him into a quiet surrender. The odds against a police visit were immense, but we were more worried that he might take it into his head to walk out. And what if Lisa had a row with him and just went home? Who'd shut her mouth then, and how? So we had to have permanent guards, even if at times they must have seemed like screws to Frank. Billy Exley and Scotch Jack took turns staying overnight with Lennie Dunn, though none of them was capable of restraining Frank, least of all Billy who was a frail fellow who had been off the scene and was only called back in for this particular job.

I'd spend most days there, sorting out any problems and reading Frank's mood. This task took me back to when I worked in the 'Ville on those psychiatric rounds. I'd kept my observational skills in good shape all these years just watching the Twins, but they came in especially handy now. First, it struck me that Big Frank was really a child. He'd been certified a couple of times but he was more simple than insane. When I went to see him, he would say, 'I want a suit like yours, Albert, with a shoulder holster.' He was the type of guy who, if somebody bumped into him in a pub – even by accident – might go berserk and kill three or four people. He wasn't so very tall maybe an inch taller than me, around six foot two but he was fantastically strong. He was very broad and very thick, with a barrel chest. He was very powerful, and all the more dangerous because he was simple.

I also realized he was in a sad state. Not 'sad' in the sense of 'unhappy' – Lisa was making him very happy – but 'sad' meaning there was already no way out. The Twins had hooked him out of Dartmoor, without thinking what they would do with him a couple of stages further on. There was no way they could control him. As the authorities had found out years before, the man could not be controlled. He was like a lovable old pit-bull terrier. He could turn on you in an instant.

During our time in the flat he went through all sorts of moods. Sometimes it would all be laughing and joking – he used to love to arm wrestle – then suddenly, he'd just 'go'. He'd look at you and 'go'. From then on it was like trying to have a row with a tree. Sometimes he'd play cards, listen to records, dance with his bird, do press-ups. At other times he'd just sit there and brood. We all feel up sometimes and down sometimes, but we can control our moods. If you're feeling miserable you try and keep busy, to do anything to counteract it, but people like Frank just fall into a mood, go with it and let it take them over. He would go from extreme confidence, when he felt the authorities were giving into him and kowtowing, to the pits of despair.

His moods didn't only affect himself. He was becoming so uncontrollably aggressive that other people's lives were in danger. After the first week Lisa's charms could still keep him happy in bed, but they could no longer tranquillize his mind. During the night one of the guards woke up to see Frank standing over him with a knife. This incident was instantly reported to the Twins who soon had a lot more to worry about.

Frank had been getting increasingly upset about what he considered their lack of respect. Reggie had come to see him just the once, while Ronnie – who'd made all the grand promises – had not come near him at all. So Frank said, 'Well, tell 'em that if they don't come round here, I shall go round there. To Vallance Road.' And that upset them.

We tried to explain that Ronnie had a good reason for not showing. He was in hiding himself, to avoid a subpoena to give evidence against a police officer Ronnie and a private detective had taped up while, according to them, he was demanding a bribe. Ronnie felt his image would be ruined if he appeared in court for the prosecution, even when the defendant was a cop. The scheme worked. Without Ronnie the case was eventually thrown out, though, of course, the mere sight of Ronnie Kray giving evidence might have persuaded the jury to clear the copper anyway. That wasn't till months later, so throughout Frank's pathetic little taste of freedom, Ronnie refused to come out of his hidey-hole to see him. This greatly upset Frank who was really a sentimental, emotionally starved child. He wanted to believe the promise Ronnie once made: that they would both go and live together in the country. He believed everything Ronnie told him. Why not? Everything else the Twins had promised, they'd done. But now he was losing faith.

He increasingly sensed the pair were giving him the runaround. He was getting wilder and wilder. He told the guards to repeat his threat to the Twins that, if they didn't come and see him pretty damn quick, he'd come and see them. There was more menace in it this time, and if the Mad Axeman menaced you, things were getting serious. OK, Frank didn't know where Ronnie was now but he certainly had Reggie's address, because he had mailed them lots of letters while he was in Dartmoor.

Now, at last, it dawned on them that they couldn't control Frank. Sure, if those letters to newspapers and tame MPs like Tom Driberg had worked some impossible magic, he would have got his release date and would soon be signing on the Firm. But the authorities could never give assurances to any escaper before he gave himself up – least of all to someone known throughout the land as the Mad

Axeman. The Home Secretary said in parliament that if he returned to prison, and there was 'good evidence that he no longer constitutes a danger to the public, fresh consideration will be given to fixing a date for his release'. When Frank heard this, he could see it meant nothing, because if anyone's going to be deemed a danger to the public, it's someone the public knows as the Mad Axeman. This wasn't the response Frank wanted, but it was predictable from the moment he escaped. Quite rightly, Frank now blamed the Twins for this mess and he was getting very mad with them.

The Twins were getting just as mad with Frank. They demanded to know everything he said and did. Their patience finally snapped when he issued what could only be interpreted as a threat. He had a row with Scotch Jack Dickson, then he told him, 'If anybody comes here, I know who it's down to.' By this he meant that if the police raided the flat and re-captured him, there were only a few people who could have betrayed him. 'I'll know where the information came from. I'll know who to deal with.'

Maybe that's just what the Twins should have done. They should have told everybody to get out, then given the cops an anonymous tip. They weren't against this on principle, they just didn't want people to know they had grassed him. There was a worse problem. If Frank did think they had turned him in, he would have told the police, 'It was the Twins who got me out.' If he was nicked, they'd get nicked as well.

Even if Frank calmed down and accepted that the Twins couldn't visit him for now, he could not be contained in this little flat for much longer. Don't forget, as well as being a nutter, he was a failed criminal. Now to prove himself, he wanted to get out on the pavement again, do robberies and wave guns about. He even asked me for guns to do robberies. Ronnie had first talked of springing him from Dartmoor a year before it happened when we were needing extra muscle against the Richardsons. The Colonel had dreamed up the entire escape just so Mitchell could be on hand to kill Billy Stayton. Nine months later Mitchell was still going on about this business, but now the Richardsons had been bagged up, and the war was never going to happen. So on top of everything, we now had a hit-man without a cause, a would-be killer surplus to requirements, a robber with no conceivable role in a firm that did not do robberies.

Everything I say about the Mitchell affair from here on has been denied by those I accuse of conspiring to kill him. When it came to court they were acquitted. Some were never put on trial. The way it all happened meant there could never be any hard evidence to support my story unless one of the conspirators had a brainstorm and confessed – but I know what I saw and heard in the coming days, and especially in the next few hours.

It was on 23 December that Scotch Jack told the Twins about Frank's latest threat. The Twins finally got the needle, and an instant decision was made. By lunch-time there was a meet at the Hackney Road flat of Harry Hopwood, an elderly family friend who'd been best man at Violet and old Charlie's wedding. I went there with Reggie and Charlie Kray. We waited for our south London friend, Freddie Foreman, to arrive. When he came in, Charlie and Reggie took him into the kitchen, leaving me and Harry outside. Then they all came in the front room again and said they had decided to move Frank.

A few minutes later Charlie approached me because he knew Frank trusted me. After all, I was the guy who took him off the moor, then I'd brought him his lovely Lisa, and since then, whenever he'd kicked up a fuss, I was the man who had calmed him down. Now I've got to split him from Lisa. I've got to get him out of the flat; I'll be met by some guys in a van, and they'll be taking him down to Kent to a farm where he'll spend Christmas with Ronnie. Then the pair of them will discuss getting him abroad.

At the time this made some sense to me, even the bit about splitting him from Lisa. There was no way Ronnie would have this girl running round his little hideaway. He couldn't stand having any woman in his domestic life except his mum. So that's how it was done. I was told by Charlie to go round that same afternoon and meet this bunch, led by Freddie Foreman, on a little slip road at the back of Canning Town Bridge. I've got to tell them where Frank is, then set up my end of the move.

So I meet these guys, and I know them: Freddie, of course, Alfie Gerard, Jerry Callaghan and a fourth man, all in the same car. Freddie had never met Mitchell. He had been in jail most of his life, whereas Freddie had not done much bird at all. He wanted to know how big Frank was. Was he so big they should bring a furniture van to move him? I said that the papers had exaggerated this 'big Frank' stuff, and a Thames van was all they needed.

I told them Mitchell was being kept in a little flat in Barking Road and gave them the address. Then I had to run them past the flat, so they could see how it was laid out. They said they would park just round the corner in Ladysmith Avenue, so all I had to do was bring Frank straight out of the flat on his own, jump into the van and away. The timing had to be exactly right. We couldn't afford to have Frank visible on the street for an extra second, so the strict arrangement was that at half-past eight that night they would definitely be parked up in Ladysmith Avenue, and I was to come out with Mitchell at exactly half-past, so there'd be no hanging about. When that was all fixed, Foreman said, 'We've got to go and pick the van up.'

Even after I'd had this chat with Freddie, I still thought Charlie's version was going to happen: Mad Frank was going to be taken off to Kent to Ronnie. Everything joined up. But now I've got to go back up to the flat and convince Frank that he's got to get ready to move but without his lovely lady. So I said, 'Well, the only way to do this is to think what's going to happen if you get a stoppo on the way down. If the Old Bill pull you, you're going to go right into one, and she's going to be involved. She'll either be hurt or nicked. You don't need that. So what we'll do, we'll set you off first, and I'll follow up with Lisa half an hour later. We'll get you there all nice and safely, you'll be with the Colonel and Merry Christmas.'

Right. He stood for that, even though by now he's saying he's in love with Lisa. She was going along with it, just so as not to upset him, but, however fond she'd become of him, she didn't love him. Then he got into the business of packing his gear. When I told him, 'You'll be going through to Kent,' he was proud that, even though he had done so much bird, he still knew the manor well enough to say, 'Oh yeah, I've got to go through the tunnel.' Even simply knowing that we'd be travelling through the Blackwall Tunnel gave him a sense of achievement. He was wearing an old jacket of mine, and he had a hat. I don't know where he got that from.

So now, while he's saying his goodbyes to Lisa, I've got to get him packed up, ready to move and out of the flat at exactly eight thirty. It's now time so I go outside to make sure they're there. As arranged, I see an old Thames van, either blue or black. It's difficult to tell at night. It's double-parked about 20 yards down on the left-hand side away from the main road. Then I go back in, tell him, 'They're here, Frank', bring him out down the path five yards to the street. As we turn right to go round the corner, who should come along but a copper on the beat!

Mitchell is on my inside, and I feel him straining up, and I nudge him and say, 'Calm down,' because if this copper says anything, like 'Excuse me, sir. . .', Frank will jump all over him. So we just walk on past him, while the others in the van must be saying, 'Whoops! Old Bill!' and waiting for everything to happen. But we're clear.

As we walk up to the van, a guy's standing on the pavement. It's Jerry Callaghan. He opens up the back door, and I see two more guys sitting on the wheel-casing on the left. They are Freddie Foreman and Alfie Gerard. The wheel-casing on the right is empty. Frank gets in first. Foreman says, 'How are you, Frank? Sit down there,' and points to the wheel-casing on the right, opposite Foreman and Gerard. I go to sit beside Frank, but Foreman says to me, 'You go up the front and tell him the best way back to the Tunnel.'

That sounds odd. These guys have found their way over here, so they must be able to find their way back. But I say, 'OK,' and I go up the front. There's a little partition through to the driving cab and, like a plum, I'm kneeling to lean over and tell the driver, 'Just go down, do a right, then a right and you're back on Barking Road.' In the meantime Callaghan's shut the back doors, he comes round to the front passenger door, gets in and sits down.

The van is running now. As he gets in, he slams the passenger door. And I'm still leaning forward, like an idiot, talking to the driver. Then 'Pow! Pow! Pow!' – the guns start off behind me. I don't know till later that slamming the door is the signal to the two guns. They just keep popping the man. He comes off the casing on to his knees, then he falls back, and these bullets are going all over him. Then he goes still, and one of the guys, Foreman, leans over and puts three more shots in around the heart. You can see the shirt jumping. And now we 're moving, travelling down Ladysmith Avenue. We do the first right, we're going up, and we've got to do the next right. He's been lying quiet for a while. He's got to be dead. Then all of a sudden there's a groan, and he lifts his head up again. I don't know what they call it – after death, the body relaxing or gas escaping – but then there's another groan. So Gerard says, 'He ain't fucking dead, give him another one. I'm empty.'

You watch gangland executions on TV, and it's one in the head and chest, and everybody dies on cue. But this guy just won't die, even though they are pumping shots into him.

Now, I'm starting thinking, I've got to 'go' as well here. I'm piggy-in-the-middle. Yeah. I'm pleased to hear one guy's empty – at least I've only got one gun to deal with now – but then Foreman goes and puts the gun right up behind Frank's ear and Pop! Pop! That's the last two shots that's fired into him. Now I'm thinking, The next thing I can do is dive into the driver's cab, among these two up front, and just start kicking and punching until I can get out. I'm firmly convinced I'm going to die. Anyway, we now come back up to the Old Barking Road so I say, hopefully and without a quiver of nerves in my voice, 'Right, drop me off here. All you got to do is a left, and the tunnel's up on your left.' So the back door is opened, and I get out. And I start walking away. I'm still waiting for one in the back of the nut, but when I hear the van pull off, that's it! I'm pleased. Boy! Am I pleased. Not pleased for poor Frank, but pleased for myself.

I recall a few more things about the killing. I heard some of the bullets hitting the van so there would have been dents around the wheel-casing. I looked to see if there was any light coming in, if any of them went through, but there weren't any holes. I don't know where the van came from. I think they told me on the first meet that they had a 'ringer' so it must have been nicked. While the shooting was going on, we were driving down Ladysmith Avenue. They stopped shooting as another van came by us in the opposite direction. When it had gone by, they started shooting again. They fired about ten shots altogether. Foreman had an automatic with a silencer. Gerard had a revolver without one.

I think Mitchell half-smelled it, because he made a dive for the driver just as they started letting go. They were going into him all the time, and he went back with his knees under him. He was hurt, but he was still groaning. When he was definitely dead, Gerard asked me if he had any money on him. I said he did, so I suppose they took that off him later. I knew he had money because the Krays had been sending him some while he was at the flat.

As they drove off I walked back to the fiat. I stank of the shooting. I could smell the fumes, the gunsmoke. During that 300-yard walk, I left my coat hanging open in the breeze, to clear it, to get rid of the fumes. As soon as I got in the door, I told the others to start to clean the place down. We had to do a 'wet-and-dry' – a wet rag and a dry rag – to wash everything in the flat and get rid of all the fingerprints. This was in case the police later came looking for Mitchell after a tip-off. As a professional criminal, you're always thinking, Old Bailey. You're always making your case before you get to court. You're constructing your defence all the time, just in case you get arrested.

Before we could get on with the clean-up, Lisa, Lennie and Scotch Jack were all going, 'Is he all right? We heard shots.' I looked straight at Jack and said, 'Shots? No. No shots. Might have been a motor backfiring or something.' I was trying to calm them down, but I couldn't convince Lisa it was anything other than a gun. She was in the bedroom, terrified and obviously thinking Frank had been murdered.

I had to get on the phone straightaway to make a prearranged call to Reggie at Vallance Road. Earlier he'd told me, 'As soon as he's clear of the flat, give me a ring and just say, "That dog has won." Don't say any more.' The Twins were always convinced the phones were bugged, so he gave me this line so I'd sound as if I'd just come from the greyhound track and won on a tip. So when I rang I said, 'That dog won.'

Later in the same call Reggie said, 'Bring the girl. I'll see you round Sam's. We'll send someone to pick you up, then he'll take you and the girl somewhere.' After my near death experience in the van, and believing I'm lucky to escape with my life, I was still thinking, Suspicious. But there's no way out of it, so now I've got to tell Lisa that she's going to see Reggie, for a debriefing. 'So stop talking about shots,' I said. 'Shut up about shots. Just say, "Frank's gone to the country, and you might be going later." If you start talking about shots, you're going to go swimming. You'll be in the river.'

Lisa wasn't stupid, and she got the point. Then Connie Whitehead pulls up, and we get in the car. As he drives along the three-mile journey to Sammy Lederman's flat where Reggie's now gone, Connie's laughing and giggling. I don't know why he's laughing. He doesn't know what's happened – he's got no idea what we've just been through, nothing's been said about the killing so for him it's a normal night out. We're just going to a party.

But Lisa thinks Connie must know what's happened, and that's why he's giggling. She decides he's a crazy twisted killer. This makes her turn to me and say something I'll never forget: 'When it's my turn, will you do it? 'Cos I think you'll do it quick.' Jesus! Imagine what frame of mind she's in! The girl was terrified. She thinks she's being taken somewhere to be done, she's going to be next, and the giggling Whitehead is going to make her death long and painful for her but highly enjoyable for himself. That's why she doesn't want him to do it.

Anyway, we got to little Sammy's flat in Stepney. Whitehead had a key. When we went in, Reggie wasn't there. He was waiting in a car outside to make sure nothing was wrong. He came in a minute after us when he knew we weren't accompanied by the police, or being followed by them. All this creeping round by Reggie made me think Lisa was right after all. Perhaps she was for the chop. So immediately I had a chat with Reggie and said, 'I think she's all right.' When he questions her, she holds her story up, doesn't mention the shots, and Reggie's satisfied. Then he tells her not to mention anything to anybody. He says, 'If you do, we will find you no matter where you go.'

Now we went to a party round Blonde Winnie's in Evering Road, Stoke Newington (practically opposite the flat where Jack the Hat later 'went'). Nobody else at the party knew what had happened, but this girl was still terrified. Then people started drifting away in the early hours, until there was no one left except us. So I said, 'Well, you better stay here for the night.' Now she started getting a little bit hysterical, and she said, 'Oh! I can't stay here on my own,' so I did the honourable thing. I slept with her. We spent the whole night together. A naughty thing to do with a lady, but I had to calm the girl down. You can imagine the state she was in. And that was that. Next day she went back West and carried on with her little life.

When I went back home that morning, my wife gave me a very cool reception. Later when it came out at the trial that I'd spent the night with Lisa, she went wild. But that morning I went straight into the bedroom. I didn't even take my coat off. I just lay on the bed, and I started a little cry. I'm not the crying type so it must have had some effect on me. It must have been some sort of a come-down. Even for a hard man like me, Frank's killing was exceptional. It was real. I can't find the words to explain how I felt, but part of this outpouring of emotion was because I had thought I too was going to go. Were the tears for Mitchell or myself? Were they tears of grief or tears of relief?

My wife must have heard something because she came in and I told her. I said they had tucked me up, and they'd shot Mitchell. She was frightened, but I said, 'Whatever you do, don't mention anything about this to anybody.' As far as I know, she never did.

I've never had nightmares. Now everyone can have counselling, to help cope with trauma and stress, though even today I shouldn't think that's available to gangland thugs involved in murders. After Mitchell, I just found that life carries you on, you calm down, and you just get on with it. I did feel sorry for Frank, but this was just the sort of thing that was happening at the time. In some crazy way it all made sense, because our whole way of life was crazy. It all had some logic, it was a natural progression, according to the climate at the time. Of course, none of it need have happened. We'd have all done better by shooting the Other Two right at the start.

Now, going back over who knew what and when. I really had no idea they were going to kill Mitchell right up to the start of the shooting. I just didn't know. When we had that meeting in Hopwood's place with Reggie, Charlie Kray and Freddie Foreman, neither Hopwood nor me could hear the conversation. That must have been when the plot was agreed, but all I was told was only that we had to get him in the van, separate him from the woman and take him down to a farm in Kent for Christmas with Ronnie.

This was how the Twins always treated individuals on the Firm. For security reasons you would never be told the whole story. You would be given just part of it. Say, you would be told to go and see a certain person, to slap or frighten him, then later you'd find out that somebody else had been doing something entirely different. And only when you matched these two things together, could you understand what the Twins had been aiming at all along. Not so much 'divide and rule' as 'divide and confuse', to minimize the risk of grassing.

So as I'd watched the whole Mitchell affair unfold since we picked him up on Dartmoor, I guess I thought it would go this way eventually. I didn't know Frank would be killed at that moment. I imagined that once they got to the place in Kent, that would be the place to do it, because they could bury him right there or do whatever else they liked. I didn't imagine it was going to happen in the van.

As for Reggie, it was only during the party at Blonde Winnie's that I told him in so many words that Mitchell had been shot to death. I also said I was surprised how much it took to finish him off. Now I could tell, by the way Reggie took this, that he knew it was going to happen – otherwise he would have expressed surprise. He would have wanted to know all the details. But it was, 'Yeah. That was the original idea.' I mentioned Foreman to him, and he didn't blink an eyelid, so of course Reggie knew it was going to happen. And so Ronnie had to know too. It was definitely a joint Reggie-and-Ronnie decision. The only people who didn't know were Mitchell and me.

So why didn't our own Firm do it? After all, Ronnie had already killed Cornell, and he was planning lots of other murders – putting more and more names 'on the list'. But Ronnie was on the trot at the time, and they were both dreadful shots. And by now each twin was an emotional wreck. Neither could have killed Frank direct because the sight of him dying would have given them nightmares. He had these big reproachful eyes, like a loyal dog. Also they'd have been worried stiff that he'd overpower them and crush them to death.

The only people on our team who could really do a shooting

were myself, Ronnie Hart and Connie Whitehead, but Frank knew all of us. Also, with all the hue and cry surrounding his disappearance, if anyone on the Firm had killed him, and his body had been found soon after, the police would have come straight for the Twins demanding to know where they were when it happened. That's another reason why it had to be farmed out to another firm: everyone on our Firm had to be at different places and have alibis. Everyone except me.

This other firm really knew what to do. They had experience of 'disappearing' bodies. They had a disposal set-up, which we hadn't. They obviously had some method of getting rid of guys without leaving a trace. If you only bury someone in the woods, a fox is quite likely to dig it up, so they probably had a furnace. Also, it was a tit-for-tat job: you do us a favour, we'll do you a favour. And this particular firm were the only outsiders the Twins could trust.

It took some time for me to get to tell Ronnie exactly what had happened, because he was tucked away in a flat over a bric-à-brac or antiques shop in Fulham. Eventually we went there, and I told him all about it. He already knew a lot because Reggie used to phone up and visit him frequently, but I had to give him all the fine details. He was so interested that I had to tell him everything three or four times. He was getting such a thrill out of it, he kept asking me, 'Tell us again. How did he look. What did he say?' He had a crazy interest in it. He was drunk at the time but, drunk or sober, he was always mad.

And now we have to start spreading the rumours. We were told to say he had gone abroad. 'Frank's in France' and this, that and the other. And somebody was sent back to settle the guy whose flat it was, little Lennie the Books. Somebody had to calm him down. And that was it. In a few weeks everybody forgot about it.

They never did find Frank's body. Where they took it, only they know to this day. There's been all sorts of nonsense about him holding up the motorway, but two or three weeks later I was given the job of taking £1000 to Freddie Foreman's pub, the Prince of Wales in the Borough, just south of London Bridge. When I got there, Fred was upstairs in the living-quarters so I went up, gave him the money, and he started talking. He said that when they took Frank to pieces, they were surprised that for such a big man, he had such a small brain, and he cupped his hands to show me. And he described how his heart was all ripped and torn from the three bullets that went through it.

They must have dismembered him to see all that stuff. Some people have suggested this was to get the bullets out, so that if the remains – even just ashes – were ever found, no one could tie the bullets to the guns. But to me, it would have been far easier to smash up the guns, or send somebody on a day trip to France and chuck them over the side. Foreman said one more bullet had stuck in his silencer, so that gun wasn't worth keeping anyway.

From what else he told me, I gather they had to keep Mitchell's body laid up somewhere for five days because they couldn't deliver it straightaway to where they got rid of it, because the fellow who owned the place had visitors over the Christmas. Foreman didn't tell me where this was. I only know what he chose to tell me. They burned him. That's all.

A few days after this conversation, I had a chat with Charlie Kray He said, 'I was talking to Fred the other day and I asked him how you'd got on. He said he was pleased. You were all right, you done your job. No panic.' I said, 'No panic! I was shitting myself. I thought *I* was going to go.' Then Charlie laughed. But, again, he and Freddie deny this.

So I didn't disappear along with Mitchell but some time later my colleague on the Dartmoor run did evaporate. Mad Teddy Smith had a row with Ronnie Kray while they were both down at the caravan site at Steeple Bay. He was never seen again.

His last known work as an author did not go unappreciated. A second of his letters from Frank appeared in the *Daily Mirror* and drew a sympathetic plea from the editor to 'take the man-to-man advice I am offering you'. This was to 'keep your word and surrender at once. By doing so you will strengthen your claim that you are entitled to a fresh consideration of your case. We've given you a fair hearing, Frank Mitchell. Now give yourself up.'

But Frank couldn't give himself up because he was murdered the day those words were published. I don't know if he even had a chance to read them. Man-to-man advice to him that day consisted of so many bullets in his head. Whatever happened to his remains – and to Mad Teddy Smith – at least one more corpse was on the way, and many more were in the planning.

10: HATS OFF FOR JACK

It's strange how soon everyone forgot about Frank Mitchell. After just a few months with no definite sighting of a man you could not miss if you did see him, everyone from the governor of Dartmoor to the guv'nors at Scotland Yard must have guessed he was dead. We thought they had given up looking for him.

One man who didn't give up was Ronnie. If the Firm could get clean away with two murders, he was thinking, there was no limit to the slaughter we could carry out. Ever since he'd finished Cornell, he'd been riling Reggie for not killing anybody. Several times I heard him say, 'I've done mine, now you do yours.' Once, right in front of me, he snarled, 'You don't have the guts to do anyone in.'

Most times Reggie would ignore these jibes, but once or twice he tried to bite back. On one occasion, not long after Cornell, we were talking about doing business with some people, when Reggie snapped, 'Well, we can't go and see them now, not after you've done the other guy, can we?' Then Ronnie sneered, 'Well, at least I had the guts to do him. When are you going to do something?' and again, 'I've done mine. When are you going to do yours?' He actually said those words. But Reggie just put it off and continued with, 'Never mind that! When are we going to get on with making some cash?' which was basically the real point of the entire organization.

Ronnie did not spend Christmas 1966 with his old friend from Dartmoor. Instead he used Frank's murder as extra ammunition in his verbal war with Reggie. The run-up was that he was getting deeper into his moods and screaming, literally screaming, 'You fucking slag! You got no guts. I've killed. Albert's killed. [Meaning, I'd been involved in the Mitchell thing, thank you very much.] You got no arsehole. When you going to do yours?' This kind of diatribe was going on more and more often. Enough to drive even a well-balanced person to violence.

Reggie was not well balanced at the best of times. And these were the worst of times, for him. His marriage was on the rocks. Frances Shea had moved back in with her parents just eight weeks after getting spliced in April 1965. None of us on the Firm had a public marriage – we were rarely seen with our wives – but Reggie's was invisible. After a wedding so publicly celebrated and snapped by no less a lensman than David Bailey, it had instantly become the marriage that never was.

This was the one thing that really split the Twins. They were always totally staunch about each other. If anyone ever said something in front of Reggie that was even faintly critical about Ronnie, Reggie would give him a look and say, 'Well? What?' and the guy would realize he'd made a big mistake and immediately retract, mumbling, 'Oh, no. What I meant was . . .' Neither twin would run the other down behind his back but, head to head, Ronnie would say, 'You slag! And that prat of a wife of yours! Why don't you go round and give her some more tablets?'

I had missed the wedding because it happened when I was in Brixton Prison over a pub fight that got out of hand after somebody said Reggie should have shot me in the head, not the foot. But later I looked at the photographs, and I saw everything she must have seen: dozens of good reasons to take a lot of pills. Where most people's wedding photos are filled with Mum, Dad, Auntie Mary and other young couples, these were dominated by big flat-noses wearing buttonholes. The reception was packed wall-to-wall with scar-faced thugs. She could not have missed them. It was obviously a happy occasion for some, but Frances was getting the drift of what was going on even then. She tried to look happy. She managed a smile, but what's a smile? You can sit in a dentist's chair and open your mouth, and it looks like you're smiling, but you're in agony.

It couldn't have got any better after the wedding. For a start, Reggie wasn't the easiest person to talk to, and there was none of this 'slippers by the fireside' business with him. She'd have been lucky if he stayed in any night. A couple of times she came out with us, but she didn't like the crowd. She didn't like the whole atmosphere. And there was something far worse: no way out. In straight marital break-ups where there are no children, most people can go through a clean divorce and hope to meet someone else, but Frances couldn't do that. Can you imagine some handsome young chap falling for her, and Reggie getting to hear about it? He's going to have the guy's legs cut off! She couldn't just say, 'That's it! I'm going out with somebody else!' because the fellow would be ripped to pieces. The girl had no chance whatever of another life, as long as Reggie was at liberty.

Nor could she have foreseen liberation in the shape of him getting nicked and locked up for a lifetime. They'd got married fresh from the celebrations when the Twins were cleared on the protection racket charges over the Hideaway Club. Like everybody else, she thought they were so well protected they would never go to jail again, a prediction that the Twins themselves trumpeted to help it come true. For her everything must have seemed hopeless. No way out here, and no escape abroad because she believed the Twins knew people everywhere. They'd always be after her, watching every move. Anyway, no East End girl in those days would dream of going abroad on her own, away from mum and dad so I don't suppose she could see any end to it.

What little hope she ever had of a proper married life was ruined by Ronnie. He was always making remarks about her that were calculated to upset his brother. As Reggie went through the motions of defending his wife, they'd suddenly burst into a fight, but all the time Ronnie was winning him back into the far stronger relationship bonding them together. These guys weren't any old pair of twins. They were so bound up together mentally, they might have been Siamese twins joined at the brain.

I think deep down Ronnie hated all women, barring his mum and Auntie May, because he was just as offensive about Charlie Kray's wife, Dolly. 'Where are you going tonight?' he'd ask Charlie. 'Staying in,' the oldest brother would reply. 'Oh, you're staying in with your lovely wife, are you? You silly prat! Yes, go home and stay in with the dopey cow!'

All right. Let's assume Ronnie had a good reason to stir his brothers, buck them up and get them doing something for the good of the family or the Firm. Fine! Do it when you're alone with them, not in a crowd – especially when you're talking about their wives. If Reggie and Charlie hadn't been family, Ronnie would have been dead years ago for making such remarks. A lone man doesn't get away with talking like that. Yet this is a man who's supposed to have got upset and killed Cornell for calling him a poof! But Ron had no sensitivity when it came to name-calling, otherwise how could he rubbish his own brothers' wives in public?

Reggie's marriage tottered on for a couple of years, but on paper only. Ever since she'd left him, Frances had been living with her parents. They'd been against him right from the start, and can you blame them? Reggie was reduced to visiting the house once a week, to take her some money. It was really bad at that stage. She wasn't mixing with him. She would look out of the bedroom window, and he would poke money through the letter-box and just say, 'How are you? Come down and talk.' 'No!'

I suspect it was a weird marriage in the first place because in the early days Reggie wasn't very interested in girls, although he and Frances had been kind of childhood sweethearts, until he developed into your typical East End tearaway and soon into a gangland boss. Then there was the wedding, and all of a sudden she was whisked off on all those trips to Greece and other lands that normal Eastenders never dreamed of visiting in those days. There was a lot of glamour attached to life with Reggie, and it must have looked nice at first, but when she got the whole drift, with Ronnie screaming in the background and going into his troughs, she must have got sick and frightened too.

I don't think the marriage ever was consummated. There were conversations I had with Reggie. He would talk to me, where he wouldn't to other people, and several times he'd asked, how do you actually touch a woman to make her excited, liven her up. He didn't know where you touched her, or how you touched her. I don't think he knew where to put it, even while he was married.

One day I spoke to the girl by herself. The three of us went out for a stroll in Victoria Park. Reggie and Frances walked ahead, and I was ten yards behind. Then they decided to sit down, and I sat down at another bench, until I was called over to join in. I still didn't speak because it wasn't my conversation, but she was talking to me about their visit to Spain. Then when Reggie left us, only for a couple of minutes, she suddenly started pouring it all out: 'I didn't like Spain. I didn't like all that travelling around,' whereas, just a few seconds before, in front of Reggie, she was saying what a wonderful holiday it had been. She was putting on a front for him, so I suppose it was some relief to her to have a couple of minutes' chat with me, but I could see the girl wasn't happy in herself.

In October 1966 she tried to gas herself to death at her parents' home. When she came out of hospital, she moved in with her brother and sister-in-law, and it was at their flat that in June 1967 she took her own life. We had all seen it coming because she was never a very strong person. Then came the shambles of the funeral, when my job was to check all the wreaths and bouquets to find out who hadn't sent flowers and make a list of those who hadn't expressed their respects. That was a bit sick. You would have thought that, if only on this occasion, Reggie could have forgotten about gangland reckonings and concentrated on asking himself why she'd done away with herself. The fact is, she did away with herself because of the same hole in his head that made him ask me to check who hadn't sent any flowers.

THE ENFORCER

I'm sure he was genuinely grieving. I'm sure that, in his own destructive way, he loved her, but he converted this into hating her family. He blamed her parents for everything that went wrong between him and Frances. Once she was gone, he drank even more. He fell back on Ronnie for moral support, which was a bit like leaning on an umbrella in a force-ten gale. And all the time Ronnie kept goading him about 'doing yours'. Who that 'yours' would turn out to be was a bit like playing, 'Eeny Meeny Miney Mo'. It could have been almost anyone but for sure, sooner, or later – unless Reggie snapped and shot Ronnie – some other poor bastard was bound to become 'Reggie's one'.

The prime candidate was not one of the enemy but one of us, and the issue had nothing to do with gangland. Nobby Clark was the fellow who had promised us his father's home to house Frank Mitchell but backed out when we showed up with the Mad Axeman. He'd made the offer to suck up to Ronnie, and it was another act of sucking-up to Ronnie that made the other one homicidally mad.

I heard the whole story from Reggie himself. It had all started back in 1965, after the marriage had first run into trouble. One day Nobby was with both the Twins, when Ronnie started slagging off Frances. Now, while it was OK for the Twins to say anything they liked to each other, it was nobody else's ground. Nobody else interfered. But instead of just shutting up like the rest of us would, Nobby chipped in and sided with Ronnie, saying, 'Yeah, Ron. That's right, Reg, he's right.'

Nothing was said or done to Nobby immediately because at that time he was still in favour, but his comments had registered with Reggie and were stored away. Two years on things had changed. Nobby had been more or less blown off the Firm – they'd finished using him – while poor Frances was dead, and Reggie was in the blackest mood. Grief-stricken. Remorseful, angry and vindictive. In short, he was looking for someone to take it out on.

So one night when he was with Ronnie Hart, Reggie stoked up

on the gin and got totally drunk. His mind went back to what
Nobby had said all that time ago, and he brooded on it. Then in the
early hours, he went round to Nobby's flat in Newington Green,
with Ronnie Hart and another guy, and they sat in a van for the best
part of the night, with a revolver on board. It was crazy. The police
could have pulled them any time.

Then about seven in the morning they knocked at Nobby's door.
His wife opened, so Reggie called him out. So far, so good. It's
normal, when you have a dispute with a man, to call him out of the
home because you don't want to hurt his family – and it was just as
understandable that Nobby was refusing to come out. So Reggie
just stood in the open doorway, shouting, until Nobby stepped out
of the bathroom and emerged at the top of the stairs. Then Reggie
fired up the stairs and hit him in the leg.

Nobby was screaming all over the place. I don't know why,
because it was only a .22, and that doesn't hurt much to start with. It
must have been fear: death was staring him in the face, and his wife
and kids might be going with him. He survived but, even so, the
punishment hardly matched the crime. After all, it was Ronnie
who'd made the original remarks, and it was only because Reggie
couldn't shoot him that he shot poor Nobby instead. The weirdest
thing was how Reggie had controlled his outrage for two years
before punishing Nobby for his 'crime'. But again, that was typical
of the pair. They saved up grievances for a rainy day.

That was personal. Back to business. Top of Ronnie's 'list' now,
and therefore a possible body for Reggie to 'do his', was Leslie
Payne, their former financial adviser. He had engineered their
takeover of Esmeralda's Barn, and he had masterminded their long-
firm frauds and stolen-bond rackets. These had brought them a lot
of money, but he also dreamed up a Nigerian development scam
that collapsed after he upset a local contractor who got him locked
up for a while in Enugu jail. During 1966 he steadily drifted off the
Firm. He wasn't coming in with any more grand scams matching

his connections with their clout. By autumn 1967 Ronnie was telling us 'the man with the briefcase' might be squealing to Scotland Yard, so he had to go.

But who should send him on his way? One evening in September we had a meet in the Grave Maurice: Ronnie, Reggie, me, Jack 'the Hat' McVitie and Billy Exley. Now Jack was on the fringes of the Firm, but he was mainly a freelance, a 'gun for hire', though he hadn't ever killed anybody. He was electric, like a puppet on a string, because he was always taking pills. He never stopped talking, and he couldn't keep still for two minutes.

The Twins were saying they wanted Payne done that very night because they'd found out he was due to show up on a meet. They gave Jack the address and told him to be there and finish him. According to Jack, Payne never showed so he came back to the Grave Maurice. Then around half-past eleven Jack and Billy went off again, this time to Payne's house on a private estate in Dulwich, south London, where they were going to cop for him. Their job was definitely murder. They were going to knock on the door and get straight back in the car before he answered. This caution was because Payne had a big dog, so they were going to shoot him from the car as soon as he opened up.

I saw them when they came back. Me, the Twins and a few more were still waiting in the Grave Maurice. We did this by way of an alibi, in case Payne did get killed, but Jack said that when he knocked it was the wife who answered. She seemed a bit worried and suspicious, and she said, 'He's not here, and he won't be back all night,' otherwise they would have waited for him. Later I was given another version, which was at least as believable: Payne lived on a private estate, and these bumbling 'hit-men' never got further than the guardhouse with the security pole.

Jack was supposed to get £250 for killing Payne. He never tried again, but early in October he was on another of the Twins' murder assignments, this time with me, Ronnie Hart and Reggie Kray who had screwed himself up again to 'do his' and level the score with

Ronnie. The target this day was a little guy out at Poplar called Bobby Cannon. While the four of us were sat in a flat in Hackney, somebody who was welcome where Cannon drank was sent to get him. He gave him a message to come to where we were, but, of course, he wasn't told that we'd be ready for him at this end, like a reception committee.

So while we're waiting in the lounge, Reggie and Ronnie Hart are in the kitchen, trying to wrap a towel round this gun to silence it. Reggie wants us to entertain Cannon till he's ready. We are to calm Cannon and put him at his ease, saying, 'Reggie'll be here in a minute,' then the great gunman will burst in the room, do the business, and we'll be left to clear it up.

So, me and Jack the Hat, we look at each other, and we can see neither of us wants to do this. So when we hear Cannon's footsteps – we don't speak in case we're heard – we just go, 'Shoo!' wave him to go, and he's gone. He doesn't need telling. But as we're doing that, we're also knocking furniture about as though there's a scuffle. Then when Reggie sticks his head out, along with this big towel wrapped round his hand, we say, 'He's bolted, he's sussed it, he's got away.' And we can still hear Bobby Cannon's footsteps on the stairs, and he shouts up, 'Bunch of bastards!' Whether that's to help us carry off the pretence or what, it certainly sounds good as far as Reggie's concerned. And he believes we've really had a fight. What a relief.

The Twins stood for that, but if we had sat Bobby Cannon down and given him some talking-to, Reggie would have walked out of that back room and shot him stone dead. I haven't got a clue what Cannon had done to upset him. If he'd done anything bad we'd have known, we'd have been told, 'That bastard's done this or that,' but he hadn't done. It was probably just that somebody had overheard him mouthing off in public against the terrible Twins.

So now Jack had been on two recent murder jobs. Neither had come off, but the Twins couldn't have held him singly to blame on either assignment. They certainly hadn't twigged we'd screwed up the Cannon job deliberately. Now the very fact that they had trusted him with both these jobs shows that there could not have been any long spell of bad feeling between him and Reggie. Throughout this time he was actually working with us. He was one of us. But in the next three weeks Ronnie turned up the emotional squeeze on Reggie even more, to the point where he had to kill somebody. Anybody. It was just a case of which duck happened to be sitting in the middle of the shooting range when he finally raised his gun. As October went on, the man most out of favour happened to be Jack the Hat.

Perhaps it was what happened at the Regency just then that condemned him to be that duck. The Regency, which was still owned by the Barrys, was a big building with a gymnasium and two bars on the upper floors and a soundproof bar in the basement, where we used to drink all our 'afters'. We were down there one night when Johnny Barry came down and said, 'The Hat's upstairs, out of his skull on pills and booze. He's carrying a shotgun, and he's asking if any of the Firm's here.' From what Johnny said, it wasn't definite that Jack was going to try and 'do' the Firm. He had simply said, 'Are any of the Firm here?' which made me think he might just want a bit of back-up on something. So I said, 'I'll go and sort him out.' Johnny said, 'No. We've calmed him down, we're going to get rid of him. We told him there's no one here.' And that was the end of that.

Some people have said he came in threatening the Firm, but that wasn't clear. It might have been a threat. If one of us had gone up, he might have shot us, we don't know, but I know for sure that the guy wouldn't shoot me. I knew Jack the Hat as a buddy. We'd go and drink together. He'd come in my club, and I'd turn my back on him with no fear of him shooting me. And I was thinking like a fox in those days. I had to smell trouble to survive, and there was no way I'd turn my back on someone I felt even half shifty about. I picked up vibes pretty quickly, but I never got any bad feedback from the Hat, and I don't seriously believe Reggie Kray did either.

A couple of nights before Jack went, we sat together on the Regency's middle floor, where there was a Chinese restaurant. Myself, Reggie, Jack and a fourth person I forget sat down and had supper together. There was no personal animosity either way that I could detect, and we would have picked it up. I'd certainly have picked it up from Reggie, but there was none – and this was after the shotgun incident.

I know Jack often said things which were 'anti' the Twins, but I pretended I didn't hear. Whenever Jack slagged them off he was just being Jack. I would never report that stuff back to the Other Two because I might have been signing his death warrant. I didn't wish the Twins' vengeance on anybody, because I'd been on the receiving end of Reggie's gun myself. Maybe other people weren't so careful, or they might have informed on him deliberately, to get him into trouble. Sure, he did have a loose tongue and maybe he deserved a slap, but nothing more. There were, as they say in court, mitigating circumstances. Jack was a pill popper. He was always downing Purple Hearts, Speed. He'd scream and rant, 'I ain't frightened of the Firm,' but only when he was full of booze and smarties. The Twins knew that – Ronnie was the same himself – so if Jack had got a talking-to, that would have been enough.

The first I knew about the Hat was one Sunday morning, 29 October, when I was due to meet Ronnie at the Blind Beggar, but instead Connie Whitehead came round to my flat in Devons Road. He said, 'They want to see you.' I asked, 'What's the matter?' He replied, 'Don't you know what happened last night?' I told him, 'No, I had a night in.' He said, 'They copped for McVitie.' I didn't quite get his drift – maybe I didn't want to – so I asked, 'How was he when he left? All right? Was he sweet with them? Did he walk away?' Whitehead said, 'He left feet first.'

Connie drove me to the Beggar, and I met Tommy Cowley. He told me, 'The Twins are off.' I pretended to know nothing and asked, 'Why?' He said, 'Well, bad news.' He took me outside, and we talked on the pavement. 'Jack the Hat's gone.' 'Oh, fucking hell! What's happening now?' I asked, so Cowley replied, 'They want you to go round, organize the clean-up and redecorate the place. They've got Tommy Brown's brother (he was a totter, a secondhand dealer) coming over from Walthamstow with furniture, carpet, curtains. They want to make sure the place is totally redecorated, and it's got to be finished by the morning. But you need to go and look at the place first.'

So I go in there. It's Blonde Carol Skinner's place over at 71 Evering Road, right opposite where I spent the night with Lisa. And there are these two women, Ronnie Hart's wife, Vicki, and Blonde Carol who lives there, on their hands and knees. Get this straight: it's no good saying there are just a few blood splashes: there's a pool of blood on the floor! They're swabbing it into buckets, tipping it into the sink and the toilet, then they're going over the whole floor with bleach and Ajax. I can't do anything till they finish. Christ! It's like one of those places where they do cattle – an abattoir. It looks as though they've done an animal and let the blood drain out.

For once I was able to put my education with the De La Salle brothers to practical use. I washed and scrubbed down the plaster, and where it crumbled, I had to rip bits off and replaster. I did the tiles and the wallpaper, which I'd picked up from the Stowe Club, but in the corner where the killing had been done, I had to stick tar paper underneath as a damp-course because this was a basement. Then I had to paint some other walls. The biggest problem was all the blood under the lino. I had to take out all the lino, then lay new felt and a new carpet.

As arranged, Tommy Brown's brother turned up with new furniture. He didn't know what it was about, he just thought there'd been a fight. So now we put everything in. I had started the job at six that night, and it took me till almost dawn the next day. Meantime this poor Blonde Carol had to stay there with her kids. She'd got nowhere else to go.

Anyway, that's my job finished. I come away. So now I get back among the boys, and I say to my partner Ronnie Hart, 'What happened?' because he was there. As he explained, it started as the normal thing. The Twins have a party somewhere, then they send some people on the outer edge of the Firm off to pick up other people. That night two second generation Bubbles happen to be around, Chrissy and Tony Lambrianou. So the Twins send them off to the Regency to tell Jack the Hat there's a party, and would he come back? They send the Lambrianous blind. They have no idea what's going to happen.

Ronnie Hart tells me that when Jack comes in the flat, Reggie tries to shoot him, but the gun is duff. Jack grabs Reggie, and he's got the gun under his arm, he's holding on to it, and he's struggling with Reggie. Then Ronnie jumps on him, and he's trying to screw an ordinary dinner knife into his back. Jack breaks away. He's in a basement, and there's a window with a grille, so he tries to smash his way through to get up and out, but they drag him back, and maybe he cuts himself in the struggle.

Then Reggie gets away, somebody comes in from the kitchen and gives him the carving knife. Ronnie's still holding him, saying, 'Go on! Do him!' Reggie does him round the body, then stabs him in the face. Then the last one goes in the neck, and he twists it round and round, and that's where all the gravy comes from.

Now, they've got to wrap Jack up, get him out of the house and get him off the manor. So, like with Mitchell, they run him over the water, south of the river, through the Blackwall Tunnel and park him up. That's the end of him, as far as the Firm is concerned.

As I found out more, I was astonished how public this killing had been. Lots of people were in the place at the time. Ronnie Bender was there, so was Connie Whitehead and so were two kids. One was called Terry, a trainee croupier at the Colony, who was only eighteen, and the other was called Trevor. This pair ran out when they saw Jack getting it, but, to show them he wasn't dead, they were told afterwards that all he needed was plenty of stitches to fix him up.

Then I went to Tommy Brown's flat at Tottenham, where the Twins were tucked away. Tommy's wife was there, but she didn't hear what the Twins were saying. Reggie was bursting to tell me how it happened, but they were both so excited that they kept interrupting themselves, each trying to explain it in his own way. They were triumphant, gleeful, and there was no remorse. In one way I was relieved to find them so cheery because I was worried they might have sussed we'd tipped off Bobby Cannon. I was thinking, Have I told anyone? Is that why Jack's gone? If so, I'm next in line. But no. Not a whiff of animosity, so I settled down and listened to their version of events, trying to pick up any differences from what I'd already heard from Ronnie Hart.

Soon after the Twins gave me their gleeful accounts, which largely tied in with Ronnie Hart's version, they fled the East End. One-armed Lou took them off to Suffolk, to stay in Lavenham, close to their friend Jeff Allen. All their clothes were burnt on a smallholding. Ronnie also had to chuck some jewellery away. The rest was washed. Meantime Jack's body was still where they'd dropped him in south London, on the back seat of his own car, awaiting collection by Freddie Foreman and company. According to Ronnie Hart, they had phoned Freddie sometime after the killing to tell him where the body was.

It seems Jack's body lay there for at least a couple of days. This was during a warm spell, and it was starting to decompose and smell. Only then was he taken away. That information came from Freddie Foreman himself, when I was sent over to his place a week after the killing. I was delivering money to him again, like I had over Mitchell. Fred told me that whoever had dropped the car off had done it a bit silly. They had left the doors unlocked, and it was near a church, where apparently a wedding had taken place because there was confetti all round the car. He said it was a miracle no one had spotted Jack because he was covered only with an old candlewick bedspread. He told me he was pleased it was Jack because he'd had a row with him at Fred's own 211 Club. He didn't say, but I was left with the impression that Jack, like Mitchell, was taken to the country and burned in an incinerator.

But there was one big difference that made Jack's killing far more dangerous for the Twins than Frank Mitchell's. With Frank, the authorities knew from the start that he had run from Dartmoor by choice, so even if he stayed out of sight for years they weren't going to worry much for his safety. But on the night Jack went, he'd been sitting happily at home reading the Saturday racing results when his wife Sylvia popped out. When she came back, he wasn't there. Then he never came home so, pretty obviously, he's gone missing against his will. Sylvia traced his movements that night to the Regency, where all anyone could honestly say was that he'd been invited to a party at Blonde Carol's place. So she went straight round there and had a row with Carol. I don't know if Carol knew he was dead. They got her out of the flat just before it happened and took her to another party. She may have guessed he was dead because of all the blood. But all she and by now Sylvia knew for certain was that the trail ended at her flat.

So what of poor Jack? A lot of the Kray fan club today talk as if he didn't deserve to live, but who are they to say who should live or die? In the Bible Jesus says, those who 'take the sword shall perish with the sword'. If that's true for Jack, it's far truer for Ronnie and Reggie. If anyone in our crowd should have died, it was that pair. In comparison Jack was a pussycat. When they told him to kill Leslie Payne, he deliberately let Payne off, and when Reggie wanted to kill Bobby Cannon we both screwed up that attack too. In a sense Jack helped save that man's life, so how can anyone say he deserved to die?

Some people have tried to justify their role in his death by trying to discredit his overall character. After all, they say, he'd thrown his girlfriend out of the car and broken her back. But even that wasn't a deliberate, 'I'm going to break your back!' job. He told me that she was yacking at him, he gave her a shove, the door flew open by chance, and she flew out. He said he had never meant to throw her out. That was his story, and you may not believe it, but there's something far sicker about far bigger East End villains, whose own record with women isn't so honourable, turning into Simon Pure defenders of women's rights just to discredit Jack. We were all rubbish, and none of us can cast a stone against him.

Jack wasn't murdered for being a woman-hater or a pill-popper or even for being a villain. He was murdered because he was available and, significantly, because he was unconnected. He had no team of his own, so killing him wouldn't cause any ripples or provoke another gangland war. We could have picked out a dozen guys who probably deserved to 'go' way ahead of Jack, if you think like that. But his killing was like one of these fun killings where they murder tramps because nobody's going to worry about them. Jack was killed because he was an easy mark. He was unconnected, he was a clown, he was a loony, and he just happened to be around.

Even the fact that he was around proves he had no intention of doing the Twins. If he really had been shouting he was going to kill them, he'd have known he had to get off the scene, otherwise he definitely would be next, but he had no such worries because he had no such plans. The Twins knew that. Jack was done only because Reggie needed 'one' of his own. Even then it wasn't a courageous solo effort, but a grubby gang bang without style, panache or dignity.

The only thing Jack really did wrong was go to the 'party', as he knew just how kill-crazy Reggie was from the Cannon business only three weeks earlier. He knew what the Twins were capable of. He also knew it could happen any time. And, of course, he never would have gone if they had sent a member of the Firm to get him. They knew that to kid him along to a party, they couldn't send a strong figure like myself, or Connie Whitehead or even Ronnie Bender because he would have suspected something. He wasn't a dummy. He'd have known it was a kid-on. Anyway, on past form the Twins knew Connie and I might tell him not to come, whereas the Lambrianous could not foresee what was coming because they had no idea then of the Twins' manipulative mentality. Chrissy and Tony were gofers, boys. They were sent to the Regency because they weren't on the Firm. They were just the right level, well enough connected to invite someone to the party but not senior enough to frighten him.

Once Jack was dead and disposed of, all that remained was to make sure no fringe witnesses could give effective evidence against the Twins. For this they devised the ritual of a statement taken down by their bent brief, Manny Fryde, even when the 'witness' was not sure any crime had occurred. So people like Blonde Carol and Tommy's brother, who'd supplied the new furniture for her flat, were called in to make statements to Fryde, just in case the cops came calling. The Twins weren't the slightest bit worried about people like me or Ronnie Hart because the thought that we might turn never entered their heads. Yet in the end it was mainly Hart's evidence, supported by people like Blonde Carol and me, that sank not only the Twins but Freddie Foreman as well.

In the weeks after the murder Charlie Kray was running the Firm, and we all went low profile. I carried on doing the Milk Round, but we didn't congregate. We scattered. But when nothing seemed to be happening, and the police weren't obviously getting stuck in the Twins returned to London and took charge again. They were more puffed up than ever, even more convinced they were untouchable, invincible. They were also far closer to each other. Now Reggie had 'done his', he felt he was back in Ronnie's favour. True, the Colonel was impressed. At last his brother had proved he was up to scratch. Now they were both accomplished killers.

Up till that point I don't think they could take themselves seriously as gangland bosses, but, with three corpses to their credit, they felt they were on a par with the Mafia. In America wiseguys 'make their bones' by killing. Now they too had killed their way to creating their own fully paid-up crime family. Before they didn't believe all the publicity they'd been getting – not surprisingly as they had invented most of it, especially the rubbish about how well organized they were. Ronnie once boasted he could put 200 armed villains on the street at the snap of his fingers, but it was a straight lie. Now they had killed Jack, they could no longer separate fantasy from reality. They had reached the stage of self-delusion that signals the fall of many top gangsters – and many 'legitimate' people too: they were believing their own headlines.

11: DOOM, GLOOM AND PARANOIA

The Twins' triumphant mood after they'd killed Jack the Hat was strong yet fragile at the same time. Sure, they were feeling secure in the belief that any police inquiry into Jack's disappearance would peter out as quickly as the one into Frank Mitchell's. This was a pretty good bet because, even when the police had a body, like George Cornell's two years earlier, the Twins had defeated them by exploiting the East End's traditional wall of silence.

They even felt cocky enough to allow a journalist, John Pearson, open access to a lot of our social gatherings. I thought this was crazy – yet another delusion of grandeur – because this guy came from a different world. His morality could not possibly be the same as ours, and he'd have to be dumb not to see what a bunch of thugs and clowns we all were. And Pearson wasn't dumb. He was clearly a bright fellow, which was a good enough reason for us to have nothing at all to do with him. But, no, the Twins wanted him to tell their life stories, to set the record totally straight after all that nasty police propaganda about them being thugs and bullies.

Pearson first showed up soon after McVitie's murder, when the Twins were still in high spirits. On one occasion Ronnie decided to play a trick on Pearson at a party in the Coach and Horses in Mile End Road. He brought in a couple of old pickpockets and then gave Pearson a sealed envelope saying something like, 'Do me a favour. Hang on to that until later. I'll ask you for it about nine but I don't want it on me.' So Pearson put it in his pocket, then Ronnie got one of the pickpockets to nick it. Then Ronnie said, 'Where's that envelope?' And Pearson searched his pockets, and then he said,

'I've lost it. Oh!' For a moment he must have been in agony, until Ronnie explained the trick. He had gone through this carry-on, partly to frighten Pearson, partly to impress him. It was a good-natured joke on one level, but at the same time only a crazy man could believe that a man like Pearson wouldn't see through him.

The Twins had so little handle on reality that they probably thought Pearson would do a whitewash job on them. It was only when these gangland Untouchables heard that Nipper Read was back in business, that they sank back into depression. It had been this tough little detective who, back in 1965, had almost put Ronnie and Reggie in jail over their extortion and blackmail rackets – only to see them acquitted in a blaze of Cockney glory.

They knew Read had been taken off their case soon afterwards, and they thought he was doomed to spend the rest of his career as a dog-handler. But now spies in Scotland Yard leaked that Nipper had been set up in Tintagel House, a top security police building on the Albert Embankment, often used for highly sensitive inquiries. He had a large staff of detectives, all dedicated to nailing the Krays. Somehow the Twins realized, however dimly, that their perpetual search for publicity had backfired on them. If a top detective keeps reading about your social and charitable activities in the papers, but at the same time he knows you're killing people every few months, you've got to expect a little heat. He's going to get angry and do something.

Now we knew that Nipper was back in business, the Firm started taking even heavier precautions against police spies than usual. One day we heard that a guy had been running round our pubs, trying to track us down. We found out that he'd recently been on remand in Brixton Prison, he'd had a couple of visits from the police, and he'd then got bail. The next thing we know he's looking for the Twins, but he didn't actually know them. To us, it's sticking out a mile that the police have told him to get into the Krays, gather information and report back to them.

So, rather than blank this guy, the Twins arrange for him to come to the Grave Maurice one night, when we'd all be in there drinking, along with a respectable guy with a clean record who would make a useful witness. So we were ready for him. Ronnie was sitting at one end of the pub, and I was sitting at the other end at a table with Reggie and the witness. When the guy came in, I pretended to be Ronnie. I was calling Reggie 'Albert', and he was calling me 'Ronnie'. He was brought up to us and searched, then I interrogated him.

I asked, 'Who sent you in?' He said, 'My wife's ill, and I need a bit of money.' This made us suspicious because the Krays never handed money out to absolute strangers. You were either known to them already or you had to show a connection, name a friend of the Firm that you'd met in jail, or come up with some believable link. This guy couldn't name anybody, nothing seemed to gel with him, and you could see he was terrified. So I said, 'You better forget all this. Just go home and do something else for them,' He said, 'For who?' I said, 'Well, the Old Bill has obviously sent you in here.' We were trying to get him to admit that he was a police spy, so the respectable guy sitting there could take notes and then claim that we were being harassed.

Then that guy went away, leaving us to take the spy round the corner at the end of the night and give him a little dressing-down. He just got a couple of good slaps and was sent on his way. I'm sure that when he reported back to the police he would have told them he'd spent the night talking to Ronnie Kray, even though the real Ronnie never said a word to him.

That night was amusing, or we pretended it was. We had to try to laugh from time to time. We even called the Twins 'Gert and Daisy' – but only behind their backs – because every day they resembled a well-known pair of women comedians more and more. They both had high-pitched effeminate voices. Whenever they said, 'How are you today, Albert?' or 'Ooh! What lovely flowers!', they sounded like a pair of drag queens rather than London's toughest villains. We'd always had a little snigger about this, but now it was becoming gallows humour.

Generally the mood on the Firm was dipping fast. The laughs were getting fewer and fewer. Ronnie was on a one-way trip, sinking deeper and deeper. He had become a slob. At the morning meets he'd sit there in a collarless shirt, with braces and baggy trousers, chain-smoking and infecting us all with his depression like a plague, barking manic orders just like Hitler must have done in his bunker during the final days. Everything was building up. We all knew. As a gangster you can go around fighting and conning people forever, and it's just part of the business, but you can't go murdering people left, right and centre, without causing some reaction among your followers as well as your enemies.

I was getting affected myself, with these bodies all over the place. I would do a lot of thinking, about where I was going and why. But I didn't let this stuff show because the Twins would be bound to say, 'Well, what's the matter with you?' and start getting concerned about your loyalty. So when anything like that was mentioned I'd laugh it off, like everybody else had to.

Around the murders the Twins were getting even more paranoid. Reggie was drinking more and more. Instead of getting drunk once or twice a week, he was drunk practically every night. Ronnie would hole up with crates of brown ale, and whether he was drunk or not, to him everybody was a spy, everybody was trying to tuck the Twins up. So while strangers were trying to get in to us, friends were trying to get away. People started making themselves scarce after McVitie's murder, which had made them realize it was all going to come together for the police and fall apart for us. So many people were drifting off the Firm that even when somebody was suffering from a genuine illness, the Twins didn't believe it.

Like when Billy Exley had a heart attack and was in the London Hospital. 'Don't believe it!' said Reggie, so we had to go and visit him in the London Hospital, to make sure he had actually had a heart attack. Even then Reggie wasn't satisfied. I was with him when he grabbed hold of the sister's clipboard on the end of the bed and started studying Billy's charts. He wouldn't have had the slightest idea how to read them, and I'm pretty sure he was holding them the wrong way up, but when he walked out of the hospital he was still convinced Exley was faking it, just to escape from the Firm. And Exley was dangerous because if he talked to the police he could cover the waterfront: from way back through the long-firms, the extortions, the attempt on Payne, as well as even Cornell and Mitchell.

We found later that it was a genuine heart attack. We also discovered that he had been talking to Nipper Read, on and off, since December 1967. When Exley eventually turned, he helped break the wall of silence. For instance, since Mitchell's murder, I'd twice been sent by the Twins to give Lisa a night out, just to keep her sweet, but when Exley finally told the cops everything he gave them a crucial lead to Lisa, who naturally told them everything. So at last the Twins' paranoia was justifying itself.

Meantime Johnny Squibb and Big Tommy Brown were noticed by their absence. And you'd certainly notice if Big Tommy wasn't around. A typical prizefighter, six foot three, big, broad, handsome and with snow-white hair, when he went missing it was as striking as if St Paul's Cathedral had disappeared overnight. He and Squibby had clearly gone AWOL deliberately. So among the rest of us on the inner Firm, there was a feeling of gloom and doom.

Ever since Cornell's murder we all knew it was going to come off. It was just a question of time. None of us was totally innocent. We were all going to get nicked – that's an occupational hazard in this game – but it was a question of minimizing our own final sentence. What can I do to cut mine down? That's all each of us could think of by this stage, so we didn't want to get involved in anything too heavy, and we covered our tracks even more carefully. That's how we had to carry on. We were walking on egg shells. I knew the hammer was coming down sometime, but it was a matter of how hard it would hit me in particular. It would do me no good going to church. Even emigrating to Australia wouldn't have got me out of it. I was still going to get nicked, but for how long?

The law wasn't the only danger. A far bigger danger was the Twins themselves. At any moment they might turn against you directly, and try and finish you off. There was always the chance that, even by accident, you could do something that would spark them off. You could be done for saying the wrong word. You might talk to somebody who, they've heard, is co-operating with the police, so they might think you were in there with that traitor, cooking something up, preparing your own destiny. We were all remembering how Jack the Hat went, for no justifiable reason, and George Cornell, so we knew we could be next, even if we'd done absolutely nothing to deserve it. They could invite me to a meet one night, then bang! I'm the next one for disposal.

It might not be a bang. It could be something in your tea, as I realized when I was sent on my next murder mission. Having killed the man who failed to kill Leslie Payne, the Twins still had the problem that Payne himself was alive and talking to the police, just like Exley. This too later proved to be true: in January 1967 he had made a 146-page statement to Nipper Read. So 'Who else is squealing?' was the question raging through the Twins' skulls now. They focused on a guy called Purvis who was one of their front-men for the long-firm frauds. He was the outwardly respectable type, used to open bank accounts, get credit and order the goods until the bust out happens, when he sacrifices his good name and liberty and goes down for three or four years. He did it with his eyes open, but early in 1968 he was in Pentonville Prison, maybe for some unrelated crime but clearly vulnerable to an approach by the dreaded Read.

He was also vulnerable to other prisoners, so we were very interested to learn that Colin 'Dukey' Osbourne was in transit from one nick to another and stopping over in the 'Ville. Dukey was one of Ronnie's former boyfriends. He was also the guy who drove me to Bow after I had been shot by Reggie. He'd since been jailed over some other business but was still considered a friend of the Firm. So with another guy I was sent into the 'Ville to sound him out on administering some poison to Purvis. If Dukey could get to him – if he was in the same wing or they ate at the same sitting – the idea was for him to put some stuff in Purvis's porridge, soup or dinner.

But would Osbourne be agreeable? We had to watch his reaction. As an old member of the Firm he was bound to say, 'Yeah,' but how keen did he sound saying, 'Yeah'? Was he enthusiastic or did he just nod? Half-hearted or all for it? In my view he was not keen. He nodded, 'Oh, yeah,' but he didn't jump at it. I reported this back to the Twins, and the scheme went no farther, not with me anyway. It wasn't my job to get the poison into the 'Ville, and, as far as I know, no one did spike Purvis's porridge. So, yet another failed murder conspiracy, thank God, but this one taught me to watch out for an attempt to do the same to me a few months later.

They say the prospect of death concentrates the mind wonderfully, which is why we cooked up our own safety codes, like the 'Jake' routine I operated with my partner Ronnie Hart. I still take precautions now sometimes. If you go on a meet somewhere, you have a look at which cars are outside and if there's anybody loitering about. You are always that aware. This caution is probably a good thing. It may be why I'm still alive. It may be why some other folk survived too. I always tried to cover for my colleagues on the Firm, like I had with Connie Whitehead that time at the Starlight, because it could happen to anyone any day. We were all on tippy-toes, looking out for each other.

After McVitie, we started wondering if the Twins were killing other people without telling us. They always operated a 'need to know' system: if you weren't supposed to hear about something, you wouldn't hear about it. So when people went missing, they could easily have been bumped off by the Twins without us knowing. We even got into thinking they'd murdered all sorts of absent friends who would confound us later by turning up alive and well. This is what happened with a driver of Ronnie's called Billy Jack Frost. We thought this little Frostie had gone, but he hadn't. On the other hand there was Mad Teddy Smith who never did come back. It was now so expected that people could be murdered, it became normal for someone just not to be around any more. Not that you ever dared say, 'So and so's gone missing. I think they've killed him.' You just accepted this sort of thing. You just went, 'Oh.'

We also noticed that the Twins were now aiming even more of their spies than usual at us who were still on the Firm. One of their *agents provocateurs* would suddenly blast off, 'I'm getting a bit pissed off with Ronnie. He's saying this and that. I think I could do him.' So we'd say to this person, 'If you feel like that, why don't you go and tell him yourself? What are you telling me for?' We knew Ronnie was slipping these little rats in to test us for loyalty. He was always looking for plots against him and Reggie.

Nowadays the word 'psycho' gets knocked about a bit – it's used too lightly and too often – but I'm sure Ronnie was a psycho. He really did enjoy 'doing' people. And when we saw his murderous paranoia at its worst, this only drove the rest of us on the Firm to thinking we might have to kill them both before they tried to kill us.

We did half-discuss popping them off. To kill them, we knew we would have had to separate them first, but that was easy. Ronnie was wide open because, when he was in a car, he would always sit in the front passenger seat. The idea cropped up once when neither Twin was with us. We were all getting in the car when, naturally enough, somebody sat alongside the driver. So someone else said, 'Oh, hello, he's in the Colonel's seat!' and we all had a laugh. Then someone else said, 'Dangerous place, when you got a couple of sharpshooters in the back like us!' Then someone said, 'Yeah, must be as easy as that. Quick trip down Rotherhithe Tunnel, and just wait till a lorry passes.'

If we had put this scheme into action, we'd have got the right driver and a couple of carefully selected people sitting in the back, then we'd take Ronnie through the Blackwall or Rotherhithe Tunnel, and bang! It's finished. Just dump him the other side of the river, in Injun Country.

We'd have had to kill Reggie straight after that, somewhere quiet, but once we'd killed them both – Reggicide and Ronnicide – we wouldn't have had to kill Charlie. We'd have frightened Charlie, but he would not have known the killings were down to us. The Twins had so many enemies we weren't going to be the prime suspects, especially when the bodies were found in south London. He might suspect it was us, but if he'd made a move he would have had to go too. If you're into killing Ronnie and Reggie, you're not going to spend any sleepless nights over killing Charlie, but that wouldn't have been necessary.

This was not idle chat. We were genuinely contemplating it as a 'What if?' but not as a conspiracy. We never reached the planning stage because no one knew if anyone who was in on the discussion might slip back and report to the Other Two. The only people we could trust to discuss it even on this level were Connie Whitehead, Ronnie Hart, myself and probably Scotch Jack. Nobody else. So it was said half-jokingly, then somebody else might say, 'Yeah, but if that happened, it'd be all over,' which took the edge off it. This meant that, if the Twins heard about it, you could tell them it was just a joke.

We weren't seriously discussing it, but we all knew inside that if together we'd have decided that killing the Twins would have worked out in our favour, they would have gone. No doubt about that at all. To get away with it completely we would have had to wait until they had had a row with another firm – someone really tasty – so they would be expecting a come-back. *Then* we could do it and pretend it was the comeback.

The other thing was that, as long as the Twins were around, we had a kind of licence for our activities. We realized that if they were popped, if we wiped them out, we would be open to all sorts of warfare. We couldn't have carried on without them. We'd have had to go into different lines of business. Once they had been killed, even by persons unknown, the police would have stamped all over us. Old Bill would definitely have walked straight in and wiped the lot of us up. The Twins were a definite benefit to us, in the sense that they had 'psyched out' the Metropolitan Police as a whole, securing a coating of immunity for themselves, and everyone who worked for them.

They had created a myth around themselves that even the police believed. If the cops had known just how chaotically the Twins ran their day-to-day business, they would have nicked them long ago, even for something quite trivial. Then when they came out of jail, they could have nicked them again and repeatedly given them a hard time. But the police thought they were some highly well-organized international gang, when they weren't at all. All this talk of 'Mafia connections' was just fantasy. They would just drop hints here and there, and people would pick it up, embroider it and spread it around. That's how a couple of characters whose entire take from extortion in London every week wasn't much over £1000 had grown into a multi-million-pound corporation in the eyes of many coppers. True, they had some spectacular one-off coups, like Esmeralda's Barn before they destroyed it, and a few good rip-offs with stolen bonds, but they would blow the proceeds, and then be back on the scrounge for tens and twenties from East End piss-holes. The only people who knew they were just penny-ante punks were the punks working with them and, ultimately, Superintendent Nipper Read and his squad.

In the early months of 1968 we could all feel the angel of death hovering over the Firm. I'm sure the strain damaged my family, though I wasn't sensitive to that. For over three years I'd been working a 16-hour day with these people. Quite often we'd spend weekends away with them too. When I look back, I can see that was wrong. It destroyed real home life, but at the time it was just my way of earning a living. I went home when I could and stayed away when I couldn't. My wife never said anything like, 'Have a nice day at the Firm.' As long as I had a clean shirt and I looked tidy that would be it. She'd say, 'While you're out, get your hair cut,' but she must have noticed how I withdrew into myself, especially after Frank Mitchell's murder.

But even I didn't know just how close I had come to being put 'on the list' myself. I was only told afterwards that Ronnie had become increasingly worried because I had gone through a few of the Firm – including Scotch Ian Barrie and Ronnie Bender – and asserted my authority over them, to the point where the Colonel thought I was planning to take over the regiment.

I didn't see my actions in that light, but I had given several of these guys a going-over. I was with a girl one night, and I looked up and there was this self-styled tough guy Ronnie Bender sticking his tongue out. So I got up, and I said to him, 'If you poke that tongue out again, I'll pull it out of your head.' Then he goes, 'What? What?' So I gave him a little smack in the head, because you can't stand arguing too long with these people. Then I just stepped away, and he collapsed. But I'd scarcely hit him! And I looked round and saw that people were all staring. So when they saw me looking at them, they made out they weren't looking. I just walked away, and he went back whingeing, 'I never did nothing!'

See, at that time Bender was getting flash. He was a big strong man but a bully. As a fighter he was a bit like that old heavyweight Brian London. If he threw the first punch, and it hurt, then he was OK, but if you hurt him, he'd back off.

Then I had to give one to Bender's brother. One night four or five of us had gone into a packed club with a crowd of girls. Then he came in on us, and somebody said to him, 'It's your turn to buy a drink.' He said, 'Oh, I'm skint. I ain't got any money.' So we say, fair enough, and as each of us bought a round we included him in. A bit later I spotted him at the other end of the bar pulling money out and buying little sneaky drinks. So I pulled him and I said, 'What's this?' And he said, 'What's it got to do with you?' He was getting all flash in front of his little pals. So I grabbed hold of him, and he just fell to pieces. I stood back. He was crying, trembling, sobbing his heart out, in a packed club. He had tried his bluster, and when that didn't work he collapsed. Why such people ever get called tough guys, I don't know.

Then there was Scotch Ian Barrie at the Regency. I walked in and I saw him sitting there with Tommy Cowley's wife, Adele, who was quite attractive. At first I thought, maybe they're waiting for Tommy to come. Then I turned round, and I see they're kissing. At first I felt embarrassed, then I said, 'Turn that in!' Now I may sound like a hypocrite because I used to play around with other women when I was married, but the difference here is that we have one member of the Firm playing with another member's wife and showing that man up. True, what they're doing is their own business really, but it's bound to cause bad feeling and might end up in murders and destroy our organization. And this was blatant, in front of other members of the Firm, not just me.

So when Adele said, 'What's it got to do with you?' I said, 'You can shut your noise up! Tommy's my mate!' because I wasn't impressed with her. Now Ian jumped up nice and smart, but he hasn't jumped up to go to the toilet, so, when he came at me, I went for him. He scuttled along the bar, and I just bundled him straight in the stock-room. I wedged him in a gap between stacks of crates, and he was squealing: 'Don't! Don't! Don't!' I was a bit disappointed – I was expecting a good fight with the man – but at that point I knew I'd done him. He was a coward.

You don't wait around having a row with these people: you just do them. I would give them a right good smacking until they asked me to stop. Then I knew that I'd done the guy in his head as well, just like I did the head of the dinner table over that bowl of spotted dick and custard back on my first day at St Benedict's approved school. Beat one, beat the lot. Just as the Twins had done on a more ruthless scale for years, before Reggie did the same to me with a shot from behind.

But this trouble with Scotch Ian wasn't over yet because, when I went outside the Regency a little while later, I saw Adele's husband, Tommy Cowley, sitting in a car opposite with another guy. I thought they knew what had happened, so I said, 'It's all finished. I've done here,' and they said, 'Get in. We'll run you home.' I thought Tommy was all very relaxed about the fact his wife had been playing around with Scotch Ian, then I realized they had been there on some totally different business. It was crossed wires, but now I had to explain what I had already let out. Well, Tommy wasn't too happy.

Next morning it's face-the-music time at the regular meet. This was now being held in the flat on the ninth floor of Braithwaite House, near Old Street in the City, where Mr and Mrs Kray had moved when Vallance Road was cleared for demolition. I was thinking, Christ. What's going to happen? I've just done Ronnie's man! None of us knew how Ron would react. We all waited till he came in but there was nothing. He never spoke about it. Reggie asked me, 'What happened there?' so I just said, 'He got a bit flash, jumped up, come at me so I done him.'

Maybe the Colonel had dismissed it as a silly quarrel over those silly things called wives. Maybe he was brooding on yet another disturbing sign of individualism and assertiveness by a mere lieutenant. He was certainly worried I was getting above myself. Yet even rows within the Firm could serve his purpose. Sure he and Reggie would smooth things over for the while, they'd take out the immediate sting, but they would carefully nurse any disagreement. Then if ever they themselves had trouble with me, they'd get hold of Ronnie Bender and Scotch Ian, and stir them up for a week by saying, 'I don't know why you stood for that, why don't you go and do him?' They'd gradually work them into the mood to do me.

Ronnie was well able to turn a dispute like that, even if it had happened a year before, into an opportunity to bring me into line. I'd seen how he stirred Scotch Jack against Connie Whitehead. I knew that was his game, but I also knew you can't just let these guys walk over you. You've got to show you have the beating of them, right from when the first row breaks out. At the same time I felt fairly secure in this side of my relationship with the Twins. They didn't trust anybody else on the Firm – Ronnie had put almost everyone 'on the list' – so they just had to trust me.

I'm not claiming I was invincible. I've had a few beatings myself. Sometimes I've been in crowd fights, and I've got done, bottled, but these were just general fights, never when I was being attacked for myself or as a member of the Firm, nothing where my own identity was on the line. But even in these encounters I often came out on top. There was another time at the Regency when someone went, 'Hold up!' and I looked round, and these three guys were coming at me. Then they split up on three sides of me. I didn't know this little firm, but I took my chances. I looked at them and went, 'Oh, well,' then I put my hand in my pocket. There was nothing in my pocket, but I just said, 'It's a nice night for dying. Who's first?' And they looked at each other, and they slunk away. I couldn't believe it. The only tool I had with me that night was a bit of bluff.

I was a lot wilder then than I am today. The fire's gone out a bit now, but I was still getting deliberately drunk every Tuesday downstairs at the Regency. In my own corner by the little door back up to the gym, I would stand at the bar with a big cut glass ashtray, and the drunker I got, the harder the smack I'd give anybody who came within reach. Everyone knew this, so they had guys standing outside range telling me jokes. I used to laugh at this myself. I was never legless. I just used to get nice and drunk, and people used to leave me alone. Then I would always walk home. I'd walk from Whitechapel to Bow with no problems. You'd probably get mugged half a dozen times now.

However bad it got on the Firm, however close we thought Nipper was getting, all I ever needed to let off steam was that one night a week. So despite everything – even the memory of Frank Mitchell's murder – I was coping pretty well. Maybe what few sensitivities I had left after half a lifetime of crime had been destroyed in three years with the Twins. One thing was certain: I was coping far better than they were.

As if Ronnie's murders, madness, manic pill-popping and near paedophile homosexuality weren't enough trouble for the Firm and his family, now Reggie was plunging more and more often into deep depressions. Both were frequently drunk, and neither could bear to be alone. They were living almost their entire lives in public. They were always with other people. They never simply went home at night. If they had nothing genuine to do during the day, they would invent reasons for sitting down at various meets until it would be, 'Right, let's get ready for tonight.' Every night!

Even on summer weekends when they went off to their mum's caravan or the Suffolk mansion, the break would turn into one long meeting. At the caravan they had a clubhouse in the grounds, but whenever I went down, there were so many people, you had to put up a trestle-bed and sleep out in the open. Not my style. I needed to get away from this crowd, but the Twins seemed scared not to have a crowd around them. This was one way of keeping an eye on people and preventing conspiracies, but what a way to live.

In London they lived like gypsies. They'd still stay with their mum and dad, even after the move to the Braithwaite House, but at the same time they were always moving in and out of rented flats, like the ones in Cedra Court, where Reggie stayed in one flat, and Ronnie had another with a four-poster bed to entertain his young boys. Sometimes they'd buy a place, but then it would be repossessed for non-payment of the mortgage. They'd have a flat for so long, and as soon as the ashtrays filled up, they'd just move out. They weren't home lovers.

What they were by now was two guys desperate never to go on trial again, which is why they went to such trouble to make sure nobody would give evidence against them. They kept calling in a solicitor to see people they'd hurt. As soon as one of their victims was coming out of hospital, they would get him to come to a pub, where the solicitor would be ready to take a statement clearing the Twins and specifically stating they had done nothing to him. The victim would be encouraged to say something like, 'It is being said that I was injured by the Krays. Since I came out of hospital I have heard this story, but I'm making this statement of my own accord to deny that.' He might write and sign this in the pub or he might be taken straight to an office.

Some victims were paid for signing these statements, not a lot but enough to persuade them it was better than giving evidence against the Twins. Sometimes people were still lying in hospital with police hovering round threatening to nick them, when an ambassador from the Twins would sneak in and say, 'We'll give you a nice few quid if you leave the Other Two out.'

Then, if the police later persuaded him to testify against them, they could produce this statement in court and destroy him. A jury might be keen to believe the Krays had done this guy, but any good brief could pop up with this statement – made soon after the incident – and throw enough doubt on the case to get it thrown out.

The Twins were convinced they would always find some way to sabotage the legal system. Once Reggie got nicked for a motoring offence. Two cops and several impartial witnesses had seen him going the wrong way down a one-way street. He showed up at the lowly magistrates' court with a barrister, when most people would defend themselves or take a dock brief. As soon as this high-powered character stood up and talked about his esteemed client, the whole case was turned round. Reggie was acquitted, and he walked out as if the incident had never happened. He thought the same would happen if Scotland Yard ever got a case together against him over Jack the Hat.

Even when they were absolutely sure Nipper and his mob were on their tails, the Twins just carried on thrashing people. I was there one night at the Old Horns pub, where we used one of the bars, when Johnny the Guitar got a belting from Ronnie. I don't know what it was about, but he was bleeding so bad I had to send him off.

Again in March or April 1968 some Scouse fellow was in there doing a bit of shouting, so Reggie belted him. This was while the Clark brothers were on the stage. Then over at the Little Dragon Reggie gave another guy a belting, because he'd been having a go at old Dutchy Sam.

But this was small-time violence compared with what they were plotting even now with their friends across the water in south London and an American hit-man who Ronnie had decided was the bee's knees.

12: GOONS FOR HIRE

Where there's a tit, there's a tat. According to me, but not to him or the verdict of an Old Bailey jury, Freddie Foreman and his firm had done us a favour by killing Mitchell and disappearing him. Now it was time for our Firm to do something in return. That's how the Twins saw it at the start of 1968, even though they knew Nipper and his chaps had been on their heels for over three months and the dust had scarcely settled over McVitie. They felt they had a licence to kill and a duty to their south London brethren.

The Foremans had a little local difficulty or, rather, a large domestic one. They had a feud going on for years with a man called Jim Evans after he had found out that his wife had been spending a lot of time with Freddie's brother, George. On 17 December 1964 Evans went round to George's flat and shot-gunned a hole in his upper inside leg and almost removed his manhood, which was the point of the exercise. Much later, when I heard the full story, I sympathized with Evans. He did nothing I wouldn't have done in the same circumstances. Not many people come out against established firms, like Evans did. He showed plenty of bottle.

Just as understandably, George was very upset too. It was a miracle he survived. In the Foreman camp his shooting was seen as a cowardly piece of work – perhaps they thought it should have been High Noon at fifty paces – so Freddie set about avenging his brother. On the night of 2 January 1965 Evans and a friend called Ginger Marks were in Cheshire Street, close by Fort Vallance, when a car drove up and someone called out, 'Ginger.' Then several bullets were pumped point-blank into Marks, including one in the head. Evans too was shot but he rolled under a parked van. There was some running around, and then the car drove off. When Evans crept out, Marks had disappeared. Everything was gone except his smashed glasses and a cartridge case. The only explanation was that the assassins had picked up Marks's body and slung him in the car, before they drove off.

This was almost two years before Mitchell disappeared in similar style, but Foreman and Co. had always denied killing Marks, just as they denied killing Mitchell. Ten years later this murder was the subject of another failed prosecution, and who should be on trial but Freddie Foreman, Alfie Gerard and Jerry Callaghan – the same three guys I say 'disappeared' Mitchell. Anyhow back in 1965 the feud with Jim Evans was continuing, as Freddie told me at the time. He said that once he'd sat up all night with his rifle on the roof of a factory opposite a house where Evans was living, but Evans did not show up. It was daylight before Fred gave up. This showed a dedication lacking in almost every other villain I knew. Most people would say, 'Oh, he's not here. Let's go round the corner and have a light ale!' but Fred had a determination that was unique in my experience.

After Mitchell's murder, Ronnie and Reggie met Freddie more often, in his pub or in our East End joints or in various West End clubs. I was at several of these meetings when Jim Evans was discussed, and the Twins offered to do him on our territory, as a return favour for Mitchell.

Saying it was easy. Doing it was the hard bit, as we foot-sloggers on the Firm soon found out. We discovered that Evans had an unpredictable trick of dropping completely out of sight. Suddenly he'd be nowhere. Then we'd get news he was moving round the East End again. Any time there was a sighting, the Twins would send one of us over to report to Foreman. Then we heard the rumour (probably untrue, but we believed it) that the police had given Evans an unofficial licence to carry a shooter – they'd turn a blind eye if he had a gun for self-defence – so killing him would now require both professionalism and guts. Jim Evans wasn't afraid of anybody – he was the most fearless man I ever met – and now he was tooled up again. If Freddie Foreman had not managed to kill him, what hope did we have?

Eventually the Twins came up with what Ronnie thought was a brilliant solution. At the time they were doing business with Alan Bruce Cooper, a rum little Jewish Anglo-American who'd first been fed into them to help get rid of stolen Canadian government bonds that had come their way. 'ABC' was flash – he had a big house in Holland Park and a pair of Rolls-Royces – but ridiculous. He had a droopy moustache, scarcely any hair, though he was only in his thirties, and a stutter. He came on our scene just as Leslie Payne was drifting off and falling out of favour. It was as if he'd taken over from Payne by mutual agreement. If you had a good introduction and a good background story, it wasn't hard to impress the Twins. Cooper spun a fantastical one: he was an international hit-man running a team of professional assassins. Ronnie was besotted with Cooper, though not sexually, as far as I know. The more extraordinary and ridiculous his schemes, the more Ronnie believed in him. He was forever praising Cooper, who struck me from the start as a fool, a con-man or a police plant. Now his bluff was called: Ronnie gave him the contract to kill Jim Evans.

This would 'kill two birds with one stone'. It would test Cooper's hit-squad and return the favour owed to Freddie Foreman. Cooper's men were supposed to be getting a grand – £1000 – for doing Evans, the same as I'd handed Foreman for doing Mitchell, which, of course, Foreman denies. But Foreman would not be asked to pay a penny. The Twins would bear the entire cost because Ronnie wanted to see if Cooper was capable of doing several other killings 'on the list'.

At the time Evans was going up at the Old Bailey for 'grievous bodily harm', but halfway through the trial he was given bail. So instead of coming up from Brixton heavily guarded, he would have to go in and out of the Bailey's main entrance every day without any protection. At last we knew exactly where he'd be and when.

When all this was explained to Cooper, he said killing Evans would be as easy as pie and came up with his scheme. He said he had a man who had won a medal in the war for assassination, who was just the guy to do Evans. Cooper then produced a briefcase with a trigger concealed in the handle. When this was squeezed, a hypodermic syringe would spring out from the case and could be thrust into the leg of the victim. Pricked, the victim would have a heart attack in two minutes because the syringe would be squirting cyanide into the victim's leg. The guy would scarcely have had time to say, 'Do you mind?' or 'What have you done?' before he'd be keeling over and collapsing.

This idea captivated Ronnie who said it would be fine, as he still wanted to vary the pattern of killing from the usual shootings. That's why he'd bought us those silly little axes to kill George Cornell's brother Eddie. Also it would be dead easy to stick the needle in at the Old Bailey because there were always a lot of people standing around. Normally you don't want people around when you're trying to kill someone, but this was different. If Evans had a crowd round him when he felt the needle, he would find it far more difficult to identify either the perpetrator or the weapon. He wouldn't even know what had been done to him until it was too late.

All this sounded fine, except that Cooper did not know Jim Evans and had no idea what he looked like. So to get his face on a photo – hear this for an act of treachery – me and Reggie went to Winston's club one evening when we knew Evans was going to be there. It was when Tony Mercer, the Black and White Minstrel who sang like Bing Crosby, was having a birthday party. Sure enough, Jim was there so we got a picture taken showing Jim Evans alongside me, Reggie Kray and an MP called Reader Harris, all chums together. This photo not only gave us Evans's face so the hitman could identify him but it would also come in handy if the police moved against us after Evans died, because it would show we were such good friends with him.

The scheme was now refined. It was decided that the best place would be inside the Bailey on the grand stairway. Then on the chosen day someone was sent in to check that Evans was definitely listed on the sheets as due up in court that day. His name was there, so the guy with the suitcase was sent in to despatch Evans on the steps. Luckily for Evans, the steps were so crowded they couldn't get the briefcase anywhere near him. That was Cooper's excuse for failing to do him, but it struck me as rubbish. Surely, the more crowded the steps, the easier it would be. If there'd been a few people around Evans, there would be no excuse for bumping into him, whereas in a real crowd you could do anything.

I don't think Cooper or his man seriously tried to do Evans. At the time I doubted if they'd even gone to the Old Bailey. Either way, Cooper had his excuse for calling off the attempt, and the gullible Twins believed him. They even believed his story about his second failure when Evans was visiting Winston's night-club again and should have been an easy target.

If at first you don't succeed, try, try again. At one point the Twins found out that Evans was living in a block called Pitcairn House in Mare Street. So me and Ian Barrie went up to Hackney Town Hall to look at the voters' lists. We were nicely dressed and went in with our usual confident bearing, and the woman in charge thought we were police. She said, 'We often get young officers in here checking up and making inquiries.' We just went, 'Oh,' in a preoccupied way. We didn't say we were gangsters trying to get someone killed.

She gave us the right sheets, and we found an Evans listed in Pitcairn House. We wrote down the flat number, then we saw the place on the left-hand side of the street going down towards Whitechapel. We told the Twins, and later Cooper came over to the Grave Maurice so I could show him the block. We drove past, and he told me he would send his assassin round to the flat pretending to ask for magazine subscriptions. If Evans came to the door, he was going to shoot him there and then. It sounded just like something out of a crime novel, which is probably where he found it.

Even this third attempt on Jim's life failed, though he really had been living in Pitcairn House. This should have destroyed Ronnie's faith in Cooper, but it was only shaken, whereas all along I had never trusted the guy. I'd always felt he was an entrapment-merchant. As well as running his joke version of Murder Incorporated, it was Cooper who had supplied the Twins with their rubbish guns, including the one that jammed when Ronnie tried to kill George Dixon and the one Reggie pointed at Jack the Hat before he resorted to the kitchen knife. Nothing Mr ABC did for the Twins ever worked.

In Cooper's favour you might claim he was deliberately screwing up the Twins' efforts in order to save lives. I certainly thought he might have been put on to the Twins just to confound their evil schemes but, on the other hand, he was half-inciting these schemes: acting as agent provocateur, supplying the weapons, writing the script! Even so, he could still have been put up to it by Old Bill.

There was one occasion when it was screamingly obvious Cooper was working for the other side. This was when the Twins had put Connie Whitehead in harness with him, driving him round on the Firm's business. One day Connie bought a gun off him. As he was coming back from Cooper's office to the East End, he stopped and went into a bank on normal business, without any intention of doing an armed robbery. Then out of the blue, he got stopped by police. They searched his car but he managed to dump the gun when they allowed him to take a pee, or so he said. Now if Connie was telling the truth, that must have been some dopey copper. Anyhow, they did find a bullet on him, which he'd said was something he'd found and kept as a memento. But why did they stop and search him? I'm sure he'd been shopped by Cooper.

Another thing proved to me that ABC had to be an informer to somebody. That was the funny business of how various Scotland Yard documents kept coming into the Twins' hands. These were top-secret crime-fighting papers concerning the Krays themselves. Ronnie and Reggie were very impressed when Cooper claimed he was getting them direct from someone he called the 'prosecutor's daughter'. Cooper said she could get in and out of her father's office, and that's how she was lifting these monthly memos of meetings between top-ranking cops. I saw two or three of these sheets. One had four or five signatures on the bottom. Superintendent Harry Mooney's was one but he had nothing to do with the leak. They weren't originals, only black and white copies, so they could have been fabricated by Cooper. If so, it's very peculiar how everything on them later turned out to be true.

Reggie really believed the documents were coming through this prosecutor's daughter, but surely she would have known Cooper would be handing them to the Twins, otherwise why should she be giving them to him at all? It must have been a deliberate set-up to appease the Twins and keep them sweet to him. The papers were certainly one reason why they stood for him for so long, but to me the whole story was baloney. I don't think there ever was a 'prosecutor's daughter'. It was all disinformation from Cooper.

Sometimes I'd use Reggie as a sounding board to express doubts about Cooper. I would wait until the subject came up then I'd say, 'I'm not so sure about Cooper. Everything he's supposed to do, it doesn't happen.' I said just enough to plant the seed, not enough to show too much interest. Then Reggie would have his own words with Ronnie and throw my words in as well. Eventually this had some effect because the Twins finally set about doing some belated investigation into the guy. They found out he was a deserter from the Canadian army, but, as they had a dreadful record during their own national service, that would have been no discredit to him in their eyes. Later it was said he had worked with British intelligence and with the FBI, which was what I strongly suspected when I heard how Cooper took Ronnie and Dickie Morgan along to the American Embassy to get visas for their long-awaited trip to New York with him to meet the Mafia.

Even I knew about the 'moral turpitude' law, which meant you couldn't get a visa to enter America if you had a criminal record. And which British criminals at liberty in 1968 displayed more moral turpitude than the Kray Firm? None, surely. But – blow me down – Ronnie and Dickie did get visas, so it was pretty clear that Cooper had to be tied up with the FBI. When he took them to the embassy, nobody interviewed them. They just sat in a waiting-room while Cooper supposedly went to have a word with 'his man'. Ronnie's faith in Cooper shot up again. He was terribly impressed: 'He took us up, sat us in the waiting-room, and he just went off and came back with the visas, didn't he Dick?' Yes, he went to see the resident G-Man, I thought.

The next thing we know, on 3 April 1968 they fly to Paris, then on to New York! Something had to be going on. I imagine the Feds – encouraged by Scotland Yard – just let them in to see who they'd meet. The trip was only allowed to proceed because it served law-enforcement's purposes. The Feds did not even have to tail them all the time because Cooper acted as their guide and chaperone, and must have been telling the Bureau everything that was going on. Not that they did any business with the genuine Mafia. That whole trip was a joke.

But oh! When Ronnie and Dickie came back, weren't they full of it! It had been such a lovely holiday. They had photos of all the famous names they'd met – Robert Preston the actor, Rocky Graziano again and a few other old fighters – all introduced to them by American gangsters, so we were told. But I could tell they had been conned because of something that was said during the homecoming party we held at the Grave Maurice. This happened to be attended by a couple of Yanks in town on other business. Right in front of them Ronnie was saying how his New York friends 'even took us round and showed us the garage where they did the St

Valentine's Day Massacre'.

Well! When I heard this I looked at one of the Yanks and screwed up my face, as if to say, 'Hold up! This cannot be right!' The Yank shook his head at me, as if to say, 'Button your lip,' so I said nothing but I thought, These guys know. The massacre happened in Chicago, not New York, so these so-called Mafiosi had been taking the piss by showing Ronnie some local garage and saying, this was where they did it.

The truth is, the Twins weren't close to the Mafia at all. The Mafia wouldn't have considered them seriously either as partners or rivak for very long, because the Twins had no real organization, and their clownish love of publicity was bound to attract 'heat' from the police in the end. The real bosses of New York's Mafia crime families were establishing their own foothold in London at the very time the Twins were at their most powerful, and for a while they were looking round for partners, but once they'd checked on the Twins, they must have realized these jokers would be a liability.

While Ronnie and Dickie were in New York they did meet a couple of second-rate mobsters, but there was only one significant crook who tried to do business with them, a guy called Joey Kaufman. He had done some work for the Mafia, but he was mainly a freelance fraudster who was coming to London with stolen bonds for the Twins. When Nipper Read closed in, Kaufman would be caught in his hotel with a lot of these bonds, so he wasn't too clever. Later, when we all got locked up in Brixton, Reggie had a fight with Kaufman and broke his chin. It was a fitting finale to the Twins' ludicrous dreams of conquering the criminal world in league with the Honoured Society. In the end it was Ronnie and Reggie who suffered worst from the Gangster Complex.

There was just one more crazy assassination plot for Cooper to cock up: one with an even more sinister twist than the cyanide briefcase. This job involved another boss of London's underworld, Bernie Silver, a man as eminent in his territory as the Krays, Foreman and the Richardsons were in each of theirs. Silver was the vice king of Soho. He was the prince of ponces. He ran the property side of prostitution. He used to let rooms to girls for as much as fifty quid a night. That was a huge amount then, but they would pick that up from five punters at £10 a trick – in their terms just one hour's work.

Silver also had clubs, for which the Twins were taking £60 a week protection money off him. This was collected by old Joe Schaffer who used to bring it over every Monday. Ronnie was now telling me they wanted a full share in Silver's clubs, and they dreamed up a wicked scheme to get it. By coincidence, Silver had just come to them with a problem he wanted solving. He didn't know that, the way they were planning to solve it, he would have a far bigger problem on his hands. It was all to do with a Maltese guy called George Caruana who, Silver said, was upsetting his business.

One evening around March 1968 we were suddenly told, 'Right, get in the car, we're going to the Gallipoli,' the Turkish restaurant off Liverpool Street where we'd nearly had a battle with some off-duty coppers a year or two before. This evening my job was to watch Reggie's back, and Ian Barrie had to watch out for Ronnie. We went in and found a couple of guys waiting: no less than Bernie Silver and his Maltese partner, Big Frankie Mifsud. Silver was Jewish, but he was running Soho in league with a lot of Malts. Then it dawned on us that Bernie Silver could not stand Ronnie. He wouldn't talk to him. He wouldn't even sit with him. Reggie and Bernie sat on one table, but Ronnie had to slum it with the rest of us. No wonder Ronnie wanted to double-cross him.

Later Ronnie filled me in on Silver's problem. According to Reggie, a Maltese called George Caruana was causing Silver aggravation. He didn't want Caruana dead, but the Twins had decided that the Malt would be killed anyway. Then, when he turned up dead, they could steam into Silver, blackmail him and finally take over his clubs. Then Ronnie added, 'So we're going to test Cooper's man on Caruana. If he does it all right, we'll give him a grand, and then there'll be other jobs for him later.'

Here we go again, I thought. Surely, we had seen enough of his work by now to know he was all mouth. Then I realized that Ronnie had begun to suss him out too. Next, we had a meet in the flat in Braithwaite House with me, Reggie, Ronnie, Dickie Morgan and Cooper himself. Ronnie gave him the contract on Caruana, then suddenly he read the riot act. He told him, 'You've had three goes at the other fella – at the Old Bailey, at Winston's and at Pitcairn House – and you blew the lot. Now this is your last chance!'

He said afterwards that if Cooper didn't do it this time, they'd know for sure he was a blow-out. But again Cooper came up with a scheme that appealed to Ronnie's love of novelty and spectacle: his international hit-man was going to wire up Caruana's car and blow him to pieces.

By now Silver had realized what the Twins were doing. He changed his mind about involving them over Caruana and tried to call them off, but the Twins wouldn't have that. They said, in effect, 'No, we're going through with it.' This way they would bring Silver into line. What's more, they were going to blow up Caruana right outside the Islet Town, Big Joe Wilkins's casino in Curzon Street. At that time there was only one clubland operator bigger than Silver, and he was Joe Wilkins. He also owned Winston's and a couple of other clubs. Doing Caruana outside the Islet Town was designed to bring him into line too. It would send him a message that he would have to pay tribute to the Twins, just like Silver. So the Twins' entire scheme now added up to putting the big squeeze on two very rich operators, killing Caruana and trying out their new hit-man. A triple coup! To them this was superb business thinking.

And what could Silver do? He was in no position to call it off because he had never called it 'on'. Who could he complain to? He must have been in a bad state: shitting himself I should think. He had nowhere to go. All he could do was offer them money. But the Twins weren't interested in money. No, they wanted him and his entire business, which was of a kind they had never got into before. They wouldn't have bothered to run it themselves. They would have found two or three faces in that game already – Greeks or Maltese – then put them to work in Silver's places, always trying to ensure most of the take came back to the Firm. That was the grand scheme, but they would have screwed it up, just like they screwed up Esmeralda's Barn.

Tommy Cowley knew Caruana slightly, so one night he took Cooper out to identify him at some spieler. Afterwards I heard Cooper talking about Caruana and telling the Twins, 'I'll make sure of this one, leave it up to me.' I thought, Ay ay!, especially when I heard the MO. Cooper's brilliant but invisible hit-man was going to buy six sticks of gelignite to fit up Caruana's car – but six sticks would have taken out the whole of Curzon Street, not just the car. If this stuff had gone off, he would have got eight years just for the gelly, and life many times over for mass murder.

But in April 1968 this crazy scheme collapsed like all the rest when, as we heard, this hit-man had gone up to Scotland to get the gelignite from a quarry. Sure, he'd got the gelly, and he still had it on him when he was captured by the police. Cooper came to the flat to confess. The Twins were a bit upset but rather more worried if the hit-man would squeal. Cooper said the man was sound, and they believed him. Then they became suspicious because there was no proof that Cooper's hit-man had appeared at any court. They got a few Glasgow papers sent down, and there was nothing in them. Later Reggie said that the hit-man had been charged, although I don't know how he found that out.

Much later, when we all got wiped up, it turned out that the hit-man, who was called Paul Elvey, was captured in Glasgow trying to board a plane for London with three dozen sticks of gelignite. This would have brought down not just Curzon Street but the Hilton Hotel too. Elvey was also the man Cooper had despatched to the Bailey to kill Evans, with the cyanide briefcase. Apparently he really had gone there twice, before giving up. He had got picked up with the gelly because Nipper Read had put him under surveillance. Nipper got him to tell all, and he named Cooper as his contact.

Nipper then cracked Cooper but kept him in play, so the Twins wouldn't know for sure if he had turned informer.

Of course, back in April 1968 we knew none of this for sure. What we did know was that we never saw Cooper again. The Twins were furious that he'd gone missing. Ronnie had his home phone number so he asked me to phone him. At first a woman answered who I assumed was Mrs Cooper. She said he was being treated for ulcers in a clinic in Harley Street.

Then I rang the clinic and put Ronnie on to speak to Cooper. They spoke about hotel bookings for Joey Kaufinan, who had just come over with their forged bonds. After this conversation there was some sense of business as usual with Cooper, but by now the Twins were very suspicious, and they believed he might already be helping Nipper Read. They said that, if they found this out for definite, he would be 'on the list'. Of course, he was well and truly in Nipper's clutches by now. Indeed it was Nipper who stuck him in the clinic, to keep him in circulation.

All this only goes to show that, when it comes to hiring hit-men and bumping people off, you should always stick to the tried and tested killer you already know. The Twins should have dropped Cooper as soon as his first schemes collapsed, and his guns failed to fire – certainly long before they started using him as a hit-man. After all, when it came to killing, there was always someone in south London ready, willing and able to do the job.

Aside from the killing of Frank Mitchell, I always had a lot of time for Freddie Foreman, and at one point I was thinking of switching companies and joining him. I'd often see him over on our side of the river. Then I'd be in his place, the Prince of Wales. We'd mix with other villains, having a drink and a chat about things like who's in the nick, who ain't, and who's coining out. Freddie was a lot more organized than the Twins ever were. He always had information. He was more alive than the Twins. He knew what was going on. He was into work, rather than just spreading fear. In fact I was looking for a way to join up with his firm, if an opportunity ever arose to leave the Twins. One of his nicknames was Brown Bread, because it rhymes with Fred. It's also Cockney rhyming slang for 'dead'.

I had done Freddie a few favours myself. One night I went in the Stork Club up the West End, and I saw him sitting on his own, looking a bit fixed. So I said, 'You OK, Fred?', and he said, 'Have you got a tool?', and I said, 'No.' So he said, 'There's a face in here: Noddy.' So I said, 'Well, just order a toasted sandwich, and they'll give you a knife – only a dinner knife but it's better than nothing.' Then I said, 'Is it going to be off, then?' – meaning, was he going to go for this Noddy and do him right there in the Stork – and he said, 'No, but just in case.' Later I was sent over to south London one Sunday to be taken round the little drinkers, including a Conservative club, to find Noddy and clock his face for future reference. Then, when everyone was nicely safe so they'd have alibis, this Noddy could be seen to. We didn't follow it through, but again that would have been in return for them doing Mitchell.

· The plot to kill Jim Evans was never called off. We were still meant to be looking to do him right till the end. In the first few days of May Ronnie Kray gave me a piece of paper with a car number on it: TVX 482E. He said, 'Take that over to Freddie, tell him that's Evans's car. It's a white Zephyr or Zodiac. He'll be able to check it through a car dealer.'

I was just choosing a good time to cross the river and take this message to Freddie when the moment we'd all been expecting finally arrived. At last Scotland Yard had got its act together.

13: BANGED UP AND OFF THE FIRM

On 6 May 1968 we were having a night up West in the Astor Club. I was sitting with Reggie, separate from the rest of the crowd. They used to have club photographers there, and one girl kept taking flash photos of me and Reggie. This was normal, except the rule was that pictures were to be taken only on request, so I asked Reggie, 'Have you asked her to take photos?' He said, 'No.' Then I said to her, 'Who's told you to take these photos?' And all of a sudden she burst into tears and ran off.

Well, even if I did snap at her, this was an extreme reaction. It was obvious she was taking the photos on someone else's instructions, and that's why she was nervous. Straight away the alarm bells are ringing in my guts. I look round, and I realize the place is crawling with Old Bill. Even in plain clothes they stick out a mile. I tell Reggie, but we're not greatly fussed because this has been going on around the Twins for three years.

In the early hours we all clear off. We're not expecting police action tonight, but we know they are definitely stepping up their surveillance. Even so, Ronnie and Reggie are very relaxed. Despite our collective paranoia, we don't decide to sleep at secret addresses or duck out of the scene for a while. That night we just go our separate ways, intending to meet up again tomorrow as usual. The Twins head off to Braithwaite House, their mum and dad's flat, though Violet and Old Charlie are away at the lodge cottage in Suffolk for a few days. Normally I'd be going back to our flat in Bow, but this particular night I peel off to visit a girlfriend and stay all night.

THE ENFORCER

Early in the morning police come to my home, but I'm not there so I don't know about this. Around eight thirty I come out of the girl's place, and I'm going off to attend the normal nine o'clock meet at Braithwaite House. I walk past the newspaper stand, and I see a placard saying something about the Krays. That's nothing out of the ordinary – they're in the papers most days. So I reach the block and get in the lift and go up to the ninth floor. As I walk along I see these two coppers outside their flat, but even that doesn't worry me too much because the police might be there for all sorts of trivial reasons.

Then I see their front door's leaning up against the outside wall and I think, Oh yeah? And, as I show I want to go inside, one of these coppers says, 'Who are you?' Well, at this time in the underworld I was generally known by my stepfather's name, Barry, and if the police are looking for me, that's the name they'll have down. So, perfectly dead-pan, I say, 'My name is Donoghue, I've got a cab firm in Bow, and I have a running account with Mr Kray. I come here once a week to collect.' The use of Donoghue throws them. They're not interested in me, so one copper says, 'Well, he won't be settling up this week, so on your bike! Piss off.' So I do piss off. I'm gone.

It was only later in the day that I read in the paper – and it was in every paper and on every news broadcast – that Ronnie and Reggie were in police custody. Nipper Read had decided to move in. His team worked from dusk till dawn, locating everybody in the Firm. Then when we were all laid down nice and quiet, they sprang the trap and wiped up the entire Firm – except me, my partner Ronnie Hart, Dickie Morgan and a few others who, by luck or judgment, weren't where they thought we'd be.

Despite our individual luck, it was now obvious that the great Kray game was over. It was just a matter of time. Each of us had to stay out of police clutches as long as we could, to get as organized as possible, for when we did get caught: clean up any loose ends of evidence, try and make provision for the wife and kids, and work out a plan for the inevitable interrogation by Old Bill.

As I listened to all the reports and read the newspapers, I could see no mention of any murders. Everybody was being held on little holding charges, so I knew they had to be looking for me too. For the time being, we didn't run away. Ronnie Hart, Dickie Morgan and me carried on as usual, but discreetly. For two weeks I still did the Milk Round, collecting from all my West End and East End protection jobs. I even visited Reggie Kray in Brixton Prison under an assumed name. He told me that Lennie 'Books' Dunn was on the missing list. Lennie was the bookseller whose flat we had used to house Frank Mitchell, and he was one of the people who heard shots after I'd taken Frank out. If he had gone missing, it was a serious business. To us that meant he was talking to the police.

There was a bit in a newspaper about a grey-haired businessman who wore glasses helping with police inquiries. This fitted Lennie, so Reggie said, 'Go and see Big Micky Regan, tell him that Lennie Books is on the missing list and to see what he can do.' So I went and saw Big Micky in his office in a gym in Marshalsea Street, close to Foreman's pub. I told him what Reggie had said, but he didn't seem interested. I had the feeling that by now people in other firms were thinking the Twins were a lost cause.

Sure, if the police really did have Lennie, then by now he'd have told them the whole story. We already believed they had Cooper, Payne and Exley, so they might also have Lisa, or they'd certainly be looking for her and obviously me as well. And what about Freddie Foreman? I was the only one who knew of his role in doing Mitchell, but, as the cops were sniffing round the McVitie killing too, they could be on his tail for disposing of Jack the Hat.

I still had to give him Reggie's note with Jim Evans's car number on it, so I went to his pub. I found out he was on the missing list too. As soon as all the Krays had been nicked, he'd gone on the run. Round the corner at Regan's gym no one knew where Freddie was. So eventually I left the piece of paper with someone who knew him. I just said, 'Give this to Fred. It's Evans's car.'

THE ENFORCER

I was still looking for Lennie Books. He was no longer living in the flat at Barking Road – who could blame him wanting to move after what had happened with Mitchell? – so he managed to exchange it for another council flat in a tower block called Albert Big Point in Stratford. I went there, it was several floors up, and I shouted for him through the letter-box. The place echoed like an empty house. It had a hollow ring, no furniture or carpets, which convinced me no one was there. I was relieved because there'd been general talk of getting him drunk, feeding him an overdose of his anti-depressant pills and letting him slip over the balcony. Back on Whitechapel Waste his dirty bookstalls were closed up too. That left only two possibilities. He was helping Nipper or he'd just run away, gone missing till everything was over.

Lots more people had left the scene. Most early Firm members had got away, including my brother-in-law Bill. He was never called in by the police, which is hardly surprising since he'd started working in Saudi Arabia by this time. Big Pat Connolly conveniently got himself nicked with a gun on the train to Glasgow. He got two years for that, which was better than going down with the Krays. Johnny Squibb also went missing, but he now had a legitimate demolition firm so he had nothing to worry about from the law. The only people being wiped up were relatively new members of the Firm.

When I realized just how many people were making themselves scarce, I figured I should get out of town too for a while. Ronnie Hart and I went down to Selsey in Sussex and stayed in a caravan, but we couldn't help looking suspicious. We stuck out so much, we weren't your typical family holiday-makers. It was lucky we decided to move on again because police raided the caravan the night after we'd headed back to London.

I wound up in Bethnal Green, hiding up a back street with Dickie Morgan in a girl's flat. We stayed there for two weeks, though we crept out from time to time. After a week Dickie and me went down the Regency, to the after-hours drinker in the basement. Ronnie Hart was there with his wife, Vicki, but that was the last we saw of him. Very soon after, the police collected them both. Nothing appeared in the papers about him being charged, so he must have turned almost as soon as he was captured. Not that we knew anything at the time. We thought he was still at liberty.

A couple of days later I was still in bed when in came the boys in blue. It was Georgie Ness and his team. We ended up sitting on the settee, just wearing trousers and a T-shirt. Georgie stood opposite us. I could see from the webbing that he was tooled up. We did a bit of acting as if we were tooled up too – 'Can we get our fags out?' – but they weren't acting. If we'd have made a wrong move, we'd have been dead.

So now almost everyone was wiped up. We were all professional criminals, so we expected to get nicked from time to time. It was the rules of the game. From now on, we just had to work on minimizing our individual sentences. We were carted off to West End Central police station and stuck in the cells. Now, for the first time, I met the legendary Detective Superintendent Nipper Read. He came in my cell with his inspector, Frank Cater. They asked me if I'd stand for an interview. I said, 'Don't want none of that.' They asked, 'Have you got legal representation?' I said, 'That's all been taken care of.' I must have sounded a bit flash, so Nipper said, 'Oh. Been taken care of, has it? Well, if you want to be Jack the Lad, you can stand up there with them, and it's our job to knock you down.' And that was it, away they went.

Next thing, I was taken out of the cell. There was no questioning, no grilling, no pressure, nothing. If I wanted a glass of water, I'd get it. Only now I'm formally charged, not with Mitchell's murder but with aiding his escape. This was a holding job, as I'd expected, enough to lock me up in Brixton on remand. It would have been no good asking for bail. I didn't even dream of that. I just worried about what else they're going to come up with, especially as I hadn't noticed Dickie Morgan getting the same treatment. Had he turned? Already? I didn't know.

It wasn't until a later court appearance on 31 May at Bow Street that Nipper Read stopped me and Reggie Kray in a corridor and said, 'I am charging you with the murder of Francis Mitchell.' This was the first of all the murder charges. We went in the magistrates' court, which had a dock specially constructed to deal with the mass of Kray defendants, and we were both formally charged.

Back to Brixton. The Krays were in D wing, which was the top-security section, the nick within a nick. Although I now had this murder charge stuck on me, I still wasn't considered worthy of top security, but I was transferred to the hospital wing. I wasn't ill, but this was normal. Anyone facing a murder rap was considered a suicide risk so I had to be closely watched. The folk on D Wing would get that level of supervision automatically, as dangerous escape risks. Not that they could have been watching Reggie closely enough. A few months later he clouted the stolen bonds man, Joey Kaufman, who was also on D Wing, and knocked out some of his teeth.

There were a few familiar faces in the hospital, including Dickie Morgan. At first I thought this was a pleasant reunion – after all, we had been arrested together – but then his being there struck me as odd because he wasn't ill, and he wasn't on a murder charge either. Then he disappeared. One minute he was walking round the hospital yard with me, the next he was gone. Later I found out he was probably put in as a spy, because he had been giving information to the police, though he didn't give evidence in open court.

While you're in jail awaiting trial, you often sit in your cell and make notes to give your brief, so he can prepare your case. Now, we'd learnt from the trial of the Richardsons, who'd been convicted and jailed for eighteens and tens a year earlier, that while they were in Brixton and left their cells to go on exercise, their notes were photocopied by someone on the prison staff. This undermined their defence. To guard against this, we carried our notes with us wherever we went.

My notes included a breakdown of various bits of evidence that the police had put together against me. For example, the people with us in the flat where we'd kept Frank Mitchell were saying that when I had rung Reggie I said, 'That dog is dead.' As I've already explained, what I really said was, 'That dog won,' according to the code that we had been using for years because Reggie thought his phone was tapped. So it would have been crazy for us to say, 'That dog is dead,' because anyone eavesdropping would immediately assume we'd killed somebody, completely destroying the point of any code.

Well, in court I couldn't admit what I'd really meant, code or not, so in the prison hospital I had been concocting a defence to explain away even the dead dog. It happened that the woman in the house where we held the party the night Mitchell was murdered, really did have her dog put down by a vet at that time, so I was going to confuse this 'dog is dead' stuff with her evidence and her vet's report. I'm not a perfectly clean, wonderful guy, but I can put up a smokescreen so the jury will have reasonable doubt. That's all I need: reasonable doubt to find the man not guilty of a murder charge. Then I don't mind getting done for some of the lesser stuff.

One day I was called up for a solicitor's visit to sort out a joint defence for all the Firm who hadn't turned. The meeting was being held in a room set aside for these conferences within the prison. I walked in the room, and there were the Twins, Charlie Kray and our brief, old Manny Fryde, already sitting down. There was an empty chair so I sat down, and they said to me, 'What do you reckon?' I said, 'Well, this is what I've written, these are the notes I've made.' Then Reggie took all my carefully prepared notes, read them and just ripped them up. When he saw this ritual, Fryde got up and said, 'I'll go get another chair.' So I'm thinking to myself, Who for? We're all sitting down. We don't need another chair. Then I realized he just wanted to be out of the room, so he didn't hear anything that might compromise his firm's formal obligation to offer a 'not guilty' plea. To do that he mustn't hear the Twins say anything that sounds like an admission of guilt. This is all rubbish, of course. Lawyers like Fryde know their clients are as guilty as sin. For gangsters such people are a vital part of the overall conspiracy. You just don't tell your brief you did the crime, in so many words.

Manny Fryde had been the Krays' legal representative in big criminal cases for years. But now in this biggest case of all, he wasn't only representing the three Krays, he was supposed to be my lawyer too. We were all under this same guy, so that the Twins would know exactly what's happening with everyone's case, and they could steer the entire case to their personal benefit. While Fryde was out of the room, Ronnie said, 'Don't bother with notes, Albert. What we're going to do is this: Scotch Jack is going to hold his hands up for Cornell, young Ronnie's going to hold his hands up for Jack the Hat, and we want you to hold your hands up for Mitchell. And we'll take all the violence and frauds.'

What a wonderful chap! How nice of the Colonel to volunteer three loyal soldiers to plead guilty to these murders, two of which he and his brother had committed, and the third they had organized. He wasn't saying, 'You go to court on your own and make your own defence.' He was saying that I must abandon my defence. I have got to say, 'They didn't do it. I did!' I have got to hold my hands up for their crimes. I've got to sacrifice myself just for them.

So I looked at Ronnie, and I said, 'No.'

Well, straight away the temperature in that room went down about ten degrees. And I looked round, and they were just staring at me. So that was it. I am now 'off the Firm'.

Then Fryde came back in – without another chair – and he smelt the change in atmosphere. It must have been like burning tyres because, without even talking to them, he leant over me and oozed, 'My boy, just because you're not a Kray doesn't mean you won't get the same treatment.' I thought, Yeah! Fat Chance! Finish.

From that point on I knew then there'd be no more happy

families. They'd scotch my every move. As for Fryde, I had no respect for him. He was a hired hand. If your washing machine breaks down, you call in the washing-machine man. And at that time if you wanted a bent brief, you called Manny Fryde. He was just someone who knew his job. And his job now was to save the Krays, even if it meant forcing another client to swear his life away.

Now some people who still think the Twins were lovely boys will tell you I was a no-good grass, but my position has always been that the Twins were grassing me. They expected me to stand up for a murder I did not commit but was down to them instead. So let's reconsider what would have happened if I had done what they were demanding.

We've just seen the Richardsons weighed off with huge sentences for crimes that did not even include murder. So if I hold my hands up for a gangland murder now, before a hanging judge, I'm going to get life. This means, if I'm lucky, I'm going to do at least 15 years, probably twice that. There's no way I'm going to risk such punishment. My own bit of intelligence won't let me stand for it. No way. Plus the fact that any defence I could put up under Fryde is going to get back to the Twins, so they're going to put the kibosh on that. Anyway, in return for my self-sacrifice, all they'll stand up for are the frauds and various little bits of violence.

But the Twins knew even these tiddly-pom items would collapse in court, if the rest of us stuck our hands up for their murders. Their minds worked this way. As soon as witnesses to these petty crimes see that they are not on the hook for any murders, they won't want to testify at all, because they know Ronnie and Reggie will be back out of jail in a couple of years at the most. Then the terrible Twins will pay them a visit and beat the shit out of them. This prospect would be enough to deter all the witnesses, so they would have walked out scotfree, or on probation at most. Then you'd have had Nipper Read committing suicide, and the entire history of the underworld would have taken a totally different shape. It would have been turned upside down. And all this time, I'd be sitting in the zoo! For 30 years! I would still be there today, while Ronnie and Reggie would be appearing on all the chat shows as lovable, warm-hearted East End celebrities.

And all for a murder I'd had nothing to do with, except to be there! What I did was blind, which was the Twins' normal way of doing business. They'd take you in, telling you only what little you needed to know. Then you did your bit and came away. Only later did you find out how your effort contributed to the bigger picture. Another thing. When the Krays laid out their grand plan, they weren't trying to con me. They still believed they had the power to instil fear. They thought Scotch Jack Dickson, Ronnie Hart and I were going to be so afraid, we would all go along with their scheme and lay down our lives for their crimes.

Anyway, unbeknownst to me and them, Scotch Jack and Ronnie Hart had turned already and were making statements before any charges were laid against them. When they eventually testified at the Old Bailey, the defence accused them of lying to save their own skins. Far from it. These guys gave a full and frank account, admitting their own involvement. It was to encourage them to tell the truth that they weren't charged, it wasn't so they would be induced to tell lies. My situation was different. I'd already been charged so if now I did a spin and laid Mitchell's murder on other people, it would look as if I was only trying to save myself.

Even though it was too late to get off serious secondary charges, I did decide to spin. Of all the people charged with the murders, I was the only one who spun. The police later told me they had tried to frighten me into grassing as soon as they arrested me but at the time I wasn't having that. Now things were entirely different. If even my own side – not just the Twins but my brief too – were demanding I plead guilty to a murder I had not committed, then I was going down, one way or the other. Fryde wasn't going to let me plead not guilty – and the Twins would stop me mounting an independent defence through a different set of lawyers – so it was none other than the Krays themselves who forced me into the police.

When that meeting with Fryde broke up, I was taken straight back to the hospital. Next day my mother came on a visit. As I was on a murder charge, I was allowed open visits. This meant I wasn't stuck behind a glass panel preventing physical contact with visitors. My mother had brought along my youngest son, a babe-in-arms, while the compulsory screw sat a few feet away. In these visits you're not allowed to hand over written material, but I had already written a tiny note to smuggle to my mother. I was holding the baby, and as I handed him back I gave her this note that said, 'Get hold of Nipper Read. Tell him I want to talk to him.'

I had to do things this way because I didn't trust the prison staff. We trusted nobody. Don't forget, I've been living in my own world of crime since I was in my teens. Now I've been living in the Twins' world for four years, among all their intrigues and conspiracies, so I'm trusting nobody. I was so indoctrinated with their system of spies and informers, so accustomed to the idea that anything I said or did would get back to them, that I really feared they could buy up any prison officer. I had no evidence for this. I was suffering from paranoid fantasies but, after all, they'd been getting top secret Yard reports through Cooper, and they had Lord Boothby and Tom Driberg MP sticking up for them at Westminster through Ronnie Kray's 'queer Mafia'. So, to my way of thinking at the time, a few Brixton warders would have been easy meat for them, even though they were probably all straight.

That's why I didn't go to the prison authorities to get a message to Nipper Read. I could not run the risk of this getting back to the Twins – because the next day I could get a funny dinner and drop down dead. When you're in the nick, whatever your location, you've got a personal officer. It may be your landing screw or, in hospital, your medical officer screw. Now if I had approached one of these officers – even one I thought I could get on with and said, 'Could you get a message to Nipper Read?' there was no doubt in my mind that, within the hour, the Twins would have heard about it over in D Wing. So that's out. So who do I turn to? Where do I go? Back to Mum! You can always trust your dear old mum, can't you?

If the Twins had heard they would have tried to kill me. There was one moment when this became clear to me, because it nearly happened. On this particular day my mother had come to see me again. While she was in the waiting-room, a blonde woman approached her and said, 'I've brought this dinner up for Reggie, but he doesn't want it, so would you like to take it in to Albert?'

Now my old mum didn't know about nick procedure, but at that time when you visited Brixton, you had to take all food and other gifts for any remand prisoner into a little room, where you handed them to a screw, before you even saw the prisoner you're visiting. The screw would then check the stuff before it was taken into the main jail and given to another screw who delivered it to your man's cell after he'd returned from your visit. The routine must be much the same today, but certainly back in 1968 there was no way the screws would have given 'Reggie's dinner' back to this blonde, because she would have finished the visit and left the jail before he would have been able to send it back rejected from his cell. There wouldn't have been time for this rigmarole, so it's clear that the dinner was never offered to Reggie. It had been brought in especially prepared for me. I wish I'd had the sense to take it and get it analysed. I'm sure they'd have found something funny inside.

I still haven't seen Nipper, remember, when one day I was getting escorted across the yard to a visit or maybe to the bath house. At the same moment I saw other members of the Firm being escorted over to A Wing, when suddenly Big Tommy Brown gave me a shout. 'Hullo, Albert. How's the missus? How's the kids?' Now I'm thinking to myself, what is this big hairy-arsed gangster asking me about my wife and kids for? He's never met my wife or kids. He's never asked about them before in his life. His normal reaction would be, 'All right, Alb? How you doing? Keep your head up!' That's it. So, whether I was feeling a bit paranoid or not, I felt this was an attempt to dribble through the message: 'Stay stumm or your family's going to get done.' So I said to myself, If that's the way the Twins are steering their dumbest supporters, then it's time for me to go my own way.

My mother went straight to Nipper, and he got straight back in touch with Brixton. Once the authorities realized I'd smuggled a message out, they got a busy-on. The next thing, my door was opened, and the governor of the entire prison was there with his chief screw: 'Did you send a message?' I didn't nod or shake my head, and I didn't say yes or no. I'm just looking at him, so he repeated himself, 'Did you send a message out?'

Then he said, 'Listen, you've got no problems, but we've been told that you sent a message out to Mr Read, and he has asked us to verify if you really did send it, or whether somebody else did.' That's how suspicious they were. So I said, 'Yeah, I sent it, yeah,' but I'd hesitated because I was thinking they're trying to nick my old mammy for smuggling the message. Nothing of the sort.

Now I'm through to Nipper. On 16 July 1968 Read and Cater showed up at Brixton, and I was wheeled in to see them. There was no sitting me down while they paced round barking questions at me. There were no glaring lights and no intimidation of any sort. In his book Tony Lambrianou says I 'cracked under questioning'. Rubbish. There was no stern interrogation, and I didn't crack. I had already decided to make a statement because of the Krays' demand over Mitchell.

Read and Cater turned out to be so different from what I'd come to expect in Metropolitan detectives that I had no difficulty in co-operating with them. In the old days a copper was at least six foot tall, three foot wide and stupid. Whenever we met anyone from the CID, we always assessed them according to our own standards and experience. We'd be thinking, Could we get into this guy? Was he bent, would he take a drink, a wad of money? But as soon as I saw Nipper, he struck me as being a straight man. He didn't come on like the traditional Yard detective: 'You're nicked, Sonny Boy!' and all that nonsense. To look at the man you wouldn't think he was a copper. He looked like a decent school teacher. Even Frank Cater didn't look like a cop. Nipper never raised his voice, he never threatened, and so I got to trust him.

On three successive days – 16, 17 and 18 July 1968 – I poured out the whole lot to Read and Cater in three long statements. First I told them the story of the Mitchell killing, then I spilt what I knew about Cornell and McVitie. Later I went through more murder conspiracies and a lot of the rackets and beatings. But in the short time available, I only skimmed the surface. I think Nipper was still smarting from his defeat by the Krays back in 1965 on the extortion charges. This time he was concentrating on the three confirmed murders. He wasn't going to spread the investigation over too many areas and risk another slate of 'not guiltys' by leaving gaps in the evidence.

In my statements I revealed my motives and anxieties: 'I'm sick of the lot of them. They talk about being loyal, but I have to be loyal to my kids.' I made it clear that the only promises given to me by the police related to protection for my wife and family. I said, 'Ronnie's got my mother's address. They haven't made threats in as many words, but I know the way they think.' I added that I had made these statements without a solicitor present. I said, 'I do not want the Krays or their solicitors to know I have made this statement at this time, because I am afraid of the consequences which might result either to myself or my family. I have reason to believe my family are in danger even now, or will be very soon.'

I was not being melodramatic. I was making these statements right there in Brixton Prison, knowing the Krays were only a few hundred feet away. Read and Cater weren't going to move me before I'd made the statements because, until they got everything, I don't think they believed I was going to do what I did.

And I really did deliver. Until I came forward, the police hadn't heard a whisper about Foreman and his crowd playing any part in Mitchell's fate. All Lisa, Scotch Jack and Lennie Books knew was that I was the one person who had taken Frank out of the flat, and then they had heard shots, so they could only assume I was the guy who shot him. To them it was straightforward: I took him out – bangs – I came back, and I cleaned the flat out. That's all anyone knew so it was reasonable to assume I was the hit-man.

I think Read and Cater wanted to believe me but, as I was telling the full story, they were wondering, How can we corroborate this? If they went straight out and grabbed Foreman or Gerard, they'd just deny it because all the cops have got is my word. Anyway, now I'd made these statements Read and Cater were convinced I had to be moved out of Brixton pronto. Next morning it was on. The door opened: 'Pack your kit, you're going.' There was a big discipline screw standing there with a brown folder and WANDSWORTH written across it, in red. This was for the benefit of any strolling cons. They'd go, 'Hello! Donoghue's being ghosted to Wandsworth.' It was just to throw the Krays off the scent because, next thing, I was on my way to Chelmsford.

I was safe there, but now my family had to be given a 24-hour man-and-woman police guard. Every minute of the night and day they had two coppers in the house, living with them on shift for five weeks. I had already told the wife I was going to turn. I said, 'You may have to change the family name, because if this doesn't work, and it goes the other way, I'll have to do the Twins. If I come head to head with either one of them, I'll just kill 'em. I'm not going to wait. It's gonna be all or nothing.' She accepted the situation. She could have disowned me if ever a Kray supporter came round, but she had a word with Nipper and Sergeant Bert Trevette and was quite happy with the police guard.

There were still some Kray folk on the streets of the East End, including Ronnie Bender. He'd been well involved with the killing of Jack the Hat. He was the one who put his ear to Jack's chest and declared him dead, but the police hadn't yet tied him in. He popped up while they were moving the family out of our home in Bow for a new secret address. When they had assembled two lorries and two cars to remove the furniture and the family, they spotted Bender sitting close by in a Mini. To confuse him, they drove off in four different directions. He must have had a brainstorm about which one to follow. He never was very bright. He must have still been working for the Twins, under instructions to do anything to destroy the case building up against them.

The strength of that case was obvious next time I went in the dock at the magistrates' court. We were about a dozen in all, but I was flanked on both sides by police. We sat in three rows, with ten more police encircling the entire structure, watching for any fights or escape attempts. As I leant back to look along all the faces, I spotted Freddie Foreman. At this stage he was only up for disposing of Jack the Hat, so he didn't yet know if I'd done him any harm. I caught his eye, and in a friendly way he mouthed to me, 'All right?' No voice, just lip-reading. So I went, 'Yeah.'

He was keen to gauge my reaction because he did know that I'd fallen out with the Twins, and I might have turned. Apparently he had blasted at them, 'What have you done with him?' He'd instantly sussed they had been up to some skullduggery. He knew I wouldn't speak to cops for the fun of it. I heard he was so upset, there was a scuffle, and he chinned Reggie. He had every reason to be wild because, without my evidence, there was nothing to link him or his team to Frank Mitchell.

At the same court hearing my obsessive fear of poisoning cropped up again. Connie Whitehead was sitting behind me to my left. At one point he offered me a Spangle sweet. I shook my head, No, but we smiled because he knew why I was refusing. At the time Connie himself was wobbling. He made a statement, which he later retracted, a decision that did him no good at all.

This time when I left court I was put in a car to go to Maidstone jail. As we were about to drive off, there was a tap on the window. It was Nipper. He passed me a note and said, 'Get in touch with this man.' It was Victor Lissack, the solicitor he was recommending to me instead of Manny Fryde. Switching to Victor proved to be the best move I ever made. He looked after me brilliantly throughout the Kray trials and later on.

When I arrived at Maidstone I was put in a little office, and the governor himself brought in the tray of tea. The screws couldn't believe it. Normally it would simply be, 'Shut up,' and they'd dump you in your cell, but I was getting special treatment because I was the only remand prisoner in the jail. They put me in solitary for my own safety.

It was only when the Twins heard I'd dumped Fryde – probably from Fryde himself – that they knew for sure that I'd spun. This seems to have driven them to do even sillier things. There was the offer from a woman friend of Reggie's to take my baby away for a holiday. Imagine: I've just turned on the Firm, and, all of a sudden, this girl is offering to take my boy away on holiday. Why? I first knew of this while I was in Winson Green Prison in Birmingham. Some police came on a visit with my wife and told me they had intercepted this letter offering to pay my mother £5 a week and to take my baby on holiday. The coppers said, 'We don't know what you want to do about this.' I looked at my wife, and I said, 'Have you seen this?' She said, 'Yes.' I said, 'You keep your eye on that baby. Don't let anybody take him anywhere.'

The impact of all this trouble on my wife and three children was immense. Even after they were moved, they still had a police man and woman with them constantly for 15 months: in the house, when the older kid went to school, when the wife went shopping or to the hairdressers, Old Bill was always there. That's not a normal way to live.

Meantime, as news spread around the East End that not just the Twins but all their main henchmen and Freddie Foreman had been scooped up, many supporting witnesses had the courage to come forward. Once they could be fairly sure that Kray hit-men weren't on the loose looking to gun them down, they were willing to give information to the police. But most still did so only on the understanding that they would not have to testify in court.

There was to be no such luxury for me. If I didn't testify against the Krays and Foreman, I would be staying in jail for a very long time. I was in emotional turmoil. Shitting myself is the correct term. For nine months I didn't know whether I was in or out, up or down. You try and think things through: what could be the possible outcome, or, how many different outcomes could there be? And you hang on to your family. I wasn't getting visits every day because I was being shifted all over the country, wherever I could be safe at any particular time. This made me feel dangerously isolated.

I didn't write a lot, I didn't send many letters because while you're sitting in your cell nothing is real. You can get carried away and start writing silly things, which may backfire on you later. The best thing is: 'Don't write,' just say what you want to say on a visit. Obviously your wife knows you so well, you don't have to say too much: just a nod, a wink, even the way you say some short sentence can express more than an hour's conversation. The family was important, and that got me through. The kids came to see me as often as possible.

Throughout this period I was mainly in solitary confinement, so I used to do silly things just to concentrate my mind and stop me going nuts. I would look at a picture of a house in a magazine and work out how many bedrooms there were; and from the position of the drainpipes, where the bathroom and kitchen were; and I used to redesign the house just to keep my old brain working. I never got any aggro from screws or other cons.

Other than the family, the only diversions were visits by police to sort out the detail in the evidence. They knew they still had severe problems establishing a case against the people I'd named as Mitchell's killers. Two had disappeared to Australia – on the Melbourne run like Ronnie Biggs – one had a convincing alibi, and only Foreman was charged, largely because they had the similar 'disposal of the body' case against him over Jack the Hat. The evidence surrounding Mitchell's escape was now overwhelming but that concerned Reggie, not Foreman. It took nine months for the police to establish even the feeblest evidence to support the murder end of my Mitchell testimony. They had no body, no guns, no van, no clean witnesses. One detective said that if I had told him the time he'd have to check with Big Ben, because I was a self-confessed accomplice giving a wholly uncorroborated version of events.

At last on 8 January 1969 the first trial began at the Old Bailey. Now there was a show: armed police all over the shop, and me being brought into the City of London from Maidstone every day. Compared with prison life, it was a pleasure going to the Bailey. Every day there was a free lunch, a glass of beer and 20 Senior Service. But I was still up to my neck in trouble. I had never been given a single promise that I was going to get any favours. When I walked into Number One Court on Day One, I was still charged with the murder of Frank Mitchell, with being an accessory after Jack the Hat's murder and with aiding the escape and harbouring and comforting Mitchell: five charges in all. So, on paper, I still had 100 years in jail in front of me.

The first trial was restricted to the murders of George Cornell and Jack McVitie. At the start Scotch Jack Dickson was allowed to plead guilty to harbouring Frank Mitchell and was given just nine months. He was then allowed to testify about driving Ronnie to the Blind Beggar to kill Cornell. Ronnie Hart also gave evidence, against every other member of the Firm present when Jack the Hat was killed. He also fingered Freddie Foreman for getting rid of the body. Ronnie Hart himself was never charged with anything.

I wasn't charged over Cornell's murder because I had nothing whatever to do with it, and I didn't give evidence either because I wasn't an eye-witness. On Jack the Hat I agreed with Victor Lissack that I should plead guilty to being an accessory. I would then sit out the trial, in the matron's quarters in the Bailey every day, until I'd testify about arriving at Blonde Carol's flat while they were cleaning up, and my own role in redecorating the entire place on the Twins' orders.

I went in the witness-box some time after Blonde Carol, when the court was still buzzing over her statement. She had told how she saw Chrissy Lambrianou crying on the stairs, saying he had no idea it was going to happen, and he had not known he was setting Jack up. This provoked Chrissy to stand up and shout, 'I never said that!' What a let-out for him that could have been, but he threw it away. He was either frightened of the Twins or self-destructively loyal. Why didn't he say, 'Get me my own brief! I want my own defence!'? This wasn't a little matter of a six-month sentence, or even five years. It's your entire adult life you're messing about with! Who could entrust that to the good faith of the Twins and Manny Fryde? Whoever did that was a bloody idiot.

The same went for Ian Barrie. If he'd had his own defence, he could have said he went to the Blind Beggar that night as blind as the Beggar himself. He didn't fire the lethal shots into George Cornell. Sure, he was acting in concert with the Colonel, but he did not commit murder himself. The sad thing was, none of these people wanted the Twins to think they weren't staunch. They thought they were being strong by standing up with the Krays, but this wasn't strength, it was weakness. You showed your strength by standing up against them.

All these people were hoping some miracle would save them. They were just like Mr Micawber, waiting for something to turn up, but it never did. Until bosh! Fifteen years of porridge. That's what Chrissy and Tony Lambrianou were given when they were convicted for Jack the Hat. Ronnie Bender got twenty, and Ronnie and Reggie Kray got thirty years each. Ronnie's sentence also applied to Cornell's murder, for which Ian Barrie got twenty. Then for cleaning up after McVitie, Charlie Kray got ten and Connie Whitehead seven. Freddie Foreman got ten for disposing of Jack's body.

Now I had to see what the judge was going to do to me for being an accessory after Jack the Hat. Which way do I go: in or out? In front of Judge Melford 'Truncheons' Stevenson my mind went completely blank, but when I came down from the dock I said to this copper, 'What? What did he say?' 'Two years!' I couldn't believe it. The copper couldn't believe it either, and he was shouting 'Two years!' Two years when I'd thought twenty.

The first trial ended on 5 March but the second, concerning Mitchell, was weeks away. I was still charged with his murder, which made the screws in Maidstone think all the more of me.

I heard one saying to another, 'Well, if he did do it, he done us a favour, didn't he?' By this he meant Mitchell had been such a pain to prison officers for years – crippling one in the hand and slashing another in the face so badly he needed over 70 stitches – that I had saved the entire service a lot of aggro. It's funny how 'straight' people's views on law and order, right and wrong, don't always lead them to condemn thugs like us.

When they found out I was claiming I hadn't killed Mitchell, and I was giving evidence against the Krays, their attitude changed to something just as funny. During my first trips to the Old Bailey in the usual small coach I was handcuffed to two screws. One would sit in front of me, the other behind, so, if you looked at us from near the front, we were all sitting in a straight line. But once they saw how the police were armed to the teeth, they took off the handcuffs and sat me in the middle all on my own, while they sat right at the front and the back, keeping well away in case someone tried to shoot me.

I had four screws and four coppers with me every day I went to the Bailey, and now at last I had to give evidence in open court. The police said the Twins had been scowling at people and upsetting them, causing hiccups in their evidence. Before I entered the witness-box they said, 'Don't look at them, don't look at the dock, because when all the other witnesses look at them, they start getting nervous.' So at first I did what they'd suggested. Then, all of a sudden, I found myself ducking and dodging so that I didn't catch their eyes. And I thought, Nah, this ain't right, so I just turned, and, with my eyes, I went up and down the line, staring at each of them in turn. I studied the lot of them, and I settled down from then on. The wife mentioned it afterwards. She said that the policewoman, sitting with her, kept on saying, 'He's looking at them! He's looking at them!' Everyone commented that this was unusual, but I found that, rather than hang my head, if I looked right along the line and dwelt on them, I was OK. And then they started hanging their heads. That was a little victory.

I spent five days giving evidence in the Mitchell case alone. When you talk to Old Bill, and you're turning Queen's Evidence, you can't leave anything out. You can't say, 'I didn't do this bit, and I didn't do that bit.' You've got to tell them what you did from the start. They weren't going to be satisfied with bits and pieces about my dealings with the Krays. They wanted all the dirt. Of course, most wasn't relevant to these Mitchell charges, and they weren't admissible in court, a curb that allowed the defence to have a field day. There were a lot of things I couldn't say but, if these lawyers could provoke, goad or jeer me into blurting them out, they would argue for a mistrial and a retrial. And all the time they were trying to lay stuff on me – 'You've done this, you've done that' – to make it look as if I were a worse villain than the murderers they were defending.

So there I was, testifying against my former employers, my senior partners in crime: men who were loved and feared throughout the East End and in south London too, my co-conspirators on the board of the most notorious criminal Firm in English history. Maybe I should have been frightened, but my most powerful emotion was anger. I was still steaming. I wasn't ashamed because I wasn't doing anything bad. I wasn't ratting on them. The ratting had already come in that solicitor's visiting-room at Brixton Prison, when they tried to turn me against myself. I still had this flaming needle.

I gave my evidence absolutely cold. I wasn't nervous. I'd rehearsed it in my own mind many times but, standing up there with all these defence barristers – five QCs plus all their juniors – hanging on every word you say, it is a bit nerve-wracking. Until you become preoccupied battling out a particular game of chess with one of these QCs as he tries to trip you up. As he suddenly hops to another subject, you think, Hello! What's he up to? You're trying to box with him all the time.

The Twins didn't squeal 'Grass!' or any other insult. Apparently some of the earlier witnesses were getting stick and hard looks and shouts of 'Slag' and 'Prat', but there wasn't a word when I went in the box. I could shout as well, and if they'd have started on me I'd have given them some back. In the so-called code of the underworld I might have been branded a grass, but the only code now was self-preservation and survival.

The defence they all mounted over Mitchell was simple: they had nothing to do with his death. At one point they claimed Billy Exley had killed him and then bolted. Billy had been one of Mitchell's minders, but the idea that he killed him was ridiculous. Sure he went missing some time after Mitchell, but that was because he had had a heart attack. Reggie and I had caught up with him at the London Hospital so there was no mystery. When he struggled into the witness-box himself, frail and seemingly at death's door, he scarcely looked like a gangland assassin. The defence were also claiming I had rowed with Mitchell, implying I might have killed him myself. This was nonsense. Even so, it had been obvious from the start that there just wasn't enough evidence against the Krays or Foreman. The jury acquitted them all of the murder, but Reggie did get five years for conspiring to effect Mitchell's escape from Dartmoor.

I knew that this result did not mean I had been lying – only that the jury had no way of knowing what really happened that night. Anyway, except in Freddie Foreman's case, the verdicts made no difference to the time these guys would spend in jail. I got two years, and the rest of them carried on doing their thirties and twenties and fifteens. Well, there you go.

Justice works in mysterious ways. Of Mitchell's other killers, Alfie Gerard returned from Australia and was eventually bagged up on a robbery and jailed for seven years. Then in 1980 he was found dead in Brighton in suspicious circumstances. Freddie Foreman did his time for Jack the Hat, then went to Spain. In 1989 he was brought back to England and given nine years for handling some of the proceeds of the 1983 Security Express robbery.

Charlie Kray was let out as early as 1975 but he never had done much to be locked up for. If it hadn't been for his brothers, he wouldn't have got dragged into crime at all. He's dead now and so are the Twins. Ronnie was the first to pass on to another place – a more durable underworld than his own, I imagine. But even if the Colonel had outlived his 30-year term, he would never have been set free. He had been in Broadmoor for so long, he was far too institutionalized to cope with life on the outside ever again. The news of his death in March 1995 left me absolutely cold. As far as I was concerned, he died years ago. I felt the same in 2000 when Charlie and Reggie died. The Krays had gone but 'Krayology' lived on.

Krayology was a coinage the prosecution used in court to describe the image that the Twins tried to project, to instil fear and exact tribute. It was a short way to explain a lot of the things that went on in the years when they ruled the underworld of the East End and a good deal of the West End too. The judge banned the word. He said he didn't want to hear it again. Yet it sums up so much of the myth, legend and bunkum that piled up around this pair when they were at their height. It even fits the bandwagon of support that these would-be serial killers have managed to get rolling for them to this day.

14: GOING STRAIGHT, ALMOST

When the Mitchell trial ended on 16 May 1969 I had already been in custody for almost a year. With remission for good behaviour, and another chunk chopped off on compassionate grounds, I was freed only three months later, in August. I had been a criminal for 20 years, I had lived several lifetimes, but I was only thirty-three and still a relatively young man. I had a wife, three children and a fresh start to make, whether I wanted to or not.

We had a family discussion about whether to change our surname. A lot of 'supergrasses' in the 1970s and 1980s changed their names, to make it more difficult for agents of the criminals they had grassed to find them and take vengeance. This argument didn't convince my wife. Must we change our name just because a toe-rag might want to impress the Twins? The kids didn't want it, the wife didn't want it, so we decided to remain the Donoghues.

Anyway, who was going to do me or my family? Of the Kray Firm there was almost no one left on the streets. Half had defected, some had gone abroad, some had died, and the rest were locked up. That only left people like Bill Ackerman who were far more frightened of me than I was of them. Also, whoever might come after me would be running after all the other defectors – Hart, Dickson, Morgan, Cooper, Payne, Exley, Lennie Books – as well as all the women on the fringe.

That only left one serious candidate, Brown Bread, and he was locked up for a ten-year stretch. Once he was out, he was quite capable of making himself busy. As I always said to the police, 'If you're looking for a danger-man, forget about the Twins, look into

THE ENFORCER

Foreman.' I never forgot what he'd said about sitting up all night on a roof, armed to the teeth waiting for Jim Evans. Even so, I never expected anything to come from him, once the first few years had passed without incident. If Foreman had wanted me, he'd have arranged for friends of his to do me while he was still in the nick. He wouldn't have waited until he came out and put himself on offer as a suspect. Or it would have been done, long after he came out, while he was living in Spain. But why should he bother? He wasn't convicted on my evidence, and he knew the Twins had done me wrong. On that basis he should have shot them, not me.

The only people who might have tried would have been some glory-seeker acting in the name of the Twins, one of those freaks who think they are the new Ronnie and Reggie, the weirdos who go round dressed like them. Or some young kid from the East End who had heard things from his uncle or dad and wanted to make a name for himself. Of course, there were the fringe people, the other firms who used to be allies of the Twins, like the Nashes, but they all went quiet, kept a very low profile and went about their own business. Even the people who tried to move in on the Krays' territory, like the Dixons, weren't going to bother about me. They detested the Twins anyway, not least because Ronnie had tried to shoot George Dixon point-blank. Rather than shoot me, the Dixons would probably have bought me a drink.

For all these reasons I felt good about earning a straight living for a while. I started a little industrial painting team, doing sub-contract work and employing a few other guys, including an old pal, Tommy Herbert, who I'd been brought up with. We'd gone to sea together and worked alongside each other for years before I got involved with the Krays.

I was feeling so sure that no one would ever come after me that, within a couple of years of testifying against the Krays, I was doing most of my business back in the East End. I didn't make detours to avoid my old haunts. I even went back into the Green Dragon, which I used to mind and collect from for the Twins, to see George

Mizel and One-armed Lou. I played a couple of games of cards there, just to show I wasn't concerned. All the same, I kept a close watch on the door.

My caution was justified a few months later, when I had a big job on, painting some timber sheds in Hackney. My HQ was the Railway Tavern in the heart of the Krays' old territory. That's where I paid the boys out and took them on. All the guys working for me – especially Tommy Herbert – knew that I was the Donoghue who'd testified against the Krays. One night I was in the Railway, nice and drunk when Tommy came in and said, 'I've brought a couple of friends to see you.' They were another Donoghue, who was no relation of mine, and a guy called Billy Amies.

'Billy Amies! You old rascal,' I said, because this was a guy I had met in the 'Ville before I'd joined the Firm. I was doing my three stretch, and he was in for armed robbery. For a while I was 'three'd up' with him – three of us in the same cell – and one day he offered me an escape. He said, 'I'm off today, do you want to come?' He was going out in a laundry basket. I said, 'No, thanks, I'm finished soon anyway.' He only had three months to do himself, but he had to get out because he was being threatened with further charges on release. He escaped as planned, sorted the witnesses so the police couldn't lay the new charges on him, then he gave himself up. It was time well spent.

I had got on well with him in the 'Ville, so I was happy now to drink with him and crack a few jokes. There was no animosity, and so we went on to a pub run by a relative of his, opposite the northern entrance to the Rotherhithe Tunnel.

Everything's just fine. We stay there for a few more drinks, until it's about one in the morning, and we decide to head for a club in the West End. Now, I'm a little bit drunker, and I wind up in a car alone with Amies at the wheel, while all the rest have piled in the other car, which is meant to be following us. Well, we end up down the Billingsgate fish market. Off to the left there are all the wharfs and slipways to the river. The place is deserted. So I say, 'Bill, what club are we going to?' He says, 'Oh, we're not going to any club.' I say, 'So what are we doing?'

He's driving along, and then he says, 'Tell me what's going through your mind right now. Where do you think we're going? Are you scared?' so I'm thinking this is some little game of Billy's, a psychological frightener just for a laugh. That's when I look up, and I see his hand thrusting down to the gear stick, but as he brings his hand back up I see something shining. So I grab the hand and snatch what proves to be a potato peeler – one of those little knives with a groove in it - and I just do him with it.

Now when this gravy – the blood – gushes out and hits the windscreen, I think I've done his throat, I think he's dead. The motor hits a bollard and stops, I slide out, I throw his tool away, and I bolt, because I'm waiting for the follow-up car, in which I'm thinking the other guys have probably got a stretcher, to shovel me dying into the river. I'm convinced this is all a set-up to kill me because I've dared to stand up against the Twins.

I remember bolting up to Fleet Street where, in those days, there was a little kiosk-type cafe for the night printers and reporters. I went in, I got 40 Senior Service and a box of matches, because I had instantly decided to give myself up. I was expecting a lie-down in a station cell overnight and a remand in jail after that. I walked on until I saw a uniform copper at one of those old *Doctor Who* police posts. I said, 'Scuse me.' He said, 'Be quiet, get away.'

I said, 'Look, none of that nonsense! I've just killed a guy down the fish market.' 'Ah! You're the one!' he said. And within minutes this motor showed up full of police, and I was taken off to Vine Street station. I told them exactly what had happened and the probable cause. I was thinking the guy's dead. They took away all my clothes and swabbed me down for forensics. I was allowed to get in touch with my solicitor, Victor Lissack. He came in, doing his usual Robert Morley act and told me, 'Don't say anything.' I said, 'It's all right, I've already said it.' I had nothing to be worried about, so I'd told them exactly what happened and why.

In the meantime other police had gone to the house in Peckham, south-east London, where I was then living with my family, to get me a change of clothes and probably search it too. When they reached there, they came across the guys who had been in the second car, the back-up mob for Billy Amies. They were at my door shouting through the letter-box, 'We didn't know Albert was going to get hurt!' Well, they must have been making this up, to escape my vengeance for them delivering me like a trussed chicken into Billy's clutches. They certainly knew I'd turned Queen's Evidence against the Krays, though it's just possible they didn't know what Amies had in store for me.

Either way, I was hopping mad because I thought my old mate Tommy Herbert had set me up. So when they dragged this crowd back to Vine Street, and a copper brought Tommy into the squad room, I just smacked him in the mouth. He went on the floor, and I thought, That's it. I'm due for a beating. Here come the sticks! But the cops didn't make a move. They just dragged him out. I didn't even get locked up. They took me on a tour of Vine Street, showed me the horses in the stables, and I sat there drinking coffee. Next morning I went to court and got fined twenty-five quid. I came out with Victor Lissack who was beaming at what was a good result, even allowing for the unique circumstances.

Billy Amies did not show up in court, even though he would have been fit enough to attend. I'd cut an artery in his lip, which was stitched up in a hospital, but then he'd bolted out of the window because there was an outstanding warrant for his arrest. The police told me, 'We want him bad because he's been running round impersonating police officers on robberies.' That was the last I heard of Billy Amies until a few years later when, ironically, he turned supergrass himself and put a lot of top robbers away. So even this tough and staunch fellow, trying to ingratiate himself with the Twins, could not be relied on. No Honour Among Thieves any more. No loyalty to the underworld code. No Omertà. Tut! Tut! What was gangland coming to?

Of course, my incident with Amies had ruined the family's cover. I had been working in the East End partly to keep the faces away from the house in Peckham. I had thought nobody knew we were living there, but now this lot had been caught shouting through our letter-box, it was clear they'd found out easily enough, so who else knew? And this was still Injun Country – Richardson territory – and Freddie Foreman too had plenty of friends in this very part of London. So we had no choice. We had to move from Peckham pronto. We packed our bags again and went to live in Kent. Whenever something happened to me, I was concerned for my wife and family, and I would move them on. Not that they were frightened. They thought I was overprotective, but you can't take chances.

After a few uneventful years in Kent, we moved to Oxfordshire where, I'm sorry to say, I went astray again. In the late 1970s I started burgling country houses: not grand places but comfortable homes, where I could pick up good antiques, gold and jewellery. I was never caught doing the burglaries. I got nicked getting rid of the stuff. I used to sell it through antiques shops in Reading, pretending it was my own. It was decent gear. In all I unloaded £56,000 worth but I got only a percentage.

It seems one of these shop owners was being leant on by the local crime squad for bodies, so he stuck my name up. One day in 1979 I went in with a couple of clocks. He said, 'I haven't got any money. I'll have to go and get it. Just wait here a few minutes,' which I did. I didn't suss it, so he had time to go off and phone the squad. They told him to stay away for ten minutes, so I'd think he really had been to the bank, and they'd have a chance to get in position. Rather than arrest me there and then, they followed me home. Then they raided the house and demanded to know who I was working with. They didn't believe I was working alone.

They searched everything, including my wife's purse, in which they found a ring I'd asked her to get repaired. That was ideal for them because now they could arrest her as well, in order to lean on me. To increase the pressure they separated us. They locked me up overnight but didn't tell me if they had let her go or not. Next morning some old uniformed sergeant out of London came into my cell and said, 'You were something hot in the Sixties. I was at Leman Street when all that Kray palaver was going on.' Later he'd transferred to the Thames Valley Police, and as soon as he saw 'Albert Donoghue' on the charge sheet, he got terribly excited. 'Wow! We've nicked Albert!' he kept saying, as if he was awestruck. He'd spread it all round the station, and then a much younger copper came in and said, 'Wow! I hear you were really something in the Sixties.' He wasn't being sarcastic. This was admiration. I thought, This guy's in the wrong job. Even coppers suffer from the Gangster Complex.

The older cop was a decent enough chap, so we sat down and got talking and I said, 'I don't want you to get involved in anything but would you do me a favour? Can you just tell me if my wife is still in the nick?' He said she was, so that was it. When the CID mob came on duty I told them, 'Right. What we do now is, you get my missus out of here – no nick at all – then you can sharpen your pencils. Get some more paper, and I'll tell you everything I've done.' They agreed, and they let her go.

I then sat down with these Regional Crime Squad guys and made a clean breast of all of my burglaries. I'd done one every fortnight for two years – 52 in all – and I'd never been caught on any of them. To prove my point I ferried the detectives round to all the houses I'd burgled so they could speak to my victims and clear their own books. I was given bail and eventually came up for trial at Oxford Crown Court.

Boy! Had my solicitor Victor Lissack laid on a good show! He had encouraged Frank Cater (Nipper Read's deputy on the Kray squad but now a Scotland Yard Commander) to come up and speak on my behalf. Then everyone on both sides of the case just walked out of the court in a huddle with the judge. They were gone for an hour, leaving the rest of us quietly sitting there: the press, me and my two screws. Then they all came back, and the prosecutor just went through the motions. He even sounded as if he was appearing for the defence by now. Then the judge said, 'You will go to prison for two and a half years.'

Why had they all been out so long? Later the detective in charge told me that at first the judge was talking terms of eight years. But then everyone including Lissack (who was a part-time judge himself by now) got to work, and they talked him down to two and a half. The judge obviously knew I wasn't going to do even that much. I was sent to an easy little C category prison at Shepton Mallet. I had only been stuck in my cell for a month when I was out painting and decorating the staff houses. I got parole as well as remission for good behaviour, and I was out in 12 months.

When I came out, the family and I moved to yet another town, but in 1985 I just packed my bags and left home. It was by mutual agreement. My wife and I were still friends, but we didn't have much to keep us together any more. She had been through hell all because of my chosen profession. It had been a crazy way of living. I'm amazed she stuck with me as long as she did. You haven't read much about her in this book, because she deserves her privacy after all those mad, mad years.

My children have survived pretty well, considering the trouble I dragged them through for 20 years. I don't think they have too many emotional scars, but I may be the last person they would tell. They haven't held anything against me. They don't blame me for a traumatized childhood, even if they should. My daughter is quite happy, and both the boys hold down straight lives. They have never spent any time in the nick. None of my kids has been in trouble with Old Bill. That's probably more important to me than the average guy. They got through it all OK. I suppose they knew that in my own twisted way I would always stand by them. I have never killed anybody, but the only way I could have killed anybody (other than in self-defence) would have been protecting my family. I would not murder for money, pleasure or revenge, but I would kill anybody who harmed my family.

After leaving my wife I poodled back to dear old London. I have tried to keep out of trouble ever since, and I've managed to survive on the tightest of funds without feeling driven to go back on the pavement and rob. My needs are simple, I roll my own cigarettes, and that sums up a life that is now very plain. Things have never been as bad for me as Tony Lambrianou claimed in a newspaper exposé. He said, 'Albert Donoghue is now living as a down-and-out in Liverpool.' When the article appeared, I was playing snooker in a London pub. Someone said to me, 'You're on the board.' I said, 'No, I'm not. I'm up in Liverpool!'

Occasionally I bump into people from the criminal fraternity who may know that I was once a member of the Kray Firm, but I don't bring it to their attention. Since Billy Amies I've never had any hostility directed at me. I've never had any verbal shit, because I can give that back. When it comes to the physical side, I'm not as quick as I used to be, but if my life is threatened, I can get a gun, and I can pull a trigger same as the next guy. Nowadays I watch not for faces but for suspicious circumstances, because if anyone's coming to kill me, it would be someone I don't know. The current watchword has to be, 'Stay well away from anyone on a motorbike. He's probably a hit-man.'

By today's criminal standards, all the Krays' antics may seem a bit quaint. Now it's all drugs, and the mobs we have running around – white, black and Asian – wouldn't put up with the Twins. They would just do them. These days people like the Krays might try and organize frauds and protection rackets, but no one would be frightened of them. Drug gangs shoot coppers down for nothing and laugh as they run away, so they wouldn't hesitate to shoot a pair of East End thugs. There are dozens of guys around now who are just as wild as Ronnie and Reggie, though they lack that certain style and glamour that surrounded our Gert and Daisy.

Sometimes I think about my four years with the Firm, and I say to myself, Christ! What did I go through? What was all that about? I wasn't dragged into anything I didn't see the consequences of. Before I ever got involved with the Twins, every criminal act I did was by my own choice. I even chose the Kray thing, despite getting shot by Reggie from behind. I can't make excuses and say, 'Oh, they conned me into it, Guv'nor, I'm really a nice boy.' I was a crook before I ever met them.

When I was at Catholic school in Devon, I had so much religion pumped into me that by the age of seven I knew enough for my confirmation. On the day there were a dozen of us little boys and girls, walking up the aisle, each dressed in white and wearing a little sash. When we approached the bishop, we knelt before him, and he blessed us one by one. Then I kissed the ruby ring on his right hand, and he confirmed me as a 'soldier of Christ'. I wonder what that old bishop would have said if he'd been told that this bonny little soldier of Christ was destined to become a soldier of the Krays?

I lived through interesting times and extraordinary events. It seems like history now, a different world. Certainly a different country.

Ronnie Kray died on 19 March 1995, Charlie died on 4 April 2000 and Reggie finally croaked on 1 October 2000. I have managed to outlive all my gangland bosses.

I can't say I was affected in any way by their deaths. They had no impact on me. There's no point in dancing on anyone's grave. On the other hand, now they've all gone, I think it's worth puncturing some myths which should have had the air let out of them decades ago but get inflated even more with every passing year.

First, there's the idea that everyone in the Kray 'firm' were chums. There's bound to be another Kray feature film one day and I wouldn't be surprised if it's based on the kind of garbage put out by the Mad Frankie Fraser fraternity portraying the entire London underworld as a bunch of pals, a folksy crowd of pearly kings all chanting the refrain, 'We wuz all one!'

But the truth, as everything in this book proves, is that few of us were pals. For me crime was just a job. I happened to be working for a firm, nominally run by Messrs R&R Kray, but in fact run by nobody with any management skills. Not the Kray Gang but the Crazy Gang. There was no real affection for the Krays even in their own neighbourhood. What show of support they ever gained at their funerals wasn't down to any fondness for them. It was a mixture of fear — you had to be seen to turn out just in case they ever made a comeback — and natural human curiosity. If a horse-drawn hearse and forty Daimlers came trundling along your street, you'd pop out and have a look, wouldn't you? It could be Winston

THE ENFORCER

Churchill, Elvis Presley, the Queen of Sheba or no one you'd ever heard of in the coffin, but you'd still spend a few minutes watching the show go by.

That's how it was with the four Kray funerals. I say four because the biggest turn out was for Violet, the boys' mum. When she died in 1982 it was reported that 60,000 people lined the route. When Ronnie went to his maker or to hell in 1995 the crowds were already on the way down. By the time Charlie took the trip from St Matthew's, Bethnal Green to Chingford Cemetery, only about 10,000 showed up and when it was Reggie's turn to go in a wooden box the numbers had fallen to 2,500, including lots of people from ethnic groups who didn't even live in the area when the brothers were still at Vallance Road.

Look at it this way. Anyone who turned up for a Kray funeral was either a hanger-on — the likes of Frankie Fraser, much of whose income these days depends on exaggerating his association with the Krays — or a 'wannabe' gangster, probably not even born when the Krays were at liberty, or a casual bystander, or a press reporter sent along to get a few chirpy cockney quotes and count the numbers.

And the reason those numbers fell so dramatically was that most people only went along to spot a living Kray. When Violet died you might have glimpsed all three, when Ronnie died there were just two to gawk at, when Charlie went there was only Reggie, and at Reggie's do, there were none at all, unless you include Reggie's second wife Roberta — a marriage that was never consummated.

When I read accounts of Reggie's funeral, I thought Roberta emerged with a lot of credit, especially for dumping all those thugs who thought they had earned the right to carry the coffin. I was tickled to see that she had written Freddie Foreman out of the script. He had written himself into it by claiming that when he went to see Reggie a week before he died, Reggie had said he wanted Fred to be one of his pall bearers. Then that spunky Roberta blanked him and chose some of Reggie's younger chums. Heaven forbid! Some weren't even criminals! Freddie was so miffed, he didn't turn up. As the Daily Telegraph put it, he said he was 'angry at being marginalised' — not the words he used, I'm sure.

Roberta also came out well for standing by Reggie throughout the month between his bizarre release in hospital and his death. I doubt if Reggie could grasp why anyone — even Roberta — could be so selflessly loyal because all his experience taught him that the only things that ever kept people loyal to him and Ronnie were fear and wages.

With her it must have been something else because in his condition he couldn't frighten anybody and he had no money. Otherwise how could he have spent his last days in a hotel room costing just £52 a night? A nice place, I'm sure, but couldn't he do better than that? What about all that money they had for the 1990 film. Some accounts put it at £100,000 each, others said a million for the lot of them. All squandered, given away to hangers-on and merchants of hard-luck stories, or just nicked by thieves masquerading as friends. I'm speculating, of course, but I know what these people are like. I lived among them long enough.

Not that the state acted any better. Imagine. They keep this guy inside for 32 years, refusing time and again to release him. Then it turns out he's got terminal cancer that can't be operated on. So they move him from Wayland jail to the Norfolk and Norwich hospital. Suddenly all his guards walk out and leave him. Then the Home Office says he's been 'freed' by the Home Secretary on compassionate grounds.

Compassion? Who are they kidding? It was cost, not compassion. They thought, We're not going to get any more time out of this guy, he's occupying valuable NHS bed space and tying half a dozen prison officers down keeping watch. Let's dump him, then his mates can look after him at his expense, not ours. A cheap ending for someone who thought he was a big 'un.

As for Charlie's death six months earlier, that was even more pathetic. He had also been shifted out of prison — Parkhurst —

after a stroke, only to get a heart attack in hospital, where they let Reggie visit him. With two sets of guards around, that must have been a pretty grim affair.

And there's another sorry thing: how Charlie ever got himself back into jail after going straight (or at least not getting caught) for twenty years. Prison is a young man's game. Doing time at 70 would be unimaginably hard, even for an old jailbird like myself, and even harder for Good Time Charlie. He should have known he would always be a target, that there would always be some toe-rag wanting to deliver him on a plate, piping hot, to the police.

On top of all that he broke the golden rule: he did business with someone he did not know.

Imagine the scene. There's this old geezer Charlie at a party in a Birmingham hotel and he gets introduced to a total stranger with a Geordie accent who calls himself 'Jack'. This 'Jack' acts as if he's wealthy, hints he's got drug connections in Amsterdam and he's looking for new sources of supply.

After that, they meet up again and Charlie tells 'Jack' he can supply him with five kilos of cocaine every fortnight for two years: £39 millions worth, of which £8 million would go to Charlie and his chums. But as Charlie tells Jack, he couldn't be at any drug handover himself, 'because I have too many eyes on me'.

Instead Charlie invites 'Jack' to a benefit evening in memory of his son Gary who had died tragically young of cancer. It's at this 'do' that Charlie introduces Jack to two runners who later deliver him two kilos of cocaine in return for £63,000 in cash.

Next thing: the runners are arrested and so is Charlie because 'Jack' turns out to be an undercover cop. Everything's on tape and poor old Charlie goes on trial without a leg to stand on. The jury convicts him but he tells the judge, 'All my life I have advised people, particularly young people, never to be involved in drugs.' He says all the claims he made on tape to the undercover team were untrue. 'It was only to get money. I swear on my son's grave I have never handled drugs in my life. Juries have got it wrong for me before and this jury has got it wrong.' Of course he squeals about entrapment, but as one of the notorious Kray clan he should have known better. He had told 'Jack' he had 'too many eyes' on him, but he wasn't sharp enough to suspect that 'Jack' himself owned two of those eyes.

So bosh! Down he goes. His own barrister described him as 'an old, skint, naïve fool — a washed-out old has-been'. What else could he say to save his client a few more years in jail? Either Charlie really was stupid, or maybe he believed he would get away with it, that somehow he would be saved by 'That Old Kray Magic' (to misquote their camp follower Billy Daniels's hit song). For sure, when he was taken through those prison gates with twelve years round his neck, he must have known he would die before he was released.

So can you have a Kray gang if there aren't any Krays?

As a practising criminal organization the Kray gang was shut down forever when all three brothers were convicted back in 1969. Now Reggie's dead, any fear still lurking in the minds of anyone who ever crossed them and survived ought to be purged for ever.

The only thing that might prevent that is what I call the 'Jesse James Thing'. It amazes me how the Twins have been turned into folk heroes. How youngsters tattoo themselves with images of Ron and Reg, and how some guy even changed his name to Ronald Kray.

But for me the oddest thing is the behaviour of those queer coves, Frankie Fraser and Freddie Foreman. Once allies in the fruit machine game and joint sidekicks of the Richardson gang, they have been acting stranger than ever now that the Kray 'industry' must struggle on with no Krays around to perpetuate it.

Fraser has become a right old circus turn, doing his tours of East End gangland, dropping into the Blind Beggar any Saturday he can scrape enough Kray groupies together to half-fill a minibus. Today he claims to have been such a friend of the Krays, ingratiating himself with Reggie before he died, and turning up at all the funerals. Yet, as I explained in Chapter Seven, in 1966 Ronnie and Reggie had assigned two of our Firm to kill him as soon they gave us the signal. He was one of their biggest enemies in the Richardson gang and he was lucky to survive because we all knew what he looked like. We had all seen him talking to the Twins because he had been the Richardsons' 'ambassador', but by this time, if Ronnie had ever caught him on our territory, he would have killed Fraser just like he killed George Cornell.

And yet in 1997 when Charlie went on trial over the cocaine, it was 'let bygones be bygones' (or 'by-guns be by-guns'!), for who shows up as a character witness but Frankie Fraser? That tells you the state of Charlie's defence: he thought this convicted torturer who's spent 41 years in jail could convince the jury that Charlie was a straight-goer. Frank did his best in a backhanded way, saying Charlie 'would not know how to pinch a penny ... he was a coward, but a lovely, lovely man. Anybody who was anybody knew he was different from his brothers. He was too nice.' No, Charlie could not deal in drugs, Fraser told the prosecutor. 'Not for a single day. You are probably more into drugs than him.'

But the man who's had the biggest rush to the head is Freddie Foreman. In 1994 I had gone on Martin Short's television series and named Foreman as Frank Mitchell's prime killer back in December 1966. He was still sticking to his story that he had played no part in Mitchell's death — just as he had when I had testified against him in court and he got off because I was the only eye-witness.

He had also never admitted disposing of Jack the Hat McVitie in October 1967, for which he got ten years at the main Kray trial. Later he pleaded not guilty to shooting and disposing of Ginger Marks when he was having his private war with the last of the independents, Jimmy Evans.

But, blow me down, in 1996 Foreman brings out his own book in which he admits everything: shooting and 'disappearing' Ginger Marks, killing Frank Mitchell, and disposing of Jack the Hat. This is how he summed up his role as a serial gangland killer:

On the following Monday I drove his body to the coast with a back-up motor minding me off. And that was the end of Jack 'the Hat' McVitie. We had a friend on the coast who wrapped him up in chicken wire attached to weights. Our contacts with certain fishermen who'd helped us with smuggling had been kept alive and they were now called in to help out again. As with Ginger Marks and Frank 'The Mad Axeman' Mitchell, Jack 'the Hat' McVitie was buried far out at sea away from the fishing lanes ... We had been told by American contacts that bodies weighted down in this way would never find their way to the surface but would be slowly disposed of by crabs and other deep-sea dwellers. Many people prefer burial at sea.

So there it was, in black and white. Freddie Foreman had come clean at last, smoked out by what I'd said on television. He whinged about me giving evidence against him over Mitchell — 'There was no need to do that, he did not have to name names' — but that isn't what really upset him. 'Donoghue told a number of lies about the incident although his description of the killing itself was fairly accurate. The worst thing was that he said I had done it for money.'

Oh dear! It's OK killing someone, or even three (or a lot more, for all we can believe this man) but it's not OK to kill for money. He goes on, 'I had no need to kill anybody for financial reward. Mitchell was a problem, a threat to all of us. I took part in his killing as a favour to the Twins. There was no financial incentive whatsoever ... So to claim he [Donoghue] handed over £1,000 after Mitchell's disappearance is an insult.'

But even now Fred is in denial. For reasons of machismo and 'respect' he's decided at last to come clean about these murders but he doesn't want to be seen as a mercenary, as the hired 'Underworld Undertaker' which he was. I know that I went to his Prince of Wales pub on the orders of the Krays to give him that £1,000 as his pay-off for getting rid of Mitchell.

THE ENFORCER

That brings me to the biggest problem I have with Foreman's tall tale about dumping all these corpses at sea. Put aside the practical difficulty of humping a huge man like Frank Mitchell on board a trawler without being seen by customs or coastguard (he says all this happened at the port of Newhaven); to try this mode of disposal time and time again would be risking discovery to a degree that a canny man like Foreman would not have run.

Then there's what he told me when I gave him the money. As I explained in Chapter Nine, 'He said that when they took Frank to pieces, they were surprised that for such a big man, he had such a small brain, and he cupped his hands to show me. And he described how his heart was all ripped and torn from the three bullets that went through it. They must have dismembered him to see all that stuff.'

That's why I'm sure Mitchell wasn't dumped at sea. I'm sure he was chopped into pieces and disposed of on land, in some incinerator or crematorium or whatever. As I said earlier, 'I only know what Foreman chose to tell me. They burned him. That's all'.

In January 2000, Foreman goes on television and recycles his fisherman's tale. He tells the same story about trussing Mitchell's whole body in chicken wire, attaching heavy weights, and turfing him into the English Channel. Some good citizens protested about him being paid for telling this gruesome saga and thereby profiting from his crimes. So, even though he had published all this four years earlier, it's only now that he gets arrested on suspicion of perjury. In other word, the police were accusing him of telling lies on oath during his McVitie, Mitchell and Marks trials. They could not try him again for murder because of the ancient protection under English law against double jeopardy: you can't be tried more than once for the same offence.

But Foreman wriggles out of the perjury rap by claiming that what he had said in court was the truth, whereas what he said on television was baloney, a pack of lies to entertain the viewers and earn a few quid.

This argument floors the police who eventually announce they aren't going to press charges. So out walks Freddie all over again. He's home free.

There is one cloud on the horizon. In March 2001 the Law Commission recommended that the double jeopardy rule should be abolished in cases of murder. So one day old Fred might have to face a retrial for murdering both Mitchell and Marks. Even then he could repeat that his book and TV confessions were lies and get 'not guilties' one more time.

Meanwhile he has suffered a far worse penalty. Recently Marilyn Wisbey, the daughter of Tommy Wisbey, the great train robber, and currently Frankie Fraser's girlfriend, has brought out her own book in which she reveals that Freddie is in big trouble. She says she's snubbed him for appearing on television with that 'grass', Albert Donoghue.

It's true. Foreman did appear on that show with me but we never met. The shots were cunningly intercut so it looked as if we were eye-balling each other, but they were filmed at different times. There wasn't any film of the pair of us together, chatting, shaking hands or even taking a swing at each other.

So for once in his life Fred Foreman, the Underworld Undertaker who's got away with so many killings, has been convicted of something he never did, by none other than Judge Marilyn.

As for me, maybe I shall meet Fred again, across a court room at the Old Bailey after they've dumped the double jeopardy rule, and he's on trial for slaughtering Frank Mitchell.

It will be just like the good old days.